Listen, Understand, Obey

Listen, Understand, Obey

Essays on Hebrews in Honor of Gareth Lee Cockerill

Edited by CALEB T. FRIEDEMAN

◆PICKWICK *Publications* · Eugene, Oregon

LISTEN, UNDERSTAND, OBEY
Essays on Hebrews in Honor of Gareth Lee Cockerill

Copyright © 2017 Wipf and Stock Publishers. All rights reserved. Except for brief quotations in critical publications or reviews, no part of this book may be reproduced in any manner without prior written permission from the publisher. Write: Permissions, Wipf and Stock Publishers, 199 W. 8th Ave., Suite 3, Eugene, OR 97401.

Pickwick Publications
An Imprint of Wipf and Stock Publishers
199 W. 8th Ave., Suite 3
Eugene, OR 97401

www.wipfandstock.com

PAPERBACK ISBN: 978-1-4982-7853-9
HARDCOVER ISBN: 978-1-4982-7855-3
EBOOK ISBN: 978-1-4982-7854-6

Cataloguing-in-Publication data:

Names: Friedeman, Caleb T.

Title: Listen, understand, obey : essays on Hebrews in honor of Gareth Lee Cockerill / Caleb T. Friedeman.

Description: Eugene, OR: Pickwick Publications, 2017 | Includes bibliographical references and index.

Identifiers: ISBN 978-1-4982-7853-9 (paperback) | ISBN 978-1-4982-7855-3 (hardcover) | ISBN 978-1-4982-7854-6 (ebook)

Subjects: LCSH: Bible. Hebrews—Criticism, interpretation, etc. | Cockerill, Gareth Lee, 1944–.

Classification: BS2775.2 L35 2017 (print) | BS2775.2 (electronic)

Manufactured in the U.S.A.   03/30/17

Scripture quotations, unless otherwise indicated, are from the New International Version of the Bible, copyright 2011, Biblica, Inc. Used by permission.

Contents

Contributors | vii
Abbreviations | ix
Introduction | xiii
Gareth Lee Cockerill: A Tribute | xv
　—MATT FRIEDEMAN

1　The Use of Psalm 8 in Hebrews | 1
　—RICK BOYD

2　"Let us draw near . . . but not too near": A Critique of the Attempted Distinction between "Drawing Near" and "Entering" in Hebrews' Entry Exhortations | 17
　—SCOTT D. MACKIE

3　Rest Now or Not Yet? Temporal Aspects of Social Identity in Hebrews 3:7—4:11 | 37
　—MATT O'REILLY

4　The Living and Active Word of God: A Theological Reading of Hebrews | 54
　—JON C. LAANSMA

5　"You are my Son": Climactic Revelation in the Son of God in Mark and Hebrews | 75
　—CALEB T. FRIEDEMAN

6　If Son, Then Priest: The Filial Foundation of Ordination in Hebrews and Other New Testament Texts | 95
　—AMY L. PEELER

7　Preexistence, Kenosis, and Exaltation in Hebrews, John, and Paul: Distinctive Explications of a Common Underlying Narrative | 116
　—CAREY B. VINZANT

8 "Son though he was, he learned obedience": The Submission of Christ in Theological Perspective (in Dialogue with Thomas Aquinas and Karl Barth) | 131
—THOMAS H. MCCALL

9 Early Methodist Theology in the Book of Hebrews | 154
—CHRISTOPHER T. BOUNDS

Bibliography of Gareth Lee Cockerill | 173
Ancient Document Index | 175

Contributors

Christopher T. Bounds is Professor of Wesleyan Studies and Gardner Professor for Promotion of Holiness at Asbury University, Wilmore, Kentucky.

Rick Boyd is Assistant Professor of Biblical Studies at Wesley Biblical Seminary, Jackson, Mississippi.

Caleb T. Friedeman is a PhD candidate in Biblical Theology—New Testament at Wheaton College, Wheaton, Illinois.

Matt Friedeman is Professor of Evangelism and Discipleship at Wesley Biblical Seminary, Jackson, Mississippi, and Pastor of DaySpring Community Church, Clinton, Mississippi.

Jon C. Laansma is Associate Professor of Ancient Languages and New Testament at Wheaton College and Graduate School, Wheaton, Illinois.

Scott D. Mackie has taught at Chapman University, Loyola Marymount University, Westmont College, and Fuller Seminary. He is the author of *Eschatology and Exhortation in the Epistle to the Hebrews* (WUNT 2/223; Tübingen: Mohr/Siebeck, 2007), and more than a dozen essays.

Thomas H. McCall is Professor of Biblical and Systematic Theology and Director of the Carl F. H. Henry Center for Theological Understanding at Trinity Evangelical Divinity School, Deerfield, Illinois.

Matt O'Reilly is pastor of St. Mark United Methodist Church, Mobile, Alabama, a PhD candidate in New Testament at the University of Gloucestershire, Cheltenham, England, and an adjunct faculty member at Wesley Biblical Seminary and Asbury Theological Seminary.

Amy L. Peeler is Associate Professor of New Testament at Wheaton College and Graduate School, Wheaton, Illinois.

Carey B. Vinzant is Assistant Professor of Systematic and Historical Theology at Wesley Biblical Seminary, Jackson, Mississippi.

Abbreviations

AB	Anchor Bible
ANTC	Abingdon New Testament Commentaries
AS	*Asbury Seminarian*
ATJ	*Ashland Theological Journal*
BBR	*Bulletin for Biblical Research*
BCOT	Baker Commentary on the Old Testament
BECNT	Baker Exegetical Commentary on the New Testament
BSac	*Bibliotheca Sacra*
BTCP	Biblical Theology for Christian Proclamation
BZ	*Biblische Zeitschrift*
BZNW	Beihefte zur Zeitschrift für die neutestamentliche Wissenschaft
CBET	Contributions to Biblical Exegesis and Theology
CBQ	*Catholic Biblical Quarterly*
CC	Continental Commentaries
CGC	Contemporary Greek Theologians
CJT	*Canadian Journal of Theology*
CUASST	The Catholic University of America Studies in Sacred Theology
EBib	Etudes bibliques
EGGNT	Exegetical Guide to the Greek New Testament
EvQ	*Evangelical Quarterly*
FAPC	Francis Asbury Press Commentary

FCNTECW	Feminist Companion to the New Testament and Early Christian Writings
HNT	Handbuch zum Neuen Testament
ICC	International Critical Commentary
JBL	*Journal of Biblical Literature*
JBLMS	Journal of Biblical Literature Monograph Series
JETS	*Journal of the Evangelical Theological Society*
JSNTSup	Journal for the Study of the New Testament Supplement Series
JTISup	Journal of Theological Interpretation Supplements
KEK	Kritisch-exegetischer Kommentar über das Neue Testament
LEC	Library of Early Christianity
LNTS	Library of New Testament Studies
LQHR	*London Quarterly and Holborn Review*
LXX	Septuagint
MT	Masoretic Text
NABPRDS	National Association of Baptist Professors of Religion Dissertation Series
NETS	Pietersma, Albert, and Benjamin G. Wright, eds. *A New English Translation of the Septuagint and the Other Greek Translations Traditionally Included Under that Title*. Oxford: Oxford University Press, 2007.
NIBC	New International Biblical Commentary
NICNT	New International Commentary on the New Testament
NIGTC	New International Greek Testament Commentary
NIVAC	NIV Application Commentary
NovTSup	Supplements to Novum Testamentum
NPNF[2]	*Nicene and Post-Nicene Fathers, Series 2*
NSBT	New Studies in Biblical Theology
NT	New Testament
NTC	New Testament Commentary

NTL	New Testament Library	
NTS	*New Testament Studies*	
OT	Old Testament	
OTP	Charlesworth, James H., ed. *The Old Testament Pseudepigrapha*. 2 vols. Garden City, NY: Doubleday, 1983–1985.	
PCNT	Paideia Commentaries on the New Testament	
PNTC	Pillar New Testament Commentary	
QR	*Quarterly Review*	
RBL	*Review of Biblical Literature*	
RNT	Reading the New Testament	
SBET	*Scottish Bulletin of Evangelical Theology*	
SBLDS	Society of Biblical Literature Dissertation Series	
SBLMS	Society of Biblical Literature Monograph Series	
SBT	Studies in Biblical Theology	
SJT	*Scottish Journal of Theology*	
SMTS	Saint Mary's Theological Studies	
SPS	Sacra Pagina Series	
SNTSMS	Society for New Testament Studies Monograph Series	
StBL	Studies in Biblical Literature	
STDJ	Studies on the Texts of the Desert of Judah	
StPB	Studia Post-Biblica	
TBl	*Theologische Blätter*	
THOTC	Two Horizons Old Testament Commentary	
TJ	*Trinity Journal*	
TynBul	*Tyndale Bulletin*	
TZ	*Theologishe Zeitschrift*	
VE	*Verbum et Ecclesia*	
WBC	Word Biblical Commentary	
WUNT	Wissenschaftliche Untersuchungen zum neuen Testament	

Introduction

IT IS MY PRIVILEGE to introduce this collection of essays in honor of Gareth Lee Cockerill, known to his friends and colleagues as Gary. Dr. Cockerill has spent his life serving the church—both in the United States and abroad—as a missionary and biblical scholar, and it is this life of faithful service that this volume seeks to honor. Dr. Cockerill is perhaps best known for his scholarship on Hebrews, which culminated in his *The Epistle to the Hebrews* in the New International Commentary on the New Testament series (2012). However, the primary mission field of his life has undoubtedly been his students at Wesley Biblical Seminary (WBS), where he has taught New Testament and made disciples for more than thirty years. It was at WBS that I first met Dr. Cockerill, initially as a colleague of my father's, and later as a professor. In addition to training me in the art of biblical exegesis, Dr. Cockerill was also instrumental in my decision to pursue doctoral work. I still have the email I received from him in November of my final year of seminary in which he encouraged me to pursue PhD work, and suggested that Wheaton College was the best place to do so. As I write this introduction from my study carrel in Wheaton's Buswell Library—now finishing my second year of doctoral work—I am reminded of the way that Dr. Cockerill has shaped not only my life, but the lives of so many students who now serve around the world as missionaries, laypersons, pastors, and scholars for the church of Jesus Christ.

The title of this volume—*Listen, Understand, Obey*—is one of the oft-repeated anthems of Dr. Cockerill's teaching. Former students will vividly recall Dr. Cockerill exclaiming, "Listen! Understand! Obey!" each word punctuated with pointed finger as the corresponding clip art appeared on the projector screen. For Dr. Cockerill, this phrase expressed a deeply-held conviction that the true goal of biblical interpretation is to live the text rather than to merely understand it. (As many of the contributors in this volume can testify, he has endeavored throughout his life to embody this belief and to help others to do so.) The emphasis on *hearing* God's word is, of course, a product of his lifelong love for the book of Hebrews, which—somewhat uniquely in the NT canon—characterizes OT Scripture as divine speech.

The essays in this volume focus on Hebrews, Dr. Cockerill's primary area of research, and are written by a mixture of his collaborators in Hebrews studies, WBS colleagues, and former students (some of whom fall into more than one of those categories). After a brief tribute to Dr. Cockerill's life and ministry by longtime fellow WBS faculty member Matt Friedeman, the book opens with four essays that contribute to Hebrews proper: Rick Boyd examines the use of Ps 8 in Hebrews, Scott D. Mackie and Matt O'Reilly each consider present dimensions of salvation in Hebrews, and John C. Laansma presents a theological reading of Hebrews. Three essays follow that focus on Hebrews as it connects to other NT books: I explore the relationship between how Mark and Hebrews each portray the Son as climactic revelation, Amy L. Peeler investigates the filial foundation of ordination in Hebrews and other NT texts, and Carey B. Vinzant notes a common narrative arc in Hebrews, John, and Paul and considers its significance. The volume closes with two essays on Hebrews from systematic- and historical-theological perspectives: Thomas H. McCall discusses the submission of Christ in Heb 5:7 in dialogue with Thomas Aquinas and Karl Barth, and Christopher T. Bounds explores Hebrews through the eyes of early Methodist theologians. We hope that this collection will serve as both a fitting honor to Dr. Cockerill and a contribution to the study of Hebrews.

A volume like this is always the product of many hands, and so I would like to extend my gratitude to those who have assisted in the process. I would first like to thank my father, Dr. Matt Friedeman, for assembling the initial contributors and providing advice at many points in the editing process. I am grateful to my mother, Mary, who graciously read over the manuscript and offered valuable suggestions. I would also like to extend my gratitude to each of the contributors for their hard work and for being so flexible on a tight editing schedule. Thanks are due to the editorial staff at Pickwick, particularly Matthew Wimer, Chris Spinks, and Brian Palmer, all of whom answered questions and assisted at various points along the way.

Caleb T. Friedeman
Wheaton, Illinois
April 2016

Gareth Lee Cockerill

A Tribute

MATT FRIEDEMAN

GARY COCKERILL HAS HAD a long and an outstanding career at Wesley Biblical Seminary. His passion for the classroom has been a hallmark of that service. Former students, now all over the world, love and admire him.

> Dr. Cockerill keeps the "biblical" in Wesley Biblical Seminary. His passion for and insights of Scripture are profound and contagious.
> —Dr. David Fry
> Lead Pastor (Frankfort, Indiana) and Adjunct Professor at God's Bible School and College

> My first experience at WBS was Dr. Cockerill's Hermeneutics class that I took one summer, and this set me on a new and positive trajectory for my life and ministry. Dr. Cockerill has had a profound influence on how I view Scripture and on how I interpret Scripture. I really appreciated how approachable and helpful he was as my teacher. I still deeply respect him as a person and as a scholar. I am grateful for his friendship to this day.
> —Dr. Mark Bird
> Professor of Systematic and Practical Theology, God's Bible School and College

Dr. Cockerill always inspires me: considerate, scholarly, disciplined, forthright, fun, energetic, skilled, devout. But the greatest impact is from our first encounter at WBS. While visiting in their home he reveled in taking our three year-old son to the park, revealing the mix of scholar and joyful servant that endears him to us all.

—Randy Huff
Interim Pastor (North Pole, Alaska)

He loves Jesus. This one thing comes shining through whether in the classroom or over a cup of coffee. His lasting impact in my life comes in hoping to love Jesus as much as he does.

—Matt Marshall
Chaplain and Professor at the Faculty of Theology, Southern Africa Nazarene University[1]

This is where Gary Cockerill has left his greatest mark—in the hearts of many hundreds of Wesley students as he dutifully taught New Testament and lived his life among these young disciples. His example of academic excellence, personal piety, commitment to the Great Commission, and devoted family life has shaped a generation of pastors and scholars.

TESTIMONY

Gary Cockerill was born in northern Virginia, in the Washington D.C. area, to a godly Wesleyan pastoral couple who kept Scripture in the forefront of their home. Many notable Christian leaders and missionaries passed through the Cockerill household during Gary's childhood, and these encounters helped expose him to a Great Commission worldview and lifestyle. Cockerill committed his life to the Lord at at a young age and solidified that commitment during his teenage years when he sensed with increasing certainty that his life would be spent in ministry.

STUDENT

Cockerill received his B.A. from Central Wesleyan College in 1966 and the Master of Divinity degree from Asbury Theological Seminary in 1969. He earned the Master of Theology degree from Union Theological Seminary in 1973. While a student he engaged in both academic study and practical ministry as he visited house to house, prayed for those in nursing homes, shared the gospel in prisons, traveled as part of gospel teams, and served as an intern and supply pastor. This blend of academic life and hands-on application would serve him well in the days ahead, both internationally and

1. Quotes from personal correspondence, February 15–18, 2016.

in the American classroom. His studies at Union culminated in a PhD in Biblical Studies with a dissertation that would forecast a lifelong interest in a particular book of the Bible: "The Melchizedek Christology in Heb. 7:1–28."

MISSIONARY

West Africa has always been on the mind and heart of this New Testament professor, and his missionary experiences are frequently referenced in his lectures, writings, and conversations. After seminary Gary met his wife Rosa, who had served as a nurse in Sierra Leone and planned to return there for further service. The young couple decided that the Lord would have them marry and go back to West Africa. Gary, Rosa, and their daughters spent three terms of missionary service in Sierra Leone, from 1969–1972, from 1976–1979, and again in 1981–1984. He served as chaplain and Bible teacher for the Kamakwie Wesleyan Secondary School and helped to build a dispensary where his wife Rosa, a registered nurse anesthetist, ministered to the medical needs of the people. Cockerill ministered through evangelism, discipleship, promoting stewardship, and counseling local pastors. He also assisted in translating the New Testament into the local dialect of the Limba language. When he arrived at Wesley Biblical Seminary immediately after his first term of missionary service, he was initially appointed Assistant Professor of Biblical Literature and *Missiological* Studies. Cockerill's work in Sierra Leone paved the way for his 2002 book *Guidebook for Pilgrims to the Heavenly City*, in which Cockerill uses his career-long specialty in Hebrews to disciple believers of Muslim background.

HUSBAND AND FATHER

Gary Cockerill met Rosa Bishop in 1970. Their two older daughters, Ginny and Allene, were born on the mission field. A third daughter, Kate, arrived while they served at Wesley Biblical Seminary. The Cockerills took seriously the scriptural mandate to diligently teach their children God's word (Deut 6:4–9). Today all three of their daughters are devoted Christians: Ginny has recently served at a Christian college and today works in higher education in Alabama, Allene teaches English and Latin at the secondary level, and Kate serves as a missionary in Central Asia. The latter two are married and are nurturing their children in the love of Christ; all are strongly committed to the church.

WESLEY BIBLICAL SEMINARY

Cockerill has served as Wesley's premier professor in New Testament for three and a half decades and in briefer stints as Vice President for Academic Affairs. His legacy is found in his passionate commitment to the inductive approach to Scripture and the use of proper exegetical methodology. He has been able to draw upon insights from multiple disciplines—rhetorical criticism, canonical criticism, and intertextuality—to enrich Bible study methodology. He is experienced in teaching Greek, knowledgeable in Hebrew, and skilled in showing students how to use the original languages to enhance the inductive process. He has taught the whole array of New Testament courses at Wesley, as well as courses in biblical theology, hermeneutics, and the biblical basis for Christian holiness. In all these disciplines, he exhibits a passionate commitment to the church's mission to communicate the gospel cross-culturally.

SCHOLAR

Cockerill has spent much of his academic career pursuing a keen interest in the book of Hebrews. His capstone academic achievement, after numerous journal articles and academic presentations, was *The Epistle to the Hebrews* (2012) in The New International Commentary on the New Testament series. This publication replaced an earlier volume of the same title by eminent New Testament scholar F. F. Bruce. Cockerill's commitment to the value of theological education resulted in *Christian Faith in the Old Testament: The Bible of the Apostles* (2014), which compiled in a single volume many of his most incisive classroom insights. Also helpful to lay and clergy was *The Wesley Bible: A Personal Study Bible for Holy Living*, for which he served as New Testament editor.

Beyond these volumes he has contributed numerous chapters for books, written extensively for Sunday school curriculum, and produced articles and book reviews for the *Bulletin for Biblical Research*, *Tyndale Bulletin*, *Missiology: A Review*, *The Evangelical Quarterly*, *The Journal of the Evangelical Theological Society*, *The Journal of Biblical Literature*, *Bibliotheca Sacra*, *Interpretation*, *Review of Biblical Literature*, *Ashland Theological Journal*, and the *Asbury Seminarian*. He is a member of the Evangelical Theological Society, the Institute for Biblical Research, and the Society of Biblical Literature. Further, he has taught concentrated courses or presented lecture series at Ohio Christian University, Patrick Henry College, Kingswood University, Oklahoma Wesleyan University, God's Bible School, and the Henry

Center for Theological Inquiry at Trinity Evangelical Divinity School. He has also taught at numerous camps and conferences and has been the keynote speaker at the Japan Holiness Association and the Evangelical Fellowship of Sierra Leone.

DISCIPLE-MAKER

Wesley Biblical Seminary has, from its earliest days, endorsed small group discipleship as a leading ideal and principal practice for her professors. All students were required to participate in a group, and all professors were expected to lead one. Cockerill's groups were always memorable and a favorite among the students. Most often, professor and students would decamp to a nearby restaurant and discuss personal challenges, disappointments and opportunities over coffee. Through the years, this simple method of what has sometimes been referred to as "life-to-life transference" impacted scores of students and stands as a strong testimony to Cockerill's consummate grasp of what it means to be a Christian scholar. For him, it was never enough to merely write high-brow academic tomes and papers, nor was it sufficient to offer outstanding classroom presentations. Throughout his career, Cockerill invested in his students and was the quintessential example in counseling them one-on-one both academically and personally.

CONCLUSION

As Gary Cockerill's longest serving colleague on the Wesley Biblical Seminary faculty I can attest that our seminary has never known a more passionate, impactful, hard-working, life-changing, and disciple-making professor. There could hardly be a more influential professor in the nation once family, scholarship, classroom performance, and one-on-one discipleship opportunities are considered. Jesus said, "Make disciples of all nations" (Matt 28:19); Gary Cockerill has, indeed, fulfilled that commission through service abroad, family discipleship, formidable scholarship, and student inspiration.

The Kingdom is a better place because of God's work through Gary Cockerill. His ears will most certainly be privileged one day to hear, "Well done..."

BIBLIOGRAPHY

Cockerill, Gareth L. *Christian Faith in the Old Testament: The Bible of the Apostles.* Nashville: Nelson, 2014.
———. *The Epistle to the Hebrews.* NICNT. Grand Rapids: Eerdmans, 2012.
———. *Guidebook for Pilgrims to the Heavenly City.* Pasadena, CA: William Carey Library, 2002.
Harper, A. F., et al., eds. *The Wesley Bible: A Personal Study Bible for Holy Living.* Nashville: Nelson, 1990.

1

The Use of Psalm 8 in Hebrews

RICK BOYD

I MET DR. GARETH Lee Cockerill at a 2006 conference on Hebrews and Theology in St. Andrews, Scotland as I was beginning to prepare for my doctoral thesis on Hebrews. Following the opening morning session, as we moved en masse toward the cafeteria, Gary came up to me, asked who I was, and offered to buy me lunch. I got to know Gary that day because that is the kind of person he is. He manifests the very character of Christ, taking the initiative and offering grace to those who are strangers to him. Gary and I became friends that day because he put his arm around me both literally and metaphorically, and we now serve together as colleagues at Wesley Biblical Seminary.

Because of our close association through the book of Hebrews, I was honored to be asked to contribute a chapter in this tribute to Gary, specifically related to our common interest in the pastor's message.[1] It is with profound gratitude that I dedicate this study to my dean, mentor, and brother, Dr. Gareth Lee Cockerill.

INTRODUCTION

Hebrews is generally regarded as containing the most sophisticated use of Greek in the NT. The author's craftsmanship is evident at every turn.

---

1. Cockerill refers to the author of Hebrews as "the pastor" (e.g., *Hebrews*, 2) because of the book's sermonic character.

Included among his[2] mastery of the Greek is his use of Ps 8 in the second chapter. This is a much debated passage, specifically as it pertains to the interpretation of the appropriated psalm. The key question is whether the author uses Ps 8 christologically, anthropologically, or perhaps both. The answer to this question has repercussions related to what may be the central theme of the book, and it is the subject of this brief essay.

In the following pages I will consider the use of Ps 8 in Hebrews in terms of its various hermeneutical emphases. I will begin by surveying the interpretation of Ps 8 in early Judaism and the NT with an eye to Hebrews, and will go on to argue that Hebrews' interpretation and appropriation of the psalm is eschatological, teleological, and filial in nature, involving both Christ and humanity. I will then conclude with some reflections on the importance of the author's hermeneutical approach and its implications for the interpretation of Hebrews and the resulting Christian praxis.

HISTORICAL INTERPRETATION OF PSALM 8

Until the first century, Ps 8 generally had been understood as a reflection on creation, although as Mark Stephen Kinzer notes, "there are few explicit references to Ps 8 in ancient Jewish literature outside the rabbinic and Christian canon."[3] The psalm was appropriated in celebration of the exalted position the human had been given by the creator,[4] a position as ruler of

---

2. The recognition of the author as male is dependent on the masculine form of the participle διηγούμενον (11:32). See Attridge, *Hebrews*, 5; Cockerill, *Hebrews*, 2; Ellingworth, *Hebrews*, 20; Johnson, *Hebrews*, 41; Koester, *Hebrews*, 45; Witherington, *Letters*, 22.

3. See Kinzer, "All Things," 12. Kinzer's focus is primarily first-century Jewish and Christian appropriation and interpretation of Psalm 8. Two documents suggest that Ps 8 was interpreted as a creation psalm: see *Sib. Or.* fragment 3.13–14 and 1QS 3.17–18 (both possibly dating to the second century BC). Additionally, possible allusions to Ps 8 and creation can be found in *4 Ezra* 6.46 (for the dating to AD 100, see *OTP* 1:520) and *3 En.* 5.10 (for the dating with connection to traditions in line with developments already begun in the Maccabean era, see ibid., 1:225–29; Evans, *Noncanonical*, 20–25). For other perspectives regarding the relationship between Ps 8 and creation, see Goldingay, *Psalms*, 159–61; Grogan, *Psalms*, 53–54; Kraus, *Psalms*, 179–80, 185; Louis, *Theology*, 57, 101–8, 121; Pietersma, "Text-Production," 487–501, esp. 490, 495; Urassa, *Psalm 8*, 59–112, esp. 72.

4. See Craigie, *Psalms*, 106. Craigie asserts that the psalm "may be classified as a *psalm of creation*," but adds, "there can be no certainty whether or not the psalm was designated in the first instance for use in the cult, in some specific act of worship." See also Kinzer, "All Things," 38, 40–41.

God's creation,[5] specifically as ruler of the animals, birds, and sea creatures (8:7–9).[6]

However, in the Second Temple period the interpretation of Ps 8 began to shift toward an eschatological hope related to the anticipated restoration of Israel and a "second Adam."[7] Israel, emerging from the exile and in the midst of varying degrees of oppression by other nations, was looking for God's promise of the restoration of his people, and Ps 8 spoke to that expectation. Israel waited with increased anticipation for the coming Messiah who would be the instrument to realize the promises God had made to his people. Psalm 8 reinforced that hope by referring to the glory with which "Adam" was once crowned, a glory to be restored in the coming days.[8]

This hermeneutical shift in the understanding of Ps 8 may have contributed an eschatological influence on both the interpretation of the psalm in first century Judaism[9] and the appropriation of the text within the NT church. One branch of Jewish interpretation saw the "second Adam" as Moses,[10] while another was focused on a variety of individual figures thought to be addressed in the psalm (e.g., Abraham, Isaac, Jacob, Moses, Joshua, David, Solomon, Samson, Elijah, Jonah, and the children of Israel),[11] but Christian interpretation identified Jesus as the main subject of the psalm.[12]

---

5. See Mowinckel, *Worship*, 85. Mowinckel refers to Ps 8 as providing a "graphic and epic description of one of Yahweh's great works—particularly of the creation." Mowinckel focuses on the use of Ps 8 in the cult of Israel.

6. The versification of the Old Testament texts used in this essay will follow that of the LXX and not the Hebrew (MT) or English text.

7. Kinzer, "All Things," 11. Kinzer attempts to establish a hermeneutical foothold over against others who deny messianic Jewish interpretation of Ps 8. See Westcott, *Hebrews*, 42: "[Psalm 8] is not, and has never been accounted by the Jews to be, directly Messianic." See also Kistemaker, *Citations*, 29. Nevertheless, the eschatological anticipation of a "new creation" can be found in texts as early as Isa 65:17–25. The idea of a future and ultimate new creation was introduced by the time of the Second Temple period and reflected in texts that date as early as 100 BC to AD 100 (*OTP* 2:252, 299). One of these texts associates Adam with the people of God, referring to them as "the holy people" (*Apoc. Mos.* 13.2–6), and it refers to a future dominion of Adam (39.2–3). Another echoes the language of Ps 8 in an eschatological sense (*L.A.B.* 13.8–9; 26.13). For more, see Kinzer, "All Things," 96–113.

8. See Pate, *Glory*. Regarding Israel in particular, see Anderson, "Exaltation," 83–110, esp. 108–10; Kinzer, "All Things," 96.

9. See Kinzer, "All Things," 96–149.

10. The association of the "second Adam" with Moses, especially in reference to Moses and the giving of the Torah at Sinai, is found in rabbinic literature with some traditions likely going back to the Second Temple period. E.g., *Gen. Rab.* 19:7. See Kinzer, "All Things," 150–208.

11. *Midr. Pss.* 8.7 (on Ps 8:5–10).

12. See Matt 21:16; 1 Cor 15:27; Eph 1:22.

Additionally, Ps 8 was being coupled with Ps 109, with both psalms being interpreted messianically,[13] to explain the exaltation of Jesus. The author of Hebrews, by utilizing both psalms, seizes the opportunity to address a believing community in need of reassurance and exhortation to persevere in the faith. Psalm 8, once understood in terms of a reflection on creation and the glorious position God gave to humanity in the beginning, was positioned to fit into the argument of Hebrews by pointing to the eschatological purpose of the human: a filial relationship with God.

HEBREWS: ESCHATOLOGICAL INTERPRETATION OF PSALM 8

The opening statement of Hebrews declares that, unlike times in the past, God has spoken eschatologically in the Christ-event.[14] The author identifies that communication as having been accomplished ἐν υἱῷ. Essentially God has given his perfect revelation "in son," not only in the person of Jesus his Son,[15] but also in the form of *sonship* and with the provision of a filial relationship for the believer.[16] This becomes evident as the opening declaration is unpacked through the rest of the epistle with references to believers as sons (2:10; 12:5–8), brothers of the Son (2:11–12, which establishes future references to believers as brothers; 2:17; 3:1, 12; 12:19; 13:22), and heirs (1:14; 6:12, 17; 9:15).

As the author builds his argument, he begins to particularize[17] his opening general statement (1:1–4) by establishing the superiority of the filial relationship to God over the relationship of angels to God.[18] Chapter

---

13. See Chester, *Messiah*, 35–37. See also Attridge, *Hebrews*, 72.

14. See among others Attridge, *Hebrews*, 39; Johnson, *Hebrews*, 63–64; O'Brien, *Hebrews*, 50.

15. Hebrews deals with sonship on two levels: The author makes reference to Jesus' ontological sonship (cf. 1:2–13; 5:8), and he also refers to Jesus as son in the flesh (2:11–14, 17; 5:7–8). The second level is the primary concern of the author, who presents Jesus, the ontological Son, as having become perfected as son in the flesh (2:10; 5:7–9; 7:28). This second level incorporates believers who are also called "sons" (2:10; 12:5–8). With this in mind, I will use the lowercase "son" to refer to sons and sonship in the flesh, whereas I will use the uppercase "Son" to refer exclusively to Jesus as the ontological Son of God.

16. See Boyd, "Sonship." The anarthrous use of υἱός in 1:2a is taken to be qualitative and foundational as the central theme of the book.

17. Particularization is a term used for a semantic structural relationship characterized by the movement from a general statement to the unpacking of the particulars of that statement. See Bauer and Traina, *Inductive*, 100–103.

18. See Boyd, "Sonship," 62–65.

one evinces the superiority of sonship and concludes by describing angels as "ministering spirits sent to serve those who will [τοὺς μέλλοντας] inherit salvation" (1:14). The author's use of μέλλω with reference to the heirs of salvation suggests an urgency that recalls the opening eschatological statement about God speaking in the Christ-event. These are the last days and the heirs are about to inherit salvation. This is further strengthened in 2:1 with a causal warning: "Therefore [Διὰ τοῦτο]"—a reference to the nearness of inheriting salvation—"we must pay the most careful attention . . . to what we have heard, so that we do not drift away."[19] Once again the author calls the recipients' attention to the opening words of the homily, to the things spoken eschatologically by God,[20] the form and content of which demand the closest of attention.

The author continues the warning by contrasting what was spoken through angels (2:2)[21] to what was spoken through the Lord (2:3). This is referred to as "so great a salvation" and one from which those who neglect it will not be able to escape. The contrast between God's former revelation and His eschatological revelation ἐν υἱῷ is unmistakable.

The final element the author employs before his use of Ps 8 comes in 2:5 as he prepares to introduce the quotation. The author returns to the use of μέλλω (1:14) in referring to the world about which he has not only been speaking, but which he is about to further elucidate through his use of Ps 8. This is the *"about-to-be* world,"[22] again suggesting an eschatological realm.[23] The author describes this realm as not being subjected to angels, continuing the contrast between son and angels that began in 1:4. According to 1:4, this one in whom God has spoken eschatologically "became as much superior to the angels as the name he has inherited is superior to theirs."[24] The author uses the rest of the first chapter to substantiate his claim that the *son* is superior to *angels*. In 2:5 the author implies that the eschatological realm he is

---

19. The Greek verb παραρυῶμεν connotes the idea of being carried away, once again emphasizing the urgency of the situation.

20. See Boyd, "Sonship," 65–66.

21. This is an apparent reference to the giving of the law on Mount Sinai (Acts 7:38, 53; Gal 3:19). This would be consistent with the revelation God gave to "the fathers" in many parts and many ways long ago (1:1). Ibid., 46.

22. My translation.

23. Note also that the use of μέλλω connects the heirs of salvation (1:14) with the eschatological realm described by the quote from Ps 8 (2:5–8).

24. Actually, the pronoun used is αὐτούς and not αὐτῶν suggesting a superiority of essential relationship and not just name. This suggests the name inherited is "son," a name superior to angels, as the author goes on to explicate.

about to describe using Ps 8 has been subjected, not to *angels*, but to the one whose name has just been proven superior, the heir of all things (1:2): *Son*.

In the actual quote from Ps 8, the author advances his argument regarding the superiority of "son" with what Kinzer calls an "ingenious" move:[25] He appropriates the words βραχύ τι temporally over against the traditional interpretation referring to the comparative position of the human to heavenly beings. Instead of understanding Ps 8:6 positionally in line with the Hebrew text ("You have made him *a little* lower than . . ."), the author of Hebrews makes use of the flexibility of the Greek to add a temporal element in turning the use of the psalm into an eschatologically hopeful assertion: "You have made him *for a little while* lower than . . ."[26] This shift is subtle but vital to his argument regarding what God has done in speaking ἐν υἱῷ. In his use of Ps 8 the author has taken a text reflecting on creation and turned it into a picture of the eschatological realm God has now provided in the Christ-event.

HEBREWS: TELEOLOGICAL/FILIAL INTERPRETATION OF PSALM 8

The key issue in understanding the use of Ps 8 in Hebrews is determining whether the author is applying the psalm anthropologically, christologically, or both, and the scholarly community remains divided on the matter.[27] The implied indirect object of 2:5, the one to whom the about-to-be realm is subjected, is the focus of the Ps 8 quotation. This object is pivotal

---

25. Kinzer, "All Things," 288. Kinzer suggests that the author of Hebrews is utilizing "creative exegesis . . . rather than [depending on] a received tradition."

26. The NIV translates this, "You made them a little lower than the angels."

27. The published material on this issue has continued to increase as evidenced by the advocates for the various positions in the current millennium alone. For an anthropological interpretation, see Blomberg, "Jesus," 88–99. For a christological interpretation, see Cockerill, *Hebrews*, 126–35; Guthrie and Quinn, "Discourse," 235–46, esp. 246; Lee, *Messiah*, 221–23; Mason, *Priest*, 19; Pietersma, "Text-Production," 494–95; Thompson, *Hebrews*, 60; Witherington, *Letters*, 141. For a dual anthropological-christological interpretation, see Caneday, "World," 28–39, esp. 35; De Wet, "Messianic," 113–25; deSilva, *Perseverance*, 108–10; Gäbel, *Kulttheologie*, 134–44; Gheorghita, *Role*, 17, 63; Hahn, *Kinship*, 284–88; Isaacs, *Reading*, 41; Johnson, *Hebrews*, 89–92; Karrer, *Brief*, 169; Keener, *Canonical*, 169–82, esp. 179; Koester, *Hebrews*, 220–21; Mackie, *Eschatology*, 45–46; Marshall, "Soteriology," 253–77, esp. 257–61; McCruden, *Solidarity*, 45–49; Mitchell, *Hebrews*, 68–69; Rascher, *Schriftauslegung*, 53–56; Rhee, *Faith*, 82–84; Schenck, *Cosmology*, 54–59; Schunack, *Hebräerbrief*, 31–32; Steyn, "Observations," 493–514, esp. 510; Westfall, *Discourse*, 101–3, 111–12; Whitlark, *Fidelity*, 143.

in determining the use of Ps 8 in Hebrews, and that object involves not only the Son but sons.

The contrast the author presents between "son" and angels in 1:4–14[28] continues in 2:5 following the brief interjected exhortation for "us" to hold to the things having been heard (2:1), a likely reference to 1:2a and God speaking to "us" ἐν υἱῷ.[29] After establishing the superiority of son to angels in 1:4–14, the author urges the recipients not to neglect so great a salvation (2:3), but to hold to what has been heard even more closely. The author then substantiates the urgent warning: "It is not to angels that [God] has subjected the world to come, about which we are speaking." This statement prepares for the use of the quotation from Ps 8 in 2:6–8a.

The use of ἀγγέλοις in 2:5 is anarthrous and may point to the quality of angels in their relationship to God over against that of "son," which has been clearly proven to be superior beginning in 1:4. It seems evident from the contrast in 1:4–14 between angels and "son" that the about-to-be realm is subjected to "son," but which son is intended by the author? Is it the Son who is seated at the right hand of the Father (1:13), or does the son to whom all things are subjected (2:8a) include the heirs of salvation (1:14), the *many sons* who follow their pioneer into glory (2:10)?

One important consideration often overlooked in the debate concerns 2:6b: "What is mankind [ἄνθρωπος] that you are mindful of them, a son of man [υἱὸς ἀνθρώπου] that you care for him?" Some who support a christological interpretation of Ps 8 in Hebrews draw support from the other two NT passages that appropriate Ps 8 (1 Cor 15:27; Eph 1:22) in combination with Ps 109 (1 Cor 15:25; Eph 1:20). In both passages the interpretation is clearly christological,[30] perhaps influencing those scholars toward a christological interpretation in Hebrews. The fact that Heb 2:6b is the *only* use of Ps 8:5 in the NT is not sufficiently appreciated by many scholars with respect to the reference to ἄνθρωπος as being more than a reference to the incarnation. Hebrews *intentionally* goes beyond the other christological uses of Ps 8:7 by incorporating Ps 8:5–7. The other NT occurrences of Ps 8:7 lack direct reference to ἄνθρωπος and, therefore, can easily be interpreted as exclusively christological. The situation in Hebrews is different. Although the author

---

28. Note the filial reference in 1:14 to those about to *inherit* salvation. See Boyd, "Sonship," 62–63.

29. The author uses ἡμῖν in 1:2a and ἡμᾶς in 2:1.

30. See Guthrie and Quinn, "Analysis," 237–38; Lee, *Messiah*, 223; Pietersma, "Text-Production," 494; Thompson, *Hebrews*, 61; Witherington, *Letters*, 141. See also Kistemaker, *Citations*, 29; März, "Zeit," 29–42, esp. 35; Vanhoye, *Situation*, 303. The common concept linking Psalm 8 and Ps 109 is the subjugation "underneath the feet" of the subject of interest (πάντα in Ps 8:7; τοὺς ἐχθρούς σου in Ps 109:1).

makes it clear that Jesus is the only one we see fulfilling the psalm (2:9a), yet he also refers to Jesus as the *"pioneer* of [the] salvation" of many sons (2:10).[31] Jesus, in fulfilling the psalm to a degree (crowned with glory and honor following a brief time of being positionally subordinate to angels), is also the trailblazer (cf. 12:2; 6:19–20) for other sons and daughters to follow into glory. With the unique reference to humanity in 2:6b,[32] serious consideration must be given to including other sons in the interpretation of 2:5 as well as 2:6–8.

Another significant factor must be considered involving the interpretation of Heb 2:5–8. If the author's use of Ps 8 should be interpreted anthropologically *in any way*, the reference to the son having been appointed heir of all things in 1:2b must be reconciled with 2:8 ("you have put everything under their feet [τῶν ποδῶν αὐτοῦ]") and the original indirect object of that statement, ἄνθρωπος (2:6). Unless Jesus alone is given reign over creation, the domain *originally* intended for humanity according to the traditional reading of Ps 8, the interpreter must reconcile the two statements in Hebrews having to do with God granting authority over all things. Is it the *Son* in whom God has spoken eschatologically in 1:2, or *humanity* who is made lower than angels "for a little while" (2:8)?

Those who interpret the use of Ps 8 christologically have no problem with reconciling these two statements. Their solution is simple: The heir of all things is Jesus. With that interpretation he would be the only one to whom God has subjected the about-to-be realm, which simplifies the need for reconciling 1:2 and 2:8. The heir of all things, by God's appointment, is the one to whom all things are subjected: Jesus. The use of Ps 109:1 (Heb 1:13) could also support this interpretation since Jesus is seated at the right hand of God, a position of authority, until his enemies are placed under his feet.

However, the context (1:4–14) of that quotation of Ps 109:1 (1:13) is the contrast between angels and *Son*.[33] As Son, not as Jesus or as Christ, he takes

---

31. The NIV translates this "many sons and daughters." However, due to the specific emphasis on υἱός in 1:2a and elsewhere, the term "many sons" has particular relevance.

32. Some scholars among those who interpret Hebrews' use of Ps 8 christologically argue for a variant reading, Τίς, at the beginning of the quote instead of the preferred reading, Τί ἐστιν ἄνθρωπος. They argue that the translation should read, "*Who is the* human that you remember him . . ." and they point to Christ who fulfils the psalm. This argument is largely rejected by the academy with but a few exceptions. See Braun, *Hebräer*, 53; Ellingworth, *Hebrews*, 148; Leschert, *Foundations*, 102–3; Zuntz, *Text*, 48–49.

33. Hubert James Keener refers to "one motif [that] dominates substantial portions of the book, including the section within which Psalm 8 is cited (Heb 1:5—2:18): the motif of Jesus' superiority in comparison with figures respected within Judaism" (Keener, *Canonical*, 172). Yet Jesus is shown to be superior to angels *as son* (1:5–13),

his seat at the right hand of God. Furthermore, a christological interpretation with Jesus as heir of all things fails to consider adequately the reference to ἄνθρωπος in the Ps 8 quotation that is unique in the NT and purposeful in Hebrews. The author of Hebrews is very careful about his appropriation of the Old Testament. For example, he leaves out καὶ κατέστησας αὐτὸν ἐπὶ τὰ ἔργα τῶν χειρῶν σου (Ps 8:7a) in his quote of Ps 8:5–7. Why would the author excise half of a verse (Ps 8:7a) that simply supports the other half (8:7b), which he quotes? The quotation of Ps 8:5–7 is continuous with the exception of 8:7a. The exclusion of Ps 8:7a could be because of the reference in Heb 1:10–12 to the works of God's hands perishing (ἔργα τῶν χειρῶν σου εἰσιν οἱ οὐρανοί· αὐτοὶ ἀπολοῦνται). If they are going to perish, they cannot be part of the future dominion of the son and must be left out of the Ps 8 quotation if it is to be understood eschatologically. Crowning the son with glory and honor and placing him over works that will perish is inconsistent with the author's eschatology. The author of Hebrews is purposeful in building his argument with his use of the Old Testament.

An exclusively christological interpretation also marginalizes the references to other sons in 2:10–11 and 12:5–11 in their relationship to God and creation. The author makes it clear that those who are being sanctified are sons (2:10) and brothers of the Son (2:11–12). Additionally, it attaches little importance to the reference to God's unchanging purpose (6:17), a reference which appears to be a character issue. According to 6:13–18, God wanted to show Abraham that his purpose does not change *because* his character does not change. God is faithful to his word, specifically his word of promise. Considering the immutability of God's nature and purpose in light of the traditional interpretation of Ps 8 (looking back to Gen 1:26–28 and creation), a problem arises for those with a christological-only view of Hebrews' use of Ps 8. If God's purpose is unchanging, what happened to God's purpose for humanity at creation? Has it been completely abandoned? Furthermore, following the Ps 8 quote in 2:6b–8a, the author writes, "yet at present we do see everything subject to them"[34] (νῦν δὲ οὔπω ὁρῶμεν αὐτῷ τὰ πάντα ὑποτεταγμένα, 2:8b). This statement must denote humanity since the referents of the pronouns in 2:7 (αὐτόν) and 2:8 (αὐτοῦ and αὐτῷ)

---

superior to Moses *as son* (3:5–6), and superior to all other priests *as son* (7:28). The eschatological revelation of God is superior to the former revelation because Jesus is superior to prophets *as son* (1:1–2a).

34. Once again the NIV translation takes liberties by softening the translation of δὲ οὔπω (but not yet . . .) and translating the singular pronoun αὐτῷ with the plural "them."

are ἄνθρωπος³⁵/υἱὸς ἀνθρώπου.³⁶ The time is apparently coming in the about-to-be realm for all things to be subjected to *humanity*.³⁷ Simon Kistemaker makes the observation that "the conclusio [in 2:9] is introduced by τὸν δέ, *which at all times* [in Hebrews] *denotes a change of subject*."³⁸ Kistemaker asserts that the subject of 2:9, Jesus, is a different subject than αὐτῷ of 2:8.

If indeed the focus of Ps 8 in Heb 2:6–8 is humanity, then Jesus, the one who fulfills Ps 8, crowned with glory and honor, must be the representative human in view.³⁹ He is the one who realizes the eschatological destiny portrayed in the psalm. Furthermore, according to 2:10, he is the *pioneer* of the salvation of *many sons*, having led them into the same glory. Jesus has fulfilled, manifested, and inaugurated the realization of the destiny and purpose for humanity: Being crowned with glory and honor.

Jesus was crowned following the suffering of death which, according to 2:10, was part of his being perfected. The realization of the eschatological realm as presented in Ps 8 involves both the death and the coronation of the *pioneer* of many sons, the one who has been perfected *as son* (7:28).⁴⁰ The perfection of the son culminates in the crown of glory and honor—for this reason he has become superior to the angels (1:4).⁴¹ No longer is he lower

---

35. See Bruce, *Hebrews*, 75; Delitzsch, *Hebrews*, 1:108; Moffatt, *Critical*, 22–23; Westcott, *Hebrews*, 45. See also Boyd, "Sonship," 71.

36. Few scholars see the reference to "son of man" in 2:6b (the only use of the expression "son of man" in Hebrews) as being explicitly messianic. Most take it as a use of synonymous parallelism with ἄνθρωπος. This position is reinforced by the fact that "son of man" is embedded in an Old Testament quote and, although Ps 8:7 was understood by the first-century church as messianic as evidenced by its use in 1 Cor 15 and Eph 1, neither use incorporates the phrase "son of man." See Attridge, *Hebrews*, 71; Buchanan, *Hebrews*, 27; Cockerill, *Wesleyan*, 59; Hughes, *Commentary*, 85; Isaacs, *Hebrews*, 40; Koester, *Hebrews*, 215–16; Lane, *Hebrews*, 1:47; Mitchell, *Hebrews*, 65; Moffatt, *Hebrews*, 23; O'Brien, *Hebrews*, 95–96.

37. See Delitzsch, *Hebrews*, 108, 112, 113. Delitzsch writes, "God has destined man to be lord over all things, [and] this destination has not yet been realized in mankind in general ... The dominion [is] assigned (Ps. viii) by God to man [sic] ... our ultimate destination ... which [Jesus has] already entered Himself." See also De Wet, "Messianic," 116, 124–25; Keener, *Canonical*, 179; Leschert, *Foundations*, 107, 113–14; Pickup, "Midrashic," 363–65.

38. Kistemaker, *Psalm*, 105; italics mine.

39. See Caird, "Just Men," 89–103, esp. 93–94; Caird, "Son," 1:73–81, esp. 1:76–78; Hurst, "Christology," 151–64, esp. 152. Hurst writes of Caird that "he taught passionately that Heb. 2 points to the destiny of mankind [sic], which he also felt is the overall theme (2:5) of the epistle." See also Hurst, *Background*, 110–11.

40. The identity of the one in whom God has spoken eschatologically (1:2a), through the quotation of Ps 8, is that of "son." Only at 2:9 is the son revealed by name: Jesus. It is Jesus, *as son*, who is perfected (2:10). Cf. 5:8–9; 7:28.

41. It is noteworthy that 2:9 refers to τὸ πάθημα (singular) τοῦ θανάτου, yet in 2:10

than angels. The "little while" is over, and he has not only entered into the eschatological realm, but he has pioneered that way for many sons to follow.[42] He has reached the goal intended for humanity: Perfected sonship.[43]

The author appears to be suggesting that what God intended in the beginning, and the subject of reflection by the psalmist in Ps 8:5–7 (omitting 8:7a) regarding God's grace given to all of humanity, is sonship. The grace of God, which was initially referred to in the context of creation, is, in Jesus, presented as redemption (Heb 2:9; 9:12, 15[44]) and reformation (9:10). The Son reaches the destiny God intended for humanity from the beginning and leads other sons as pioneer of their salvation.[45]

If the proposed solution is correct, then the reference to the son being appointed by God as heir of all things (1:2) has more to do with reaching the purposed destiny of humanity than his unique and eternal position as the one and only Son of God. The son in whom God has spoken is appointed heir because he has pioneered and perfected the faith (12:2).[46] He has become son in the way God designed for humanity and, therefore, reaches the destiny God intended for humanity, becoming heir of all things as God purposed for humanity. The filial relationship God intended all along is what God spoke ἐν υἱῷ in the Christ-event, according to the author of Hebrews.[47]

Jesus is perfected διὰ παθημάτων (plural). This suggests the perfection takes place over a much larger span of life than the cross. Cf. 2:18; 5:7–9 (which also includes the plural ἀφ' ὧν ἔπαθεν).

42. The term "sons" is borne out of the text. No evidence exists of any gender exclusion among those of faith. The expression "sons and daughters" could just as easily be used, as it is in the NIV.

43. See Schenck, *Cosmology*, 51–77, esp. 71–72. Schenck writes, "In Hebrews, something is perfected when it has attained its appropriate status within the purposes of God . . . perfection is by definition final." See also Boyd, "Sonship," 129–46.

44. Note the connection in 9:15 between redemption (ἀπολύτρωσιν) and sonship (τὴν ἐπαγγελίαν τῆς αἰωνίου κληρονομίας) through the mediation of Christ in the new covenant (διαθήκης καινῆς μεσίτης ἐστίν). See Boyd, "Sonship," 194–97, for more.

45. The keys to understanding this reference to the destiny of humanity are found in 2:5 (the about-to-be realm), 2:6 (the inclusion of ἄνθρωπος in the quotation of Ps 8), and the temporal use of βραχύ τι interpreted as "for a little while" (2:7). See Kinzer, "All Things," 287–96. Kinzer concludes that the unique temporal use of Ps 8 by the writer of Hebrews is "ingenious" with respect to the eschatological destiny of humanity. It is clear, however, that it is only "sons" who realize this destiny, based in part on Heb 2:10–11. The sons of 2:10 follow their pioneer, Jesus, the son whom believers *see* crowned with glory and honor (2:9). See also France, "Expositor," 245–76, esp. 262.

46. Note the articular use of faith, τῆς πίστεως, coupled with the second use of ἀρχηγός (2:10; 12:2).

47. See Rissi, *Theologie*, 45. Rissi, in reference to 1:1–2, writes, "das Kommen des Sohnes den Unterschied der Zeiten der göttlichen Offenbarungen markiert. Im Unterschied zu den Offenbarungsträgern der Zeit vor seinem Erscheinen spricht Gott

Filiation is only perfected, however, because of the suffering of death (2:9). The destiny is reached through the perfect completion of the flesh and blood (2:14; 5:7) life of the son.

The realization of God's purpose for humanity is perfect sonship, crowned with glory and honor.[48] God has subjected the about-to-be realm to the perfected son, not to angels. Furthermore, the perfected son is the one who is leading other sons (his "brothers" according to 2:11–12) to that very destiny (2:10), the glory of perfected sonship, a new and living relationship with God as Father.

Sonship in the flesh is experienced in an arena where the son is *lower* than angels for a little while, yet *only* for a little while (βραχύ τι). The ultimate relationship that the eternal Son, who has taken on flesh, has entered into and inaugurated is perfected sonship. Sonship begun in the flesh must be completed in the flesh.[49] It must be perfected and reach the goal intended for the flesh. This kind of sonship is superior to angels, something God designed for the human and realized initially by Jesus, according to the author's use of Ps 8 in Heb 2:6–8 and his temporal interpretation of βραχύ τι. The perfected son realizes the destiny God planned for ἄνθρωποι (2:6–9) but only those who are referred to as πολλοὺς υἱούς (2:10)—those who follow their pioneer to glory—attain.[50] The statement that the human was made lower than angels for a little while (2:7) implies that inferiority to angels will not last *for the human*. The glory and honor of perfect sonship is the destiny God intends for humanity,[51] sonship that was pioneered and perfected in Jesus.

FINAL THOUGHTS

Hebrews' use of Ps 8 is instrumental in the author's "word of exhortation" (13:22). He encourages the recipients to persevere through the sufferings of this realm (2:18; 4:14–16; 10:32–39; 12:1–11) for a "little while," (cf. 2:7, 8) knowing that doing so will lead to the realm of glory and honor God

---

nun durch den Sohn, der nicht nur am Ursprung der Welt beteiligt ist als Mittler der Schöpfung, sondern auch an deren Ziel (1,2)." Rissi refers to the son participating in the realization of the *goal* of creation.

48. Along with the commentaries, see Boyd, "Sonship," 231; Caird, "Method," 44–51, esp. 49; Caird, "Just Men," 93; Gäbel, *Kulttheologie*, 137; Kögel, *Sohn*, 43; Vanhoye, *Situation*, 282–83.

49. See Boyd, "Sonship," 129–46 for more.

50. Sons are referred to as those being "set apart" by the Son (2:10–11), those perfected by the ἐφάπαξ offering of Jesus (10:14).

51. See Caird, "Method," 46; Caird, "Son," 73–81, esp. 77–78.

intended for humanity all along, the perfected filial relationship pioneered and perfected by Jesus (12:2). We presently "see" that realm realized in Jesus (2:9), the perfected son who, as the ontological Son of God (5:8), calls his brothers (2:11–12) to obedience (5:9) and to continue to persevere. The manifestation of Ps 8 through Jesus urged the original recipients to live in the reality of an accomplished yet about-to-be hope. However, it also encourages the present reader of the text to come to the Father with confidence (10:22; 4:14–16), to hold on to the now-visible hope without wavering (10:23; 2:9), and to live in close fraternal relationship with one another in Christian love (10:24–25), The promise that we do see realized in the perfected son is a promise set aside for God's children, a realm characterized by joy, and it makes us ask: What is the human that God should care for us, visit us, and crown us with the glory and honor of perfected sonship?

BIBLIOGRAPHY

Anderson, Gary A. "The Exaltation of Adam and the Fall of Satan." In *Literature on Adam & Eve: Collected Essays*, edited by Gary A. Anderson, Michael E. Stone, and Johannes Tromp, 83–110. Leiden: Brill, 2000.

Attridge, Harold W. *The Epistle to the Hebrews: A Commentary on the Epistle to the Hebrews*. Hermeneia. Philadelphia: Fortress, 1989.

Bauer, David R., and Robert A. Traina. *Inductive Bible Study: A Comprehensive Guide to the Practice of Hermeneutics*. Grand Rapids: Baker Academic, 2011.

Blomberg, Craig L. "'But We See Jesus': The Relationship between the Son of Man in Hebrews 2.6 and 2.9 and the Implications for English Translations." In *A Cloud of Witnesses: The Theology of Hebrews in its Ancient Contexts*, edited by Richard Bauckham et al., 88–99. London: T. & T. Clark, 2008.

Boyd, George R., Jr. "Sonship: Central Theological Motif and Unifying Theme of Hebrews." PhD diss., London School of Theology, 2012.

Braun, Herbert. *An die Hebräer*. HNT 14. Tübingen: Mohr/Siebeck, 1984.

Bruce, F. F. *The Epistle to the Hebrews*. Rev. ed. NICNT. Grand Rapids: Eerdmans, 1990.

Buchanan, George Wesley. *To the Hebrews: A New Translation with Introduction and Commentary*. AB 36. Garden City, NY: Doubleday, 1972.

Caird, George B. "The Exegetical Method of the Epistle to the Hebrews." *CJT* 5 (1959) 44–51.

———. "Just Men Made Perfect." *LQHR* 191 (1966) 89–98. Reprinted in *Resurrection and Immortality: Aspects of Twentieth-Century Christian Belief*, edited by Charles S. Duthie, 89–103. London: Bagster & Sons, 1979.

———. "Son by Appointment." In *The New Testament Age: Essays in Honor of Bo Reicke*, edited by William C. Weinrich, 1:73–81. Macon, GA: Mercer University Press, 1984.

Caneday, Ardel B. "The Eschatological World Already Subjected to the Son: The Οἰκουμένη of Hebrews 1:6 and the Son's Enthronement." In *A Cloud of Witnesses: The Theology of Hebrews in its Ancient Contexts*, edited by Richard Bauckham et al., 28–39. London: T. & T. Clark, 2008.

Chester, Andrew. *Messiah and Exaltation*. WUNT 207. Tübingen: Mohr/Siebeck, 2007.
Cockerill, Gareth Lee. *Hebrews: A Bible Commentary in the Wesleyan Tradition*. Indianapolis: Wesleyan, 1999.
———. *The Epistle to the Hebrews*. NICNT. Grand Rapids: Eerdmans, 2012.
Craigie, Peter C. *Psalms 1–50*. WBC 19. Waco, TX: Word, 1983.
De Wet, Chris L. "The Messianic Interpretation of Psalm 8:4–6 in Hebrews 2:6–9. Part II." In *Psalms and Hebrews: Studies in Reception*, edited by Dirk J. Human and Gert Jacobus Steyn, 113–25. New York: T. & T. Clark, 2010.
Delitzsch, Franz. *Commentary on the Epistle to the Hebrews*. Translated by Thomas L. Kingsbury. 2 vols. 1871. Repr., St. Paul: Klock & Klock, 1978.
deSilva, David A. *Perseverance in Gratitude: A Socio-Rhetorical Commentary on the Epistle "to the Hebrews."* Grand Rapids: Eerdmans, 2000.
Ellingworth, Paul. *The Epistle to the Hebrews: A Commentary on the Greek Text*. NIGTC. Grand Rapids: Eerdmans, 1993.
Evans, Craig A. *Noncanonical Writings and New Testament Interpretation*. Peabody, MA: Hendrickson, 1992.
France, R. T. "The Writer of Hebrews as a Biblical Expositor." *TynBul* 47 (1996) 245–76.
Gäbel, Georg. *Die Kulttheologie des Hebräerbriefes: Eine exegetisch-religionsgeschichtliche Studie*. WUNT 2/212. Tübingen: Mohr/Siebeck, 2006.
Gheorghita, Radu. *The Role of the Septuagint in Hebrews*. WUNT 2/160. Tübingen: Mohr/Siebeck, 2003.
Goldingay, John. *Psalms*. Vol. 1, *Psalms 1–41*. BCOT. Grand Rapids: Baker Academic, 2006.
Grogan, Geoffrey W. *Psalms*. THOTC. Grand Rapids: Eerdmans, 2008.
Guthrie, George H., and Russell D. Quinn. "A Discourse Analysis of the Use of Psalm 8:4–6 in Hebrews 2:5–9." *JETS* 49 (2006) 235–46.
Hahn, Scott W. *Kinship by Covenant: A Canonical Approach to the Fulfillment of God's Saving Promises*. New Haven: Yale University Press, 2009.
Hughes, Philip E. *A Commentary on the Epistle to the Hebrews*. Grand Rapids: Eerdmans, 1977.
Hurst, Lincoln D. "The Christology of Hebrews 1 and 2." In *The Glory of Christ in the New Testament: Studies in Christology*, edited by L. D. Hurst and N. T. Wright, 151–64. 1987. Repr., Oxford: Clarendon, 2002.
———. *The Epistle to the Hebrews: Its Background of Thought*. SNTSMS 65. 1990. Repr., Cambridge: Cambridge University Press, 2005.
Isaacs, Marie E. *Reading Hebrews and James: A Literary and Theological Commentary*. RNT. Macon, GA: Smyth & Helwys, 2002.
Johnson, Luke Timothy. *Hebrews: A Commentary*. NTL. Louisville: Westminster John Knox, 2006.
Karrer, Martin. *Der Brief an die Hebräer: Kapitel 1:1—5:10*. Gütersloh: Gütersloher, 2002.
Keener, Hubert James. *A Canonical Exegesis of the Eighth Psalm: YHWH's Maintenance of the Created Order through Divine Reversal*. JTISup 9. Winona Lake, Indiana: Eisenbrauns, 2013.
Kinzer, Mark Stephen. "'All Things Under His Feet': Psalm 8 in the New Testament and in Other Jewish Literature of Late Antiquity." PhD diss., University of Michigan, 1995.

Kistemaker, Simon J. *The Psalm Citations in the Epistle to the Hebrews.* Amsterdam: Van Soest, 1961.
Koester, Craig R. *Hebrews: A New Translation with Introduction and Commentary.* AB 36. Garden City, NY: Doubleday, 2001.
Kögel, Julius. *Der Sohn und die Söhne: Eine exegetische Studie zu Hebräer 2:5–18.* Gütersloh: Bertelsmann, 1904.
Kraus, Hans-Joachim. *Psalms 1–59.* CC. Minneapolis: Fortress, 1993.
Lane, William L. *Hebrews.* 2 vols. WBC 47A–B. Dallas: Word, 1991.
Lee, Aquila H. I. *From Messiah to Preexistent Son: Jesus' Self-Consciousness and Early Christian Exegesis of Messianic Psalms.* WUNT 2/192. Tübingen: Mohr/Siebeck, 2005.
Leschert, Dale F. *Hermeneutical Foundations of Hebrews: A Study in the Validity of the Epistle's Interpretation of Some Core Citations from the Psalms.* NABPRDS 10. Lewiston, NY: Mellen, 1994.
Louis, Conrad. *The Theology of Psalm 8: A Study of the Traditions of the Text and the Theological Import.* CUASST 99. Washington, DC: Catholic University of America Press, 1946.
Mackie, Scott D. *Eschatology and Exhortation in the Epistle to the Hebrews.* WUNT 2/223. Tübingen: Mohr/Siebeck, 2007.
Marshall, I. Howard. "Soteriology in Hebrews." In *The Epistle to the Hebrews and Christian Theology*, edited by Richard Bauckham et al., 253–77. Grand Rapids: Eerdmans, 2009.
März, Claus-Peter. "'... nur für kurze Zeit unter die Engel gestellt.' (Hebr 2,7): Anthropologie und Christologie in Hebr 2,5–9." In *Von Gott reden in säkularer Gesellschaft: Festschrift für Konrad Feiereis zum 65. Geburtstag,* edited by Emerich Coreth et al., 29–42. Leipzig: Benno, 1996. Reprinted in *Studien zum Hebräerbrief,* 81–96. Stuttgart: Katholisches Bibelwerk, 2005
Mason, Eric F. *"You Are a Priest Forever": Second Temple Jewish Messianism and the Priestly Christology of the Epistle to the Hebrews.* STDJ 74. Leiden: Brill, 2008.
McCruden, Kevin Barry. *Solidarity Perfected: Beneficent Christology in the Epistle to the Hebrews.* BZNW 159. Berlin: de Gruyter, 2008.
Mitchell, Alan C. *Hebrews.* SPS 13. Collegeville, MN: Liturgical, 2007.
Moffatt, James. *A Critical and Exegetical Commentary on the Epistle to the Hebrews.* ICC. 1924. Repr., Edinburgh: T. & T. Clark, 1952.
Mowinckel, Sigmund. *The Psalms in Israel's Worship.* Rev. ed. Grand Rapids: Eerdmans, 2004.
O'Brien, Peter T. *The Letter to the Hebrews.* PNTC. Grand Rapids: Eerdmans, 2010.
Pate, C. Marvin. *The Glory of Adam and the Affliction of the Righteous: Pauline Suffering in Context.* Lewiston, NY: Mellen, 1993.
Pickup, Martin. "New Testament Interpretation of the Old Testament: The Theological Rationale of Midrashic Exegesis." *JETS* 51 (2008) 353–81.
Pietersma, Albert. "Text-Production and Text-Reception: Psalm 8 in Greek." In *Die Septuaginta—Texte, Kontexte, Lebenswelten,* edited by Martin Karrer and Wolfgang Kraus, 487–501. Tübingen: Mohr/Siebeck, 2008.
Rascher, Angela. *Schriftauslegung und Christologie im Hebräerbrief.* BZNW 153. Berlin: de Gruyter, 2007.
Rhee, Victor (Sung-Yul). *Faith in Hebrews: Analysis within the Context of Christology, Eschatology and Ethics.* StBL 19. New York: Lang, 2001.

Rissi, Mathias. *Die Theologie des Hebräerbriefs: Ihre Verankerung in der Situation des Verfassers und seiner Leser.* WUNT 41. Tübingen: Mohr/Siebeck, 1987.

Schenck, Kenneth. *Cosmology and Eschatology in Hebrews: The Settings of the Sacrifice.* SNTSMS 143. Cambridge: Cambridge University Press, 2007.

Schunack, Gerd. *Der Hebräerbrief.* Zürich: Theologischer Zürich, 2002.

Steyn, G. J. "Some Observations about the Vorlage of Ps 8:5-7 in Heb 2:6-8." *VE* 24 (2003) 493-514.

Thompson, James Weldon. *Hebrews.* PCNT. Grand Rapids: Baker Academic, 2008.

Urassa, Wenceslaus Mkeni. *Psalm 8 and Its Christological Re-Interpretations in the New Testament Context: An Inter-Contextual Study in Biblical Hermeneutics.* Frankfurt: Lang, 1998.

Vanhoye, Albert. *Situation du Christ: Hébreux 1 et 2.* Paris: Cerf, 1969.

Westcott, Brooke Foss. *The Epistle to the Hebrews: The Greek Text with Notes and Essays.* 3rd ed. 1889. Repr., London: Macmillan, 1920.

Westfall, Cynthia Long. *A Discourse Analysis of the Letter to the Hebrews: The Relationship between Form and Meaning.* LNTS 297. London: T. & T. Clark, 2005.

Whitlark, Jason A. *Enabling Fidelity to God: Perseverance in Hebrews in Light of the Reciprocity Systems of the Ancient Mediterranean World.* Colorado Springs: Paternoster, 2008.

Witherington, Ben, III. *Letters and Homilies for Jewish Christians: A Socio-Rhetorical Commentary on Hebrews, James and Jude.* Downers Grove, IL: IVP Academic, 2007.

Zuntz, G. *The Text of the Epistles: A Disquisition Upon the Corpus Paulinum: The Schwiech Lectures of the British Academy 1946.* Oxford: Oxford University Press, 1953.

2

"Let us draw near . . . but not too near"

A Critique of the Attempted Distinction between "Drawing Near" and "Entering" in Hebrews' Entry Exhortations

SCOTT D. MACKIE

THE EPISTLE TO THE Hebrews is renowned for both its inspired novelties and its interpretative quandaries. Examples of the former include the mysterious Melchizedek who surfaces in chapter seven, the high priest Christology which dominates chapters 7–10, the curious blend of Platonic metaphysics and Jewish apocalypticism, and the dramatized voicing of scripture by the triune God. The two most important interpretative *desiderata* involve determining the nature of the author's metaphysical thought-world and the provenance of his high priest Christology. Given these many attention-grabbing novelties and seemingly insolvable interpretive tasks, it should come as no surprise that many interpreters underemphasize (and sometimes even overlook) the actual intent of this self-proclaimed "word of exhortation": to encourage a small community of embattled and weary early Christians to persevere in their commitment to Jesus. As might be expected, the author's primary hortatory solution to this crisis of commitment is also inadequately appreciated: the community will find the strength and resolve to persevere in their commitment by "drawing near" to Jesus in the heavenly sanctuary (4:14–16; 10:19–23).

It was my great pleasure to find Gary Cockerill's recent commentary on Hebrews so fully focused on the author's main intent. In fact, as I noted in my review, Gary repeatedly emphasizes both the pastoral purpose of this self-confessed "word of exhortation," as well as its emotional and suasory power.[1] Throughout, the author is referred to as "the pastor," whose "sermon" evinces "consummate skill" in its passionate appeal to "the faltering people of God," who are "beleaguered and humiliated," "intimidated," and whose "own suffering corresponds to Christ's."[2] Moreover, this sermon seeks to bring "encouragement to believers suffering the rejection and the shame heaped upon them by an unbelieving world."[3] Conversely, it issues a "warning to believers of every age" who are "pressured by rejection from the unbelieving world and enticed by its offer of immediate, though temporary, gratification."[4]

My greatest pleasure, however, was derived from Gary's insightful handling of Hebrews' rich experiential soteriology. And of these experiential elements, Gary places the greatest emphasis on the author's exhortations to "draw near" to Jesus in the heavenly sanctuary. Thus, Gary notes that the pastor's "primary picture of the situation of its readers is as the people of God entering his presence."[5] This intimate and immanent access is "vital because life in God's presence is the essence, means, and end" of the community's "existence"; in fact, it "encompasses the entire orientation of the life of faith."[6] Drawing near and accessing God in the heavenly sanctuary represents the "polar opposite" of the community's greatest threat, a "willful persistence in neglect of what Christ has provided."[7] This access to God is "intimately related" to the community's most urgent need, perseverance, since "drawing near to God through Christ is the means of perseverance."[8]

---

1. Mackie, "Review."

2. Cockerill, *Hebrews*, 3, 8, 11–16, 134–38, 252–53, 347, 462–63, 489–90, 505, 586–87, 603, 647, 663, 702. Gary's comments on 6:11 ("But we yearn for each of you to demonstrate the same zeal for full assurance of faith until the end") are illustrative: "Nothing shows the writer's pastoral heart like the intensity of longing revealed in this verse" (282). An extended demonstration of Gary's perceptive grasp of Hebrews' powers of persuasion can be found in his discussion of 10:26–39 (481–514). Hebrews' literary virtues are also well appreciated, with a fine example occurring in Gary's treatment of 11:32–38: "The very meandering style that the pastor has adopted for this section communicates the homeless wandering of those described" (594).

3. Ibid., 165.

4. Ibid., 277.

5. Ibid., 6.

6. Ibid., 472, 476.

7. Ibid., 484–85.

8. Ibid., 476. Gary elsewhere contends that "drawing near" offers both the "reason and resource for perseverance" (383).

Gary helpfully distinguishes between "two types of imagery" used "to describe the place where God's people enter his presence. When he is urging them to persevere . . . he uses Promised Land language," including "rest," "homeland," and "City." When Hebrews exhorts the community "to draw near in the present so that they can receive grace for perseverance, he speaks of the Most Holy Place."[9] This extraordinary hortatory motif is also repeatedly enlisted in Hebrews' dialectic of superiority/inferiority. Gary insists "faithful believers" enjoy a level of "direct access to God" that "was not available before Christ," even for the Levitical high priests.[10] Thus, believers "have 'authorization' of the 'entryway' into the very presence of God. The way to God that was not even revealed under the old system (cf. 9:8) is now fully open to the people of God. God's own enter freely and continuously . . . They need not 'slink' into his presence."[11]

Gary's keen and comprehensive focus on Hebrews' ultimate hortatory goal should come as no surprise, however, given his own effusive testimonies of the "pastor's" power to inspire and exhort him to greater levels of devotion to Jesus and deeper dimensions of intimacy with God. As those who know him will attest, Gary freely and emotionally testifies to profound transformative encounters with our great high priest, encounters which occurred in the course of his (nearly) life-long study of Hebrews. A true Wesleyan, Gary has obviously *lived in* and *from* this remarkable inspired text. His example has been an inspiration to me and it was with pleasure that I accepted this opportunity to contribute to this much-deserved *Festschrift*!

In this present work, then, I will address a common misinterpretation connected with the two most important verbs that are used in conjunction with Hebrews' theology of access and entry: προσέρχομαι ("to draw near") and εἰσέρχομαι ("to enter"). A number of scholars, including John M. Scholer, Marie E. Isaacs, Hermut Löhr, and David A. deSilva, contend that the author of Hebrews maintains a careful and deliberate distinction between these terms, with προσέρχομαι representing "drawing near," and εἰσέρχομαι reflecting actual "entry" into the inner sanctum of heavenly sanctuary.[12]

9. Ibid., 197.
10. Ibid., 327, 372.
11. Ibid., 466. Gary also repeatedly correlates soteriological benefits and life-giving access: cf. ibid., 17, 77–79, 143, 149, 197, 224–26, 228, 269–72, 291, 362–63, 443, 452.
12. Scholer, *Proleptic Priests*, 11, 144–45, 149, 201; Isaacs, *Sacred Space*, 219; Löhr, *Umkehr und Sünde*, 269; deSilva, "Entering God's Rest," 28; deSilva, *Perseverance*, 337. Johnson (*Hebrews*, 131, 139) believes the entry terminology, when applied to believers, represents not an "entry" into a "physical-spatial reality," but an "internal, moral transformation of persons." When applied to Jesus, however, it denotes "the full and ontological entry of the human Jesus, through his resurrection . . . and his exaltation . . . into the power and glory that are proper to God."

More specifically, for Scholer, προσέρχομαι denotes the "proleptic," "incomplete," and "preliminary access into the holy of holies" which is the province of the "living," while εἰσέρχομαι describes the full access "afforded those who have died."[13] In this "thoughtful and intentional distinction," the preliminary access denoted by προσέρχομαι will be eventually "superseded by a still future and greater access," indicated by εἰσέρχομαι.[14] While Scholer primarily focuses on the differing spheres of access attained by living and dead "saints," Isaacs instead contrasts the access attained by believers with that of Jesus. Near the conclusion of her monograph on Hebrews' "theology of access," she contends that προσέρχομαι represents "the language of approach rather than attainment. Only Jesus has entered (εἰσέρχομαι, 6:20; 9:12, 24, 25) the presence of God. As yet for the people of God that entry remains in the future (4:1, 3, 4, 9)."[15]

Though this distinction between προσέρχομαι and εἰσέρχομαι seems both exegetically sound and theologically well-reasoned, ultimately it fails to withstand close scrutiny for at least three reasons:

(1) The author's hortatory goals and suasory logic typically are not adequately appraised, and often they are even ignored. For example, far from making a strong distinction between the community's access and that attained by Jesus, Hebrews instead repeatedly exhorts the community to mimetically replicate Jesus' entry into the heavenly sanctuary (cf. 2:9–10; 4:14–16; 6:19–20; 10:19–23).[16] Furthermore, the verbal and oral/aural "confessional" goals of the two main entry exhortations (4:14–16; 10:19–23) require and even demand that the community occupy a position "within earshot" of God and his Son. Their expected confession represents both an affirmation of Jesus' sonship, and a reciprocal acknowledgement of the Son's prior conferral of family membership on the community (2:12–13).[17] It is truly a family-creating act of "saying the same things" (ὁμο-λογία) that Jesus has said to the community. However, this twice repeated and clearly stated

---

13. Scholer, *Proleptic Priests*, 11; cf. also 149, 183, 201.

14. Ibid., 11, 201. Cf. Löhr, *Umkehr und Sünde*, 269: "Umgekehrt wird von den Addressaten ein 'Hinzugetretensein' . . . ausgesagt, nicht jedoch ein 'Eingetretensein.'"

15. Isaacs, *Sacred Space*, 219. DeSilva ("Entering God's Rest," 28) similarly distinguishes between the approach of the community and the full entry of Jesus.

16. See, e.g., Thompson (*Hebrews*, 30) who notes that the community is "consistently invited to follow where Jesus has gone (4:14–16; 10:19–23; 12:1–2)" (cf. also 73, 76–77, 114, 140).

17. On this confession of Jesus' sonship and its hortatory significance, see my essays, "Confession of the Son of God in Hebrews," 114–29; "Confession of the Son of God in the Exordium of Hebrews," 437–53; and my monograph, *Eschatology and Exhortation*, 223–30.

hortatory goal would be frustrated if the alleged προσέρχομαι-εἰσέρχομαι distinction was indeed valid.

(2) The immediate context in which the verbs occur is often inadequately evaluated. Thus, the thoroughgoing emphasis on a full and confident entry in 10:19–23, which is based on profound architectural, psychological, and mystical/experiential changes effected by Jesus' high priestly accomplishment, is severely attenuated by appeal to a dubious reading of one word, προσέρχομαι.

(3) The author's overarching imagery, particularly his depiction of the cultic and regnal aspects of the heavenly sanctuary/throne room, is not accorded an appropriate level of prominence in the discussion.[18] Instead, his often sparse and suggestive imagery is suffocated and supplanted by cultic architectural imagery imported from more elaborately detailed OT texts. These cultic texts, which use προσέρχομαι in their LXX translations, are then forced back on the context of the entry exhortations in Hebrews, warping their intended shape. It is surely significant that the cultic sacrifices of Leviticus are generally depicted as entirely "speech-less" acts.[19] Given the prominence of aural/oral elements in Hebrews' entry exhortations, more appropriate LXX texts should then be sought, texts which use προσέρχομαι to represent the attainment of communicative and relational proximity to the deity.

As we will see, these three issues will recur, and somewhat overlap, in our discussions of the three most significant occurrences of προσέρχομαι (4:14–16; 10:19–23; 12:22–24), and the one pertinent use of εἰσέρχομαι (6:19–20).[20]

---

18. On the author's use of visually oriented rhetorical techniques to stir the community's visual imagination, and thus encourage their substantive participation in his hortatory program, see my essay, "Heavenly Sanctuary Mysticism," 77–117; esp. 99–116.

19. In Lev 5:5 a "confession of guilt" is required before bringing a prescribed offering to the priest; however, this confession is not explicitly directed toward God. On the Day of Atonement Aaron "confesses all the iniquities and transgressions of the sons of Israel" over the scapegoat, thereby "laying them on the head of the goat" (Lev 16:21). Though this act is to be performed "before the Lord" (16:10), communication with God does not appear to be occurring, or intended to occur.

20. Two additional occurrences of προσέρχομαι, in 7:25 and 11:6, are not treated in this essay. Though these texts focus on access to God, their brevity and relatively undeveloped hortatory implications limit their relevance to the discussion.

ΠΡΟΣΕΡΧΟΜΑΙ IN HEBREWS 4:14-16

> Therefore, because we have a great high priest who has gone through the heavens, Jesus, the Son of God, let us hold firmly to our confession. For we do not have a high priest who is unable to sympathize with our weaknesses, but we have one who has been tempted in every way, just as we are, yet without sin. Therefore, let us approach [προσερχώμεθα] the throne of grace with confidence, so that we may receive mercy and find grace to help us in time of need.[21]

Though Scholer contends that "every occurrence of προσέρχεσθαι has its setting within a cultic context," this text offers an almost perfect "50/50 blend" of cultic and regnal elements.[22] After surprisingly connecting Jesus' exaltation to both of his two primary christological titles, High Priest and Son of God, the author neatly folds together descriptions of Jesus' high priestly and divine qualifications, attainments, and compassionate disposition.[23] Furthermore, the architectural details of the tabernacle have been "altered," as the heavenly sanctuary's altar has been unexpectedly replaced with a regnal "throne of grace."[24] Since this "throne of grace" is obviously occupied, an instance of metonymy is intended. Thus, the "throne" *itself* does not impersonally dispense grace and mercy, rather the *person* seated on it, Jesus "the Son of God," is the one dispenses the salvific benefits of grace and mercy "in times of need."[25] And far from making a distinction between the community's level of access and that attained by Jesus, as Isaacs contends, the author instead encourages a mimetic replication of Jesus' full and con-

---

21. Here, and in the introductory quotations of 6:18-20, 10:19-23, and 12:22-24, I follow the translations offered in Gary's commentary. Unless otherwise noted, all other translations are my own.

22. Scholer, *Proleptic Priests*, 11.

23. It is surely significant that Scholer fails to include the phrase, "Jesus, the Son of God," whenever he quotes or paraphrases 4:14 (cf. ibid., 104, 106). Perhaps even more egregious: his lengthy discussion of 4:14-16 contains only one mention of that all-important title (106) and never once considers its implications (103-13; cf. also 193).

24. Scholer's (ibid., 104-6) discussion of the divine throne only briefly considers its regnal implications, i.e., as symbolizing the place where God reigns as king.

25. In my article, "Ancient Jewish Mystical Motifs," I contend that Hebrews deliberately transforms and re-purposes a number of motifs found in ancient Jewish visionary accounts of the heavenly throne room, so as to encourage the community's substantive entry into the heavenly sanctuary. These formerly fearful and repelling motifs—which in addition to the throne of God include the temple veil, the glory of God, and participation in angelic worship—are reconfigured by Hebrews so as to encourage and facilitate the community's full entry into the heavenly throne room, where they are welcomed into the immediate presence of God and his Son.

fident entry into the heavenly sanctuary, a mimetic pursuit which is found in a number of other texts, including 2:9–10; 4:14–16; 6:19–20; 10:19–23; 12:1–4.[26]

The principal point of this text's imagery, and the even more significant hortatory goal of the larger context (i.e., 3:1—4:11), however, is the attainment of a sufficiently close communicative and relational proximity to the sympathetic figure seated on the throne. The attainment of this proximity will then afford the divine impartation of the transformative benefits which will evoke and sustain perseverance. The putative imagery of the community passing through architectural "checkpoints" and eventually hoping to address an empty, impersonal throne (though at safe remove) is incorrect and insufficient from a hortatory and soteriological standpoint. This misinterpretation, in fact, would more closely adhere to Josephus's description of the holy of holies, rather than Heb 4:14–16. The "holy of holies," according to Josephus, is an "innermost recess . . . screened . . . from the outer section by a veil. In this innermost recess stood nothing whatsoever, unapproachable and inviolable, invisible to all" (*J.W.* 5.219).

A host of LXX texts that employ either προσέρχομαι or access imagery, and which occasionally blend cultic and regnal imageries, can be appealed to as illuminating the imagery attending Heb 4:14–16. In these LXX texts, however, the primary point is not the temple architecture, and thus the attainment of full entry into holy of holies. Rather, the principal point is the attainment of communicative and relational proximity to God, regardless of geographic context. Thus, in Exod 16:9–10, the "grumbling" Israelites are commanded to "draw near before God [προσέλθατε ἐναντίον τοῦ θεοῦ], for he has heard your grumblings." The "whole congregation of the sons of Israel" then "turned toward the wilderness and the glory of the Lord appeared in the cloud." The community's complaints are then addressed through the miraculous provision of life-sustaining manna (16:12–21). Following the sacrificial inauguration of the Sinai covenant, Exod 24:9–11 recounts a celebratory meal enjoyed in God's immediate presence. Though προσέρχομαι is not used in this context, the imagery of approach and close communion is prominent. Moses, Aaron, Nadab, Abihu, and seventy elders "went up" (ἀνέβη) Mt. Sinai, and in this "close encounter of the visual kind," this large group "saw the place where the God of Israel stood." Though this was a potentially dangerous "close encounter," "not a single one of the elect ones of Israel perished." Rather, they gazed upon God as they safely "ate and drank" in his presence.

---

26. Isaacs, *Sacred Space*, 219. I discuss this mimetic aspect of Hebrews' hortatory agenda in my forthcoming essay, "Visually Oriented Rhetoric."

Similarly, the imagery of approach and close communicative communion is ascribed to Moses, in his role as Israel's mediator, in the Deuteronomist's account of the events following the giving of the decalogue. In this account, προσέρχομαι is used to emphasize the immanence attained by Moses, as he reminds the Israelites, that at Sinai,

> when you heard the voice from the midst of the fire, while the mountain was burning with fire, you came near to me, all the heads of your tribes and your councils. You said, "Behold, the Lord our God has shown us his glory, and we have heard his voice from the midst of the fire. On this day we have seen that God speaks with humans, yet they live ... who has heard the voice of the living God ... as we have, and remained alive? Go near [πρόσελθε] and hear all that the Lord our God says, then tell us whatever the Lord our God tells you, for we will listen and do it." And the Lord heard the sound of your words when you spoke to me, and the Lord said to me: "I have heard the sound of the words of this people ... all that they have spoken is correct. Who shall grant a heart in them that will fear me and to always obey all my commandments, so that it might go well with them and with their children forever!" (Deut 5:23–29)

Furthermore, Lev 9 recounts a sacrificial/cultic "close and communicative encounter" between the Lord and the Israelites, one which issues in a vision of God and the impartation of a divine "blessing" upon the people. Most significantly, God twice disregards the "rules and restrictions" of the tabernacle architecture in his desire to manifest his glory to the "whole congregation." After "summoning ... Aaron and his sons and the elders of Israel," Moses told Aaron, "offer before the Lord" a "calf for a sin offering and a ram for a whole burnt offering ... for today the Lord will be seen in your midst." The "whole congregation" then "drew near and stood before the Lord" (προσῆλθεν πᾶσα συναγωγὴ καὶ ἔστησαν ἔναντι κυρίου) and "Moses said, 'This is the thing that the Lord has spoken. Do it, and the Lord's glory will be seen in your midst.' Then Moses said to Aaron, 'Draw near [πρόσελθε] to the altar and sacrifice ... and make atonement for yourself ... and for the people ... as the Lord has commanded.' Aaron drew near [προσῆλθεν] to the altar," and after offering the sacrifices which were commanded, he "lifted his hands toward the people and blessed them." Thereafter "Moses and Aaron entered the tent of testimony, and when they came out, they blessed all the people; and the Lord's glory appeared to all the people. Fire came out from the Lord and consumed everything on the altar ... all the people saw it, were amazed, and fell on their faces."

Finally, after circumcising "the whole nation" and celebrating Passover, Josh 5:13–15 recounts a "close and communicative encounter" between Joshua and "the captain of the Lord's host." Joshua "looked up with his eyes and saw a man standing before him with his sword drawn in his hand." Despite the fearful prospect raised by the "drawn sword," Joshua responded by immediately and confidently "drawing near" (προσελθών) to the armed man, and brusquely asking him, "Are you one of us or are you with our adversaries?" The "armed man" replied,

> "Neither; but as commander of the army of the Lord I have now come." And Joshua fell on his face to the earth and said to him, "Master, what do you command your servant?" The commander of the army of the Lord said to Joshua, "Loosen your sandals from your feet, for the place on which you stand is holy."

With these LXX texts informing our reading of Heb 4:14–16, a fruitful examination of this latter text's hortatory goals can now be offered. The attainment of close proximity to Jesus and God in the divine throne is commended with the exhortation "draw near with confidence/boldness" (μετὰ παρρησίας, 4:16). Like Joshua, their approach is not "halting, with fear and trepidation." Most significantly, an oral/aural outcome to the approach is twice stated: "let us hold firmly to our confession," and "let us approach the throne of grace . . . so that we may receive mercy and find grace to help us in time of need." This pair of hortatory subjunctives clearly indicates that God and his Son are within earshot of the worshippers who have drawn near. Like the God who "hears" the "grumblings" of the people (Exod 16:8–9, 12) and who acknowledges that he "has heard the sound of the words of this people which they have spoken" (Deut 5:28), and the communicative interactions of the "commander of the army of the Lord" with Joshua (Josh 5:13–15), the community addressed by Hebrews can be certain that God and his Son hear their "confession" and requests for "mercy" and "grace" in "times of need" (4:14, 16). Furthermore, like Joshua and Moses, "boldness" (παρρησία) characterizes their speech (as well as their approach).[27]

Entirely misguided is the idea that the community has come to a place resembling the dystopian bureaucracy of Terry Gilliam's film, *Brazil* (1985), a place where hopeless requests are repeatedly lodged in a dizzying variety of offices, offered in vain to a host of disinterested bureaucrats. Such a world might be inferred from an astonishing assertion made by Scholer:

---

27. On the bivalence of παρρησία, as characterizing both the "bold speech" and "confident approach" of the community, see my monograph, *Eschatology and Exhortation*, 228–29, and Weiss, *Hebräer*, 53, 251–53, 298.

"the readers are not yet in direct contact with the Lord."[28] A comparable bureaucracy appears to be envisaged by Craig R. Koester, who contends (while discussing 7:25) that "for a person to approach God 'through' Jesus means that he or she lodges a request with Jesus, trusting that he will bring it before God for a favorable response."[29] Though Hebrews fails to fully "map out" the seating arrangements of the throne room, it is explicitly stated in 1:13 that God is present there, standing or sitting beside Jesus' throne, as God has invited his Son to "Sit at my right hand" (cf. 10:13). Any requests made before the divine throne(s), therefore, are audible to both divine personages, rendering unnecessary any imagined bureaucratic relay of requests and responses. Moreover, the author all but guarantees a sympathetic and empowering response: "we do not have a high priest who is unable to sympathize with our weaknesses, but we have one who has been tempted in all ways, just as we are, yet without sin. Therefore, let us therefore approach the throne of grace with boldness, so that we may receive mercy and find grace to help us in times of need" (4:15–16).

ΠΡΟΣΕΡΧΟΜΑΙ IN HEBREWS 10:19-23

> Therefore, brothers and sisters, since we have authorization for entrance into the Most Holy Place, by means of the blood of Jesus, an entrance which he inaugurated for us, a way new and living through the veil, that is, [through] his flesh, and since we have a Great Priest over the house of God, let us keep drawing near [προσερχώμεθα] with true hearts in fullness of faith, having allowed our hearts to be sprinkled from an evil conscience and our bodies to be washed with pure water. Let us hold the confession of our hope firm, for the One who has promised is faithful.

In his most elaborate entry exhortation, the author of Hebrews emphasizes the architectural, psychological, and mystical/experiential changes effected by Jesus' high priestly accomplishment, changes which wholly function to promote and evoke the community's confident and substantive entry into

---

28. Scholer, *Proleptic Priests*, 144. This comment is offered while commenting on 12:22–24, and is based on his reading of 12:10–17: the divine discipline the community is presently experiencing would be presumably unnecessary if they had really "arrived" at the "heavenly Jerusalem."

29. Koester, *Hebrews*, 365. Admittedly, a "bureaucratic" process can be potentially surmised from Heb 7:25: "[H]e is able comprehensively to save those who draw near [προσερχομένους] to God through him, since he always lives to make intercession for them."

the "most holy place." (1) *Architectural* changes abound in this text, as the community has received divine "authorization" (παρρησία) to make use of an "entrance" (εἴσοδος), and follow "a new and living path" (ὁδός) which has been "inaugurated," one which ultimately passes "through the veil," and into the most holy place (10:19–20). It is surely significant that this text, which provides the most architectural detail of the entry exhortations, singularly and forcefully utilizes this wealth of architectural detail to convince the community of their ability to freely and confidently access God and his Son in the heavenly sanctuary. (2) *Psychological* transformations are also prominent. The community has previously enjoyed and is presently experiencing a sanctifying "sprinkling" (ῥαντίζω) of their "innermost beings" (καρδία) "from an evil conscience" (ἀπὸ συνειδήσεως πονηρᾶς), and a "washing" (λούω) of their "bodies with pure water" (10:22).[30] The profundity and novelty of these psychological transformations, and the aforementioned architectural changes, are most readily apparent when one compares them with the psychological trauma and architecturally-enforced limitations experienced by "Enoch" in his throne vision: after being commanded by God to "draw near," Enoch (who "until now was on" his "face, prostrate, and trembling") was "lifted up," by either God or an angel, and carried to the doorway leading to the divine throne room. His heavenly journey finds its terminus in that doorway, as the radiant and repellent glory of God disallows all but a few angels closer access (*1 En.* 14.24–25). (3) Finally, as I have previously argued, the *mystical/experiential* effects delineated in 10:22 are of preeminent importance to the success of this whole exhortation. The author's descriptions of these cultic soteriological experiences, therefore, must be entirely consonant with the community's own experiences of them, or this most important entry exhortation will fall flat, perceived by the community as either rhetorical flourish or wishful thinking.[31] The author's awareness of this "all or nothing" hortatory gamble is readily apparent, as he connects the climax of this entry exhortation, "let us draw near," directly with the community's past and ongoing experiences of a decisively cleansed heart and conscience (10:22). It is doubtful that a rhetor as adept as the author of Hebrews would wager the success of his entire "word of exhortation," unless he was convinced that these transformative cleansings were experientially verifiable by the community.

In addition to these architectural, psychological, and mystical transformations, this text also commends a mimetic replication of Jesus' entry

---

30. Heb 10:14 similarly characterizes the community as "those who are presently being sanctified" (ἁγιαζομένους) by Jesus.

31. On this, see my essays, "Heavenly Sanctuary Mysticism," 84–87; "Eschatological Experience," 93–114, esp. 112.

into the heavenly sanctuary. The more suggestive account offered in 6:17–20 of the community's ability to mimetically follow Jesus' passage "through the veil" is now augmented by a clearer affirmation: "we have authorization for entrance into the Most Holy Place, by means of the blood of Jesus, an entrance which he inaugurated for us, a way new and living through the veil" (10:19–20).

As we have seen, this text almost approaches excess in its repeated and diverse affirmations of the community's ability to access God in the most holy place. Moreover, the author's previous reminders of the frustrated and futile "approach" of the high priest in the tabernacle/Temple (9:6–14, 25; 10:1–4) were surely intended to heighten the impact of these abundant affirmations of confident and full access. In fact, a number of elements in 10:19–23 constitute the climax of an overarching "comparative critique" (*synkrisis*) which persuasively contrasts the frustrated and futile entry of the high priest with the confident access presently enjoyed by the community: (1) It is a "new [πρόσφατος] and living [ζάω] pathway," and completely unlike the old path, which had the potential to lead to an ignominious destruction, as Nadab and Abihu discovered, this new path is not a path fraught with life-threatening dangers. Of particular interest to the present discussion is the cause of Nadab and Abihu's demise, as described by Lev 16:1: "The Lord spoke to Moses after the death of the two sons of Aaron, when they drew [too] near before the Lord and died."[32] (2) That a "confident" and "authorized" (παρρησία, 10:19) approach is commended further serves the author's primary point: an attitude of fear and the need to maintain a reverent distance from God in the holy place are no longer necessary. (3) That Jesus has "inaugurated" (ἐγκαινίζω, 10:20) the many architectural transformations he engineered and constructed further serves the author's intended old/new contrast. (4) Finally, and perhaps of greatest significance, is the fact that this "path" passes "through the veil" (διὰ τοῦ καταπετάσματος, 10:20), the final and most significant architectural barrier in the tabernacle/Temple.[33] The community's actual presence in the heavenly sanctuary therefore represents the irrefutable proof and rhetorical climax of the author's comparative critique. Moreover, the access experienced by the community must qualitatively supersede that of the Jewish cultus. The often-encountered contention that the entry terminology refers metaphorically to prayer or worship, or represents an "imaginal" and/or "spiritualized" entry, is altogether inad-

---

32. Anderson, "'Nadab and Abihu,'" 11. Anderson notes that the ignominious end of Aaron's sons vividly illustrates the fact that "every approach to the altar constitutes a potential danger" (16).

33. On the veil in ancient Jewish traditions, see my essay, "Ancient Jewish Mystical Motifs," 93–95.

equate when contrasted with the vivid and tangible cultic experience of the tabernacle/temple priests (9:1–10, 18–21; 10:1–4).[34]

As should now be apparent, allowing a tendentious reading of a single word, προσέρχομαι, to smother out these profuse affirmations of the community's full access to the most holy place is exegetically unsound and represents a failure to appreciate the significance of not only the author's comparative critique but also his primary hortatory agenda. An oral outcome to the approach is strategically located at the conclusion of this entry exhortation: "let us hold the confession of our hope firm." This aural/oral outcome assumes that the community has approached close enough to speak with God and his Son, and so confess their commitment to Jesus, as God's Son, and affirm their membership in the family of God. This confession, so enacted, represents the author's ultimate hortatory goal.[35]

Despite the apparent reservations of those circumscribing the extent of this approach, we can be sure that the author does not intend that this entry exhortation would be misconstrued by the community as inviting and authorizing a "total immersion expedition" into the holy of holies, one involving a "hands-on encounter" with the accoutrements of that most holy place, e.g., climbing up on and swinging from the wings of the cherubim, popping open the lid of the ark and having a nibble of some manna, playing "sorcerer's apprentice" with Aaron's rod, and perhaps cracking off a souvenir chip from the two tablets.[36] The author has other goals for the community's substantive and full entry, clear goals that cohere with his overarching hortatory agenda: to enact the community's faith-filled commitment to Jesus and inspire dogged perseverance in an adverse and sometimes hostile environment.

---

34. Among those who believe that the entry exhortations represent metaphors for prayer and worship are: Rissi, *Theologie*, 97; Scholer, *Proleptic Priests*, 11, 107–8, 111–12, 127–28, 144, 182–83; Löhr, *Umkehr und Sünde*, 253; deSilva, *Perseverance in Gratitude*, 329; Koester, "God's Purposes," 372; Thompson, *Hebrews*, 105.

35. That the community's confession centers on Jesus' sonship, and occurs in a familial context, the "household of God" (οἶκον τοῦ θεοῦ, 10:21), serves to slightly attenuate the predominant cultic imagery of 10:19–23.

36. The original draft of this essay also mentioned "cooking a burger on the altar of incense, bunching up the veil into a rope and using it to swing onto the cherubim, planting a listening device under the throne (so as to keep abreast of the 'goings on' in the throne room) . . ." These additional details were deemed excessive and omitted from the final version of this essay.

ΠΡΟΣΕΡΧΟΜΑΙ IN HEBREWS 12:22-24:

> But you have come [προσεληλύθατε] to Mount Zion, and to the City of the living God, heavenly Jerusalem, and to myriads of angels, a festal gathering, and to the assembly of the firstborn enrolled in heaven, and to a judge who is God of all, and to the spirits of righteous persons made perfect, and to the Mediator of the New Covenant, Jesus, and to blood of sprinkling that speaks better than Abel.

In this triumphant announcement of the community's present and full access (προσεληλύθατε, perfect tense) to God and his Son in the heavenly realm, an oral/aural outcome is evident a third time. The worshippers have drawn near enough to hear the "blood of sprinkling that speaks better than Abel." It is also surely significant that they are close enough to "hear" the "speaking blood" over the exuberant praise emanating from the "festal gathering of innumerable angels." Moreover, the community's participation in the aforementioned angelic praise can be easily imagined.[37]

Most significantly, it is in this text, which *presently* places the recipients in the immediate proximity of dead saints, that Scholer's alleged distinction between living and dead saints comes to ruin.[38] The futility of his attempted distinction is apparent in his assertion that "the assembly of the firstborn who are enrolled in heaven" (12:23) refers to "dead Christians," while "the spirits of the righteous made perfect" (12:24) represents "the deceased Old Testament faithful."[39] That Hebrews would carefully differentiate between these two groups of deceased saints in this manner is highly improbable, especially given the extent of his recent effort at closely linking the entire Christian community with the OT saints (11:1–12:4). Those saints, who all lived "by faith," are figured as a "cloud of witnesses" that "surrounds" the community, observing and cheering for them as they run their race of faith (12:1-2). Though Scholer claims that "the current earthly predicament of living saints excludes them from this festal assembly in heaven," it is much more probable that "the assembly [ἐκκλησία] of the firstborn who are enrolled in heaven" (12:23) refers to the community, who, *because* of the gravity of their "current earthly predicament," are emphatically and explicitly described as "having entered" (προσεληλύθατε) this heavenly milieu.[40] As I

---

37. On this, see my "Ancient Jewish Mystical Motifs," 99–103.
38. Cf. Scholer, *Proleptic Priests*, 11, 144, 149, 201.
39. Ibid., 146–47.
40. Ibid., 147. Cf. also 107, 112, 144, 168–69, 174–75. Though Scholer's rare admissions of the community's grave earthly circumstances are consistently interpreted as

have noted elsewhere, "in addition to dissolving the barriers dividing living and dead saints, this remarkable passage also closes the eschatological gap separating angels and humans."[41] Finally, this προσέρχομαι text envisages an "open-air" "festal gathering," occurring on "Mount Zion," a mountain presumably found within "the city of the living God, the heavenly Jerusalem" (12:22). This imagery fails to comport with Scholer's contention that "every occurrence of προσέρχεσθαι has its setting within a cultic context."[42]

ΕΙΣΕΡΧΟΜΑΙ IN HEBREWS 6:18–20

> ... we might have strong encouragement, we who have fled for refuge to take hold of the hope laid before us. We have this hope as an anchor of the soul, sure and indeed steadfast and entering [εἰσερχομένην] into the inside of the veil, where the forerunner on our behalf has entered in [εἰσῆλθεν], Jesus ...

Complicating the interpretation of this text are a somewhat confusing blend of unrelated images, which include nautical, cultic, and the imagery of fugitives seeking asylum.[43] These disparate images, however, may be suggestively pieced together with the assistance of 6:13–14, 18 and 7:19–22. In 6:18, the author contends that God's trustworthiness is proven by "two immutable things": the oaths made to Abraham (6:13–14) and Jesus (concerning his eternal priesthood, 7:19–22).[44] Therefore, the community's hope functions as a rope, connecting them to Jesus and his eternal high priestly ministry.[45]

---

proof of their inability to substantively access God and his Son in the heavenly realm, these circumstances should be seen instead as *motivating* the author of Hebrews' exhortations to fully and freely "draw near" to God and find the necessary "help" in "times of need" (4:16).

41. Mackie, *Eschatology and Exhortation*, 205.

42. Scholer, *Proleptic Priests*, 11; cf. also 141, 143, 145, 148–49.

43. Johnson (*Hebrews*, 172) notes that 6:18–20 is "exceptionally complex, not because of the syntax, which is straightforward, but because of the use of metaphors that overlap and blend. The author makes use of three distinct conceptual domains, one nautical (hope is an anchor), one cultic (heaven is a temple), and one athletic/military (life is a race/war). They are drawn together by the verb 'entering.'"

44. Though Ellingworth (*Hebrews*, 342) argues against this interpretation, 6:13–20 and 7:19–22 contain two significant points of contact: (1) the instrumentality of "hope" in entering into the holiest place (6:19) and drawing near to God (7:19); (2) the unchangeable plans of God that come to expression in self-sworn oaths (6:17–18; 7:21).

45. Scholer (*Proleptic Priests*, 180) helpfully observes that this "hope" possesses both objective and subjective dimensions. It is an "objective reality centered in the Christ event ... which provides the believer with the 'subjective confidence' or 'hoping.'"

That ministry is carried out within "the innermost reaches" of the heavenly sanctuary, beyond the "curtain" (εἰς τὸ ἐσώτερον τοῦ καταπετάσματος, 6:19), where Jesus has "entered" (εἰσέρχομαι, 6:20). As for the community, when they "flee" (καταφεύγω) into the security of the heavenly sanctuary, they will find this hope within their grasp, and when they "seize" it (κρατέω, 6:18), it will become "securely and reliably anchored" (ἄγκυραν ... ἀσφαλῆ ... καὶ βεβαίαν) within their innermost being (ψυχή, 6:19), firmly fastening them to their "forerunner" (πρόδρομος, 6:20) Jesus.[46] Moreover, by this hope the community is presently "entering" (εἰσέρχομαι) "the innermost reaches" beyond the curtain (6:19).

Also worth noting, and further mitigating attempts at assigning a purely cultic context to this passage, is the "fugitives seeking asylum" imagery which surfaces in the characterization of the community as "having taken refuge" and "seizing the hope set before us" (6:18). This imagery recalls the "six cities of refuge," to which those who have unintentionally killed someone may "flee" (φεύγω, Num 35), and "seize" the horns of the altar (1 Kgs 1:50; 2:28). A number of other illuminative texts are worth mentioning. For example, Aeschylus claims, "Stronger than a castle is an altar, it is an invulnerable shield" (*Suppl.* 190). Plutarch (*Sol.* 12.1) offers an interesting account of Cylon and his "fellow-conspirators who had taken sanctuary at the temple of Athena." They were talked into leaving the sanctuary, so they might stand trial. Before they left the sanctuary, however, they "secured a braided rope to the image of the goddess and kept a tight grip on it." Unfortunately the rope broke, which was seen as a sign that the goddess had revoked her protection. Some of the conspirators were immediately stoned to death, while others ran back to the altar for refuge, where they were slaughtered. According to Herodotus (1.26), the Ephesians applied similar logic in an attempt to fend off an attack from King Croesus, ca. 560 BCE. They ran a rope from the temple of Artemis to the city walls (nearly a mile away), hoping to extend the temple's asylum to the whole city. Croesus, apparently failing to appreciate the logic, attacked the city. Gregory Stevenson has identified the primary convictions underlying this practice: "the god owns whatever is in his sanctuary, thus the supplicant becomes his property and is not to be violated or seized."[47]

---

46. Quite comparable language and imagery is found in Philo, *Flacc.* 53: "Flaccus seized our houses of prayer ... and turned to another exploit, the destruction of our polity, so that our ancestral customs and participation in political rights, to which our life was anchored, was cut off ... having no cable to which to hold on to for our safety."

47. Stevenson, *Power and Place*, 105. Cf. also Sinn, "Greek Sanctuaries," 88–109. Plutarch critiques the logical shortcomings of this practice in his treatise *On Superstition* 166e.

Of greatest significance, however, is this text's participation in the author's large-scale program of hortatory mimesis. This program is evident in a number of contexts, where it encourages the mimetic replication of Jesus' perseverance (12:1–4), as well as his ascent and entry into the heavenly sanctuary (2:9–10; 4:14–16; 10:19–23). Though Isaacs mistakenly contends "entry" is solely predicated of Jesus in 6:18–20, this text in fact forges a mimetic and linguistic link between the community and Jesus their "forerunner," as both parties are described, using the same verb εἰσέρχομαι, as attaining full entry.[48] Indeed, this text's description of the community's entry in a manner that linguistically mirrors Jesus' own full entry represents a final "nail in the coffin" of the alleged distinction between προσέρχομαι and εἰσέρχομαι.

CONCLUSION

The principal point in all four of these entry and access texts is hortatory: the author of Hebrews is convinced that the community's faithful perseverance is dependent upon them coming within communicative and relational proximity of God and Jesus in the heavenly sanctuary. Coming in such close proximity to the Father and the Son will surely issue in their transformation, and perhaps even the transformation of their circumstances. Hebrews is not concerned with establishing an elaborate and restrictive architecture of the heavenly sanctuary, with the putative goal of reminding the recipients that although they experience a "preliminary access" to God in the present time, "a still future and greater" level of access awaits them "in the sweet by and by."[49] Despite its seeming reasonableness, such a hortatory strategy would utterly fail to evoke and sustain the perseverance that this struggling community needs in the present and immediate future.

Though those circumscribing the extent of the community's access in the present would presumably contend that their interpretive efforts represent an attempt at properly balancing the "now" and the "not yet" aspects of Hebrews' eschatology, they are in fact *underestimating both elements*.[50]

---

48. Isaacs, *Sacred Space*, 219. DeSilva ("Entering God's Rest," 28) ignores this occurrence of εἰσέρχομαι, while Scholer (*Proleptic Priests*, 181–84) spiritualizes it.

49. Scholer, *Proleptic Priests*, 11.

50. Scholer (ibid., 206) believes that the community was part of a "charismatic movement" that "embraced a realized eschatology, rife with problems." The author of Hebrews is then seen as responding with an eschatology that places proper emphasis on the "not yet." However, a number of key hortatory elements in Hebrews are inexplicable if this was the actual *Sitz im Leben*. The author's accounts of the community's eschatological experiences, which are principally located in the crucial warning passages,

In contrast to the impoverished experience of the supernatural and supra-rational in our present time (particularly in North American and European churches), the early Christian church was convinced by the close conformance of their many experiences with prophecies like Joel 2:28–32 and Jer 31:31–34, that they were living in the promised "last days," a time in which God was "pouring out" his miraculous and salvific pneumatic charisms on "all flesh," radically transforming "hearts" and "minds," and "effecting" an entirely efficacious "new covenant" with his people (cf. Acts 2:16–21; Heb 8:8–12; 10:15–17). Thus, by all accounts, the early church's experience of God's "now" appears to *even surpass* our meager expectations of the heavenly "not yet." Texts like Acts 2:1–13, 4:29–33; 5:12; 6:8; 7:55–56; 8:6–8, 13; 9–10; Rom 8; 1 Cor 12–14; 2 Cor 3:18; 5:17; 12:1–12; Gal 3:1–5; 4:6; Eph 1–3; 1 Thess 1:5–6; and Heb 2–4; 6–10; 12:22–24 testify to a widespread experience and immersion in the supernatural and supra-rational, one which is only recently receiving an appropriate level of critical attention. The early church's expectations of the future, heavenly life appear to have been extrapolated from their present experiences, though with the clear recognition that the future heavenly world would elude all earthly human attempts at comprehending and expressing its wonders.[51] As Paul observes, "we know" and "prophecy only in part," and like children, who talk and think in "childish ways," our apprehension and articulation of the heavenly is similarly immature and inadequate to the task (1 Cor 13:9–12). A comparable admission is made in 1 John 3:2: though "we are now the children of God, what we will become has not yet been revealed; but we know that when Jesus is revealed, we will be like him, for we will see him as he truly is."

It is within this evaluative framework that Hebrews' entry exhortations begin to make sense. These astonishing exhortations to presently and fully "draw near" to God and his Son in the heavenly sanctuary closely correspond to the actual experience of the author and the community, and this powerfully transformative (and even ecstatic) experience also dimly foreshadows

---

would then be counterproductive (2:1–4; 6:4–5; 10:32). The listed experiences function therein as potent *reminders* of the "great salvation" that the endangered community is neglecting. Hebrews' characterization of the community as "drifting away" (2:1), "neglectful" (2:3), "sluggish" (6:12), spiritually immature (5:12–14), "growing weary" and "losing heart" (12:3) is similarly baffling, as these are inapt attributes for a charismatic community. Charismatics are typically characterized as "enthusiastic," albeit with misguided enthusiasm.

51. A similar "experiential extrapolation" is evident in Plutarch's elaborate account of the afterlife, which is based on the mystical "experiences of those who are undergoing initiation into great mysteries" (frag. 178). Plutarch further notes, "in this world we are without knowledge" of the afterlife, as "the gods keep it concealed from human awareness."

an entirely superior form and experience of access, one which is solely the province of those who have persevered "to the end" in their commitment to Jesus (cf. Heb 3:14; 6:11).[52] The theologian who wrote Hebrews undoubtedly possessed a firm grasp of what eschatological experiences belonged to the "now," and which pertained to the "not yet" (2:8–9). His knowledge and experience in pastoring endangered and threatened early Christian communities, however, led him in this instance to more heavily emphasize those eschatological experiences and resources which were presently available. The preservation of this eschatologically rich "word of exhortation" perhaps testifies to its success in exhorting and effecting the addressed community's substantive and full entry into the transformative presence of God and his Son.

This discussion has demonstrated that the indispensable role of transformative experience in Hebrews is only beginning to be appreciated. As is evident in our extended account of Gary's experientially-rich discussion of the entry exhortations, his contribution to the prestigious New International Commentary on the New Testament series represents a landmark first step in that direction.

BIBLIOGRAPHY

Anderson, Gary A. "'Through Those Who Are Near to Me, I Will Show Myself Holy': Nadab and Abihu and Apophatic Theology." *CBQ* 77 (2015) 1–19.

Cockerill, Gareth L. *The Epistle to the Hebrews*. NICNT. Grand Rapids: Eerdmans, 2012.

deSilva, David A. "Entering God's Rest: Eschatology and the Socio-Rhetorical Strategy of Hebrews." *TJ* 21 (2000) 25–43.

———. *Perseverance in Gratitude: A Socio-Rhetorical Commentary on the Epistle "to the Hebrews."* Grand Rapids: Eerdmans, 2000.

Ellingworth, Paul. *The Epistle to the Hebrews: A Commentary on the Greek Text*. NIGTC. Grand Rapids: Eerdmans, 1993.

Isaacs, Marie E. *Sacred Space: An Approach to the Theology of the Epistle to the Hebrews*. JSNTSup 73. Sheffield: Sheffield Academic, 1992.

Johnson, Luke T. *Hebrews*. NTL. Louisville: Westminster John Knox, 2006.

Koester, Craig R. "God's Purposes and Christ's Saving Work according to Hebrews." In *Salvation in the New Testament: Perspectives on Soteriology*, edited by Jan G. van der Watt. NovTSup 121. Leiden: Brill, 2005.

———. *Hebrews: A New Translation with Introduction and Commentary*. AB 36. New York: Doubleday, 2001.

---

52. Gary's comments on Heb 12:22–24 are particularly relevant here. He contends that this text "unites in one" both "the present preliminary privilege and future ultimate destiny of God's people." The author's "emphasis is on the present privilege—'you have come.' Yet this is also his most comprehensive glimpse of the future that God has for his own" (*Hebrews*, 653).

Löhr, Hermut. *Umkehr und Sünde im Hebräerbrief.* BZNW 73. Berlin: de Gruyter, 1994.
Mackie, Scott D. "Ancient Jewish Mystical Motifs in Hebrews' Theology of Access and Entry Exhortations." *NTS* 58 (2012) 88–104.
———. "Confession of the Son of God in Hebrews." *NTS* 53 (2007) 114–29.
———. "Confession of the Son of God in the Exordium of Hebrews." *JSNT* 30 (2008) 437–53.
———. "Heavenly Sanctuary Mysticism in the Epistle to the Hebrews." *JTS* 62 (2011) 77–117.
———. "Early Christian Eschatological Experience in the Warnings and Exhortations of the Epistle to the Hebrews." *TynBul* 63 (2012) 93–114.
———. *Eschatology and Exhortation in the Epistle to the Hebrews.* WUNT 2/223. Tübingen: Mohr/Siebeck, 2007.
———. Review of *The Epistle to the Hebrews* by Gareth Lee Cockerill. *CBQ* 76 (2014) 347–48
———. "Visually Oriented Rhetoric and Visionary Experience in Hebrews 12:1–4." *CBQ* (forthcoming).
Rissi, Mathias. *Die Theologie des Hebräerbriefs: ihre Verankerung in der Situation des Verfassers und seiner Leser.* WUNT 41. Tübingen: Mohr/Siebeck, 1987.
Scholer, John M. *Proleptic Priests: Priesthood in the Epistle to the Hebrews.* JSNTSup 49. Sheffield: Sheffield Academic, 1991.
Sinn, Ulrich. "Greek Sanctuaries as Places of Refuge." In *Greek Sanctuaries: New Approaches*, edited by Nanno Marinatos and Robin Hägg, 88–109. London: Routledge, 1993.
Stevenson, Gregory. *Power and Place: Temple and Identity in the Book of Revelation.* BZNW 107. Berlin: de Gruyter, 2001.
Thompson, James W. *Hebrews.* PCNT. Grand Rapids: Baker Academic, 2008.
Weiss, Hans-Friedrich. *Der Brief an die Hebräer: Übersetzt und Erklärt.* KEK 13. Göttingen: Vandenhoeck & Ruprecht, 1991.

3

Rest Now or Not Yet?

Temporal Aspects of Social Identity in Hebrews 3:7—4:11

MATT O'REILLY

THAT THE LETTER TO the Hebrews reflects the already/not yet eschatology found throughout the NT is widely recognized.[1] Despite this general agreement, elements of Hebrews' eschatology continue to be debated. Not least among these contested matters is the theme of "rest" (κατάπαυσις) in 3:7—4:11. Most interpreters of Hebrews take the promise of rest in this passage as a future reality experienced by believers after death.[2] In this view, believers may anticipate or have a foretaste of the eschatological rest in the present life, but entrance into that rest is reserved for the life to come, not this one.[3] Andrew T. Lincoln and William L. Lane have argued against the majority that "rest" in Heb 3:7—4:11 is not portrayed solely as a future experience. Rather, it reflects the already/not yet tension found elsewhere in Hebrews and the NT. Believers are said to enter that rest presently (4:3) and

---

1. Cockerill, *Hebrews*, 25–28; cf. Barrett, "Eschatology," 364; Lane, *Hebrews 1–8*, 10; O'Brien, *Hebrews*, 93–94; deSilva, *Perseverance*, 30; Ellingworth, *Hebrews*, 77; Gaffin, "Sabbath," 34; Dumbrell, *Search*, 323; Lincoln, *Guide*, 92–100.

2. Cockerill, *Hebrews*, 197, 200–201; cf. Bruce, *Hebrews*, 110; deSilva, *Perseverance*, 168; Witherington, *Letters*, 189; O'Brien, *Hebrews*, 165. Käsemann understood the rest to be a future heavenly experience, though he argued that Gnosticism formed the background for it (*Wandering*, 68–75). Käsemann's argument with regard to the Gnostic background has been refuted in Hofius' book *Katapausis*, which demonstrated that Jewish apocalyptic literature was the background for the language of rest in Hebrews.

3. Witherington, *Letters*, 181.

yet are exhorted to strive to enter the future rest as well (4:11).[4] To put the debate in the form of a question: Does "rest" in Hebrews 3:7—4:11 refer to an experience available to believers in the present or is it a fully future experience reserved for the life to come? May believers enter this "rest" now, or not yet?[5]

I am inclined to answer that question with the affirmation that believers may begin entrance into rest in the present—though full realization of that rest awaits—and I will introduce additional evidence to support that reading. The goal of this essay is to consider the psychological impact that this understanding of the rest motif may have had on the recipients of Hebrews and its function with regard to their self-understanding as members of the people of God. The tool for gauging that impact will be the hermeneutical lens of social identity theory (SIT). More specifically, I will draw upon the work of Marco Cinnirella, a social identity theorist who has given specific attention to the function of temporal dynamics in social identity formation. While much of the previous discussion has focused on what is meant by "rest," the concern of this essay is the function of that language with regard to the recipients' perception of themselves as members a Christ-following community. How might their group identity have influenced them to persevere in faith and stand firm in the face of the opposition they appear to have experienced? Let me be clear that I am in no way suggesting that a social-psychological reading of this passage is to be preferred over against a theological reading. Theology and social identity are not mutually exclusive categories, and we have no reason to take them as such. To the contrary, theological and social dynamics of the text are simultaneously in play and careful readers will be attentive to each and to their relationship, not only with regard to the way theology might influence identity but also with regard to the possibility for identity and self-perception to influence theology.

In what follows, then, I begin with an outline of Cinnirella's approach to temporality and SIT. Second, I will argue that the recipients of Hebrews were facing opposition and were perceived by the pastor to be in danger of apostasy.[6] Third, drawing on Cinnirella, I will analyze Heb 3:7—4:11 through the lens of SIT giving special attention to temporal aspects of the passage. As we shall see, the weaving together of past-, present-, and future-oriented language to describe the concept of rest in Heb 3 and 4 justifies this approach and points toward its potential for yielding a fruitful reading. As

---

4. Lincoln, *Guide*, 94–95; cf. Lincoln, "Sabbath," 210–12; Lane, *Hebrews 1–8*, 99.

5. Closely connected with this question is the different question of whether this rest is a place or a state of being (see Cockerill, *Hebrews*, 199–200).

6. Following Cockerill, I will refer to the author of Hebrews as "the pastor" throughout this essay (Cockerill, *Hebrews*, 2–3).

the argument unfolds, it will become increasingly clear that the language of "rest" in Heb 3 and 4 functions in part to construct and maintain a temporally coherent social identity among the recipients which has the potential to influence them to stand firm in the face of persecution.

TEMPORAL DYNAMICS OF SIT

The relationship between time and social identity has not been studied extensively by social identity theorists. Nevertheless, a series of essays by two researchers in particular—Marco Cinnirella and Susan Condor—points to the importance of considering diachronic processes in the formation and maintenance of social identity and provides a framework for getting started.[7] In particular, Cinnirella highlights the need for a "theory of social identity which adequately encompasses the temporal nature of identity maintenance and the quest for coherence amongst past, present, and future identities."[8] Working toward that end, he articulates a series of hypotheses that are useful for assessing diachronic processes in identity formation. His work draws heavily on the concept of "possible selves" developed by Hazel Markus and Paula Nurius.[9] According to Markus and Nurius, possible selves involve a sort of self-knowledge which "pertains to how individuals think about their potential and about their future. Possible selves are the ideal selves that we would very much like to become, and the selves we are afraid of becoming."[10] Possible selves theory also accounts for the way an individual might have thought about the self in the past.[11] The theory provides a framework for analyzing behavior because individuals tend to act in a way that they believe will help them attain desired positive selves and avoid undesired possible selves.[12] Cinnirella argues that "one particular kind of possible self is a *possible social identity*," by which he means an individual's perception of present or potential group memberships.[13] To put it another way, one possible self is the self as member of one group or another. Cinnirella argues that "Ingroup members are concerned to persuade both other ingroupers *and also outgroupers*, to endorse the desired possible social identities of the ingroup

---

7. Cinnirella, "Temporal Aspects"; Condor, "Social Identity and Time"; Condor, "Temporality and Collectivity."
8. Cinnirella, "Temporal Aspects," 227–28.
9. Markus and Nurius, "Possible Selves."
10. Ibid., 954.
11. Cinnirella, "Temporal Aspects," 229.
12. Ibid., 229
13. Ibid., 230; emphasis original.

i.e. [sic] to accept positively valued 'visions' of what might happen to the ingroup in the future."[14] He further hypothesizes that ingroup members develop "life stories" or accounts that give coherence to the past, present, and desired future of the group. The potential exists that group identity will be strengthened by the perception of a temporally coherent representation. Group members may also accept or adopt a particular aspect of the potential future social identity, including behaviors and practices that correspond with the desired identity.[15]

In what follows, I argue that the rest motif in Heb 3:7—4:11 functions in part to develop and maintain a temporally coherent group identity.[16] The prospect of achieving a future experience of rest (Heb 4:1, 6, 9) can be described as a positively evaluated future possible social identity; the pastor is attempting to persuade the recipients to see themselves as members of the group that will enter into rest. I shall argue further that the use of Gen 2:2 and Ps 95:7–11, which evokes the narrative of Num 13:1—14:45 and the rebellion of the wilderness generation at Kadesh-Barnea, functions together to give shape to the "life story" of the group and create a sense of coherence between the history of the people of God and the possible future the pastor holds before them, even though the wilderness generation is also portrayed in contrast to the recipients of Hebrews. Such coherence has potential to strengthen the pastor's effort to persuade them. Given a coherent representation of past and future, the likelihood is increased that group members will behave in the present in such a way as to achieve the desired future identity; that is, they are likely to act in such a way so as to achieve entrance into God's rest. In particular, they would have to remain faithful in the face of any persecution they might experience. To restate my central thesis: the "rest" motif in Heb 3 and 4 functions in part to form and maintain a temporally coherent social identity that has potential to strengthen the resolve of the recipients to resist the temptation to commit apostasy and instead to persevere against any opposition they have encountered or might yet encounter.

Before giving an account of the situation faced by the recipients, it bears emphasizing that the model outlined above is not intended to be a frame into which the text must be made to fit. The goal is not to align bits

---

14. Ibid., 235; emphasis original.

15. Ibid., 235–36.

16. To be clear, I am not making the anachronistic suggestion that the pastor had modern social-scientific models in mind as he wrote. Rather, I am reading Hebrews through the lens of SIT with a view to understanding the extent to which it might function to form and maintain Christian social identity. The theory is a heuristic that stands in dialectic relationship with the text. It is descriptive, not prescriptive.

of text with bits of theory. The question is not whether text and theory fit seamlessly together, but whether and to what extent the theory may be said to accurately describe the text or to shed some light on it by enabling a fresh reading. In some cases a model may fit quite nicely; in other cases evidence from the text may push back against the model. This does not mean that the theory is useless; instead, it should lead us to ask why the text makes such a move when the model might lead us to expect some different move. The relationship between text and theory is more dialectic than it is a game of matching. Keeping that methodological point in mind, we turn to the possibility that the recipients were facing persecution and the temptation to apostatize before proceeding with our analysis of the language of rest in Heb 3 and 4.

THE SITUATION OF THE RECIPIENTS AND THE POSSIBILITY OF APOSTASY

Evidence from the text of Hebrews indicates that the recipients underwent a significant degree of persecution after their initial conversion to Christian faith and practice.[17] The pastor exhorts them to, "Remember those earlier days after you had received the light, when you endured in a great conflict full of suffering" (10:32). The "insult and persecution" they experienced were, at times, public matters (10:33). The text suggests that this persecution involved the confiscation of their property (10:34) and imprisonment (12:4). The extent of their suffering had not, however escalated to the point of martyrdom (12:4). The pastor responds to their experience of suffering by exhorting them to persevere in the face of hardship (10:23, 36; 12:7, 12).

DeSilva suggests that Hebrews' recipients faced opposition because they had adopted a lifestyle that appeared to subvert larger cultural and social norms.[18] Christian devotion to the one God meant ceasing to participate in numerous political, business, and other social occasions that included the worship of pagan deities as a regular practice.[19] Such worship symbolized personal dedication to structures that ensured a stable society, and refraining from such practices was seen as a threat to society itself. The public nature of the antagonism meant the recipients would have lost honor and acquired shame in the eye of the larger society.[20] Such disgrace functioned

---

17. Cf. Cockerill, *Hebrews*, 16–18; deSilva, *Perseverance*, 12–16; Lincoln, *Guide*, 54–55.

18. deSilva, *Perseverance*, 12.

19. Ibid.

20. Cockerill, *Hebrews*, 18.

as a means of social control that would have discouraged the recipients from maintaining their association with the community of Christ-followers.[21] From the perspective of SIT, we have at least two social identities competing for salience among the Hebrews: (1) there is the group identity oriented around the norms of Hellenistic society and (2) there is the Christ-oriented group identity expressed through faith in and devotion to the one God.[22] If the pastor's effort to keep the recipients from committing apostasy is to be effective, the Christ-oriented social identity must become and remain salient among the recipients. The question is whether the rhetoric of Hebrews can overcome the shame imposed by the larger society in order to maintain the salience of Christ-oriented identity. This paper takes up the more specific matter of how the rest motif in chapters 3 and 4 relates to that larger task.

REST AS FUTURE POSSIBLE SOCIAL IDENTITY

The argument that rest is appropriately described as a future possible social identity depends on two key pieces of evidence. First, it must be shown that rest in Hebrews 3 and 4 is indeed a future possible *social* identity; that is to say, it is perceived by members of the group that they will attain this rest *as members of the group*. Second, since individuals tend to embrace positively valued future possible identities, we need to consider the extent to which "rest" is portrayed in a desirable light.[23]

---

21. deSilva, *Perseverance*, 14.

22. Individuals have a variety of social identities that become salient in different settings. When I am in an ecclesial setting, my identity as a member of the clergy is salient. When I am at an academic conference, my identity as a member of the academic guild is salient. When I am at the table for a meal with my wife and children, my identity as a member of the family is salient. In light of that, and given the view held by some scholars that Hebrews was written to keep Christ-following Jews from reverting to reliance on the Jewish cultus, readers will be justified in questioning how a Jewish social identity relates to the questions raised in this essay. First, the ethnicity of the recipients is a contested matter. For the view that the recipients were predominately a Jewish-Christian group, see Ellingworth, *Hebrews*, 21–27. For the alternative view that the recipients are both Jewish Christians and Gentile Christians, see deSilva, *Perseverance*, 2–7. Second, a focus on Christian identity in contrast to the Greco-Roman cultural identity facilitates the aims of this essay to consider the maintenance of Christian identity, whether Jewish or Gentile, in contrast to an identity shaped by the values of the larger society (cf. deSilva, *Perseverance*, 11–16).

23. Readers might also expect attention given to the *future* orientation of the social identity. That this rest is *at least* future is not largely contested. What is debated, as indicated above, is whether and to what extent believers may be said to enter into this experience in the present. For the future orientation of rest, see Heb 4:1, where rest is portrayed as a "promise" (ἐπαγγελία) for the future, Heb 4:9 where entrance into rest

With regard to the first matter, several features of the text indicate that rest should be understood as it relates to the group. First, Heb 3:7—4:11 is characterized by familial and group-oriented language.[24] The first appearance of "rest" language in this passage comes in 3:11, which forms part of a quote from Ps 95:7–11, which indicates that the wilderness generation did not enter into God's "rest" because of their hardened hearts and unfaithful rebellion. This is immediately followed by the pastor's instruction that the recipients consider their hearts to ensure they are neither sinful nor unbelieving, leading them to turn from God (3:12). In issuing this exhortation, the pastor addresses the recipients as ἀδελφοί. The use of familial language reinforces the social-orientation of the instruction and fortifies bonds between group members.[25] That bond is further strengthened in the following verse by the imperative to "encourage one another daily" (παρακαλεῖτε ἑαυτοὺς καθ' ἑκάστην ἡμέραν, 3:13). Entrance into rest is not left to individual effort; to the contrary, group members are responsible for assisting each other in reaching this goal. In 4:3, the substantive plural participle οἱ πιστεύσαντες ("we who have believed") once again reinforces the group-oriented nature of entrance into rest. It is for those who are members of the group of believers. The social nature of the future "rest" is restated again in 4:9 where the "Sabbath-rest" that remains is said to be specifically "for the *people* of God" (τῷ λαῷ τοῦ θεοῦ, emphasis mine). The group nature of the future experience of rest is evident throughout the passage.

The group orientation of the rest motif is further apparent in that it functions as a boundary marker between ingroupers and outgroupers. Those who believe will enter rest (4:3), but those who do not believe will not (3:12, 19).[26] While disobedience characterizes those who do not enter rest (4:6), those who are striving to enter rest must take care that they do not follow the "example of disobedience" (4:11). Non-entrance into rest is associated with sin and hardness of heart (3:12, 15), which the faithful are instructed to resist (3:15). These instances indicate that the rest motif functions in part to identify a social boundary. This means that entrance into eschatological

---

"remains" (ἀπολείπω), and Heb 4:11 where the recipients are exhorted to "make every effort to enter that rest," which suggests they have not entered it in the present but may do so in the future. Cf. Cockerill, *Hebrews*, 196–97; Lincoln, *Guide*, 94–95.

24. For familial language elsewhere in Hebrews, see 2:11–12, 17; 3:1; 7:5; 10:19; 13:22. Cf. Muir, "Social Identity," 432.

25. So Cockerill, "By addressing his hearers as 'brothers and sisters' the pastor reminds them that they are part of the family (v. 6) of God acknowledged by the Son as his 'brothers and sisters' (2:11–12)" (*Hebrews*, 182); cf. Muir, "Social Identity," 432.

26. As Cockerill notes, "'Unbelief' is the most comprehensive description of the sin of the wilderness generation" (*Hebrews*, 183).

rest does indeed function in part as a social identity: members of the group perceive themselves as entering into rest while members of outside groups do not. Further, the use of rest language as a boundary marker that highlights intergroup differentiation has potential to strengthen the bond of the recipient ingroup and increases the likelihood that individuals will continue to identify themselves with that group against pressure from outgroupers.[27]

Having established that "rest" can here be accurately described in terms of a future possible social identity, we turn now to the extent to which it is given a positive evaluation in Heb 3:7—4:11. The key insight is that the future possible identity, which is characterized by rest, is portrayed positively by association with divine rest on the seventh day of the creation narrative. In Heb 4:4, the pastor establishes this association, quoting this material from Gen 2:2, "on the seventh day he rested from all his work." The work from which God rested is the work of creation.[28] And while understandings of divine rest certainly underwent development by the time Hebrews was written, we should not assume that "rest" in Gen 2:2 means the cessation of all effort.[29] John Walton has argued that the "rest" of Gen 2:2 reflects the broader ancient near eastern notion that "rest is what results when a crisis has been resolved or when stability has been achieved."[30] He further explains, "This is more a matter of engagement without obstacles rather than disengagement without responsibilities."[31] Further, the place of divine rest should be understood in terms of a temple.[32] Temples in the ancient near east were not primarily places of worship; rather, "When a deity rests in a temple, it means that he is taking command."[33] Divine rest in Genesis thus involves God taking up the posture of cosmic control from the temple which is the space from which that control is exercised. If we allow these observations to shed light on the material in Hebrews, the notion of entrance into rest as a state of resolution or stability would certainly amplify the desirability of the future possible social identity.[34]

---

27. Cf. Hogg and Abrams, *Social Identifications*, 23.
28. Cockerill, *Hebrews*, 207.
29. For the development of the concept of "rest," see Lincoln, "Sabbath," 213.
30. Walton, *Lost World*, 72. Cf. Walton, *Ancient*, 157–60.
31. Walton, *Lost World*, 72.
32. Ibid., 77–85; cf. Beale, *Temple*, 60–80.
33. Ibid. Cf. Beale, "Eden was the first archetypal temple" (*Temple*, 80).

34. The question might be raised as to what is meant by the pastor's comment that, "anyone who enters God's rest also rests from their works" (4:10). Elsewhere in Hebrews, when the cessation of works is in focus, it is "dead works" (νεκρῶν ἔργων, 6:1; 9:14) that are in view. It is through faith that they move from dead works to obedient rest (4:3); cf. Lincoln, "Sabbath," 213.

People tend to be drawn to positively evaluated future possible social identities, and we can now conclude that the notion of rest in Heb 3:7—4:11 is accurately described in those terms. It is regularly associated with familial and group terminology. It functions in part to mark the boundary between the faithful and the unfaithful. And it is positively associated with the divine Sabbath-rest and the cessation of persecution. We are ready now to consider the extent to which the story of the people of God is portrayed to cohere with the pastor's vision of the future.

REST AND THE STORY OF THE PEOPLE OF GOD

According to Cinnirella's hypothesis, people tend to embrace temporally coherent social identities. In order to create the sense of temporal coherence, they may emphasize aspects of their group's history that resonate with their vision of the group's future while giving less attention to features of their past that do not stand in coherence with their vision of the future. Given that rest functions as one possible future social identity in Heb 3:7—4:11, we should then ask whether and to what extent the group's past is portrayed to cohere with the future hope for rest. Does the pastor tell the story of the people of God in a way that stands in continuity with his vision of their future?

Of no small importance is the association developed between the promise of rest and the creation narrative in Heb 4:3b–5. The significance of the creation narrative for the story of the people of God would be difficult to overstate. It defines the relationship between Creator and creation, not least the relationship between the Creator and his human creatures. And inasmuch as it is the beginning of the story of the people of God, it is foundational to their history and identity as a people. As we have just seen, the future rest that the recipients are to strive to enter is associated with the divine rest on the seventh day of creation in Gen 2:2. But this does not function solely to lend positive value to the rest motif; it also creates coherence between the past and the anticipated future. A key point for the pastor is that this all-important narrative comes to its climax with God's own Sabbath-rest, "And yet his works have been finished since the creation of the world. For somewhere he has spoken about the seventh day in these words: 'On the seventh day God rested from all his works'" (Heb 4:3b–4). In making this point, the pastor portrays the history of the people of God in terms of the anticipation and realization of rest going all the way back to the beginning. God's creative work anticipates his coming Sabbath-rest, which is then realized on the seventh day of creation. This pattern of work leading to rest corresponds with the pastor's hope for the recipients, "for anyone who enters God's rest also rests from their works, just as God did from his" (4:10). The divine pattern is prototypical of what the faithful can expect to experience. Portraying the past in this way establishes diachronic continuity between the group's past as reflected in one of its foundational narratives and its anticipated future. The group's past is, therefore, presented in a way that maintains the integrity of the group identity over time. They are the people of the God who rested after his work; likewise, they too shall rest from their work. Taking it through the lens of SIT, this sort of coherent representation across time increases the potential of the rest-oriented identity to strengthen the salience of their identity as part of the people of God in contrast to the larger Greco-Roman society, the members of which have inflicted suffering upon them. Such a temporally coherent representation could serve to mitigate the effects of the shame-oriented efforts of social control deployed by the larger society. If this diachronically consistent and distinct social identity becomes and remains salient among the recipients, they are more likely to be motivated to behave in a way that accords with the full realization of that identity.

As noted above, we need also be open to the question of whether and to what extent the textual evidence might cut against the grain of the model. Given that our model leads us to expect the past to be portrayed in terms of continuity, it is significant that at least one chapter in the group's story is portrayed in rather pronounced discontinuity with the pastor's hope for his recipients. I am referring to the account of the rebellion of the wilderness generation, which is portrayed both in terms of continuity, as we might expect, *and* discontinuity, as we might not, given the theory outlined above. Continuity is asserted between the wilderness generation and the recipients in that both groups "have had the gospel preached" to them (Heb 4:2). The message given to the Hebrew people in the wilderness is the same message the pastor gives to the Hebrews that are his recipients. The message in both cases involved the promise of deliverance into rest.[35] For the wilderness generation this was an anticipation of the entrance into the land; for the pastor's recipients it is the eschatological promise of entering the divine Sabbath-rest. In both cases, scholars have recognized that the rest-oriented nature of the promise establishes continuity across time. As Cockerill remarks, the pastor affirms "the relationship of his hearers with God's people of old. In the divine economy they are one with God's ancient people because they too have received God's invitation to enter his 'rest.'"[36] Ellingworth puts it

---

35. deSilva, *Perseverance*, 163.
36. Cockerill, *Hebrews*, 196.

this way: "continuity is maintained between the people of God in the old and new dispensations: there is for the writer of Hebrews only one λαὸς τοῦ θεοῦ."[37] As the model suggests, we have continuity thus far. But the pastor couples the comparison with contrast. The promise of rest in the land was of no benefit to them because they did not receive it with faith (4:2). The promise was conditioned on faithful obedience, and the condition was not met. As a result, God declared that they would not enter rest. This, of course, is discontinuous with the pastor's hope for his recipients. The question is why. DeSilva suggests that the pastor, in describing the wilderness generation with the language of "distrust" or "unbelief" (ἀπιστία, 3:19) and "disobedience" (ἀπείθεια, 4:6), casts the ancient people in a shameful light. Their memory is disgraceful and dishonorable. They are to be censured, not honored or emulated. DeSilva concludes, "The author hopes that, by arousing shame especially in the hearts of the wavering, they will be all the more motivated to remain committed to God's promise."[38] Reading from the perspective of SIT, the pastor has crafted a social comparison between two subgroups: the recipients and the wilderness generation. By emphasizing the shameful behavior of the earlier group along with their lack of trust in the promise of God, he highlights the distinction between the values of the recipients (i.e., honor and faithfulness) and the behavior of the wilderness generation, which should function to strengthen the future possible social identity set forth by the pastor. The recipients thus acquire positive distinctiveness and the wilderness generation negative distinctiveness.[39] And since it is their sense of honor that might tempt them to give in to the pressure of their society to abandon their Christian identity and return to pagan practices, the pastor's argument that appeals to honor and the avoidance of shame carries potential to redirect the values that might tempt them to abandon the faith toward keeping it instead. Further, in the eyes of the recipients, the negative distinctiveness of the wilderness generation lends itself to the perception by the recipients that apostasy involves a feared possible social identity, which has the potential to motivate them to behave in such a way as to avoid that feared identity.[40]

The life story of the group is thus marked by general diachronic continuity with regard to the hope of participating in the divine rest. However, that same story includes examples of discontinuous deviants able to function as negative examples that reinforce the group's primary identity. The

37. Ellingworth, *Hebrews*, 255.
38. deSilva, *Perseverance*, 169.
39. Hogg and Abrams, *Social Identifications*, 23.
40. Cinnirella, "Temporal Aspects," 240–41.

presence of some discontinuity does not mean the model itself is useless or unhelpful. To the contrary, the evidence from the text is further illumined by our SIT lens precisely because it pushes back against the model to some degree.

REST NOW OR NOT YET?

We have considered how the past and the future relate to the identity-forming function of Heb 3:7—4:11, but our passage places significant emphasis on the present also. This emphasis can be seen in the repetition of the term σήμερον ("today") five times (3:7, 13, 15; 4:7). Three times the pastor extends the imperative of Ps 95:7-8 to his recipients: "Today, if you hear his voice, do not harden your hearts" (Heb 3:7, 15; 4:7). The expectation is that the recipients will not sin like the wilderness generation but will instead faithfully strive to enter God's rest. To that end they are instructed to "encourage one another daily," so that none of them fall victim to sin and fall away and fail to enter the rest that remains for them as the people of God. (Heb 3:13). The temporal continuity between the promise of rest in the past and future is thus maintained in the present. And they are expected to behave in a way that aligns with their group's life story and with the pastor's vision of the future.

The question remains, however, as to whether the recipients may actually enter into the promised rest in the present or whether that entrance into rest is reserved entirely for the future. The key verse in the debate is 4:3, "Now we who have believed enter that rest," (Εἰσερχόμεθα γὰρ εἰς [τὴν] κατάπαυσιν οἱ πιστεύσαντες). The present form of εἰσέρχομαι would seem to suggest that entrance into rest is not limited to the future but is also available to some degree in the present by faith. This is the view taken by Lincoln, who argues that it makes sense of the repetition of "Today" in the passage. The pastor, he notes, can apply the "Today" from Ps 95 to his recipients because, as Heb 4:3 indicates, the time for entrance into rest is the present. Holding the already/not yet dimensions in balance, he writes, "On this new day the rest has become a reality for those who believe but remains a promise that some may fail to achieve through disobedience, so that all are exhorted to strive to enter it."[41] DeSilva criticizes this reading, saying that it reflects a tendency to read the present εἰσερχόμεθα with perfect

---

41. Lincoln, "Sabbath," 212. Cf. Barrett, "The 'rest', precisely because it is God's, is both present and future; men enter it, and must strive to enter it. This is paradoxical, but it is a paradox which Hebrews shares with all primitive Christian eschatology" ("Eschatology," 372).

force. DeSilva suggests instead that the verb should be read as a "true present" with emphasis given to the "progressive" or "continuous" aspect. He suggests that, "Such a reading allows the verse to impact the hearers with the all the immediacy that the author desires, while at the same time not violating the future aspects of entering that rest that are so clearly indicated in the surrounding context."[42] For deSilva, this means that believers are on the "threshold" of rest but do not enter it in this life.[43] The problem here is that a straightforward translation which emphasizes the present *as a true present* can be rendered "we enter" or "we are entering." It nowhere reflects the tendency to introduce the perfect tense, and it reflects precisely the interpretation for which Lincoln argues.[44] To affirm both the present entrance into rest alongside the instruction to "make every effort to enter that rest" (4:11) carefully holds the balance between the already/not yet. To say "we are entering" into rest means that entrance into rest is presently available and not limited to the future, though it remains a future promise also.

The argument is further substantiated by the close connection between rest and temple discussed above with regard to the creation narrative in Genesis, a connection which should be brought to bear on Heb 4, since the pastor makes direct appeal to that narrative. Immediately following the passage under consideration in this essay, Jesus is described as a "great high priest who has ascended into heaven" (4:14). The proximity of the language of "rest" earlier in chapter 4 to cultic language here should not surprise us given the OT notion discussed earlier of the temple as the place of divine rest. Having ascended into heaven, Christ is enthroned and "serves in the sanctuary, the true tabernacle" (8:2). As we have seen before, the heavenly temple is pictured as the place of cosmic control where Jesus is engaged as ruler and mediator. It should be remembered that in the OT divine rest in the temple does not mean cessation of activity or effort. Rather, as Beale remarks, "God's rest both at the conclusion of creation in Genesis 1–2 and later in Israel's temple indicates not mere inactivity but that he had demonstrated his sovereignty over the forces of chaos (e.g., the enemies of Israel) and now has assumed a position of kingly rest further revealing his sovereign power."[45] This could just as easily describe the movement of Christ in Hebrews. Having taken a lower position for a time so that he could suffer and "taste death for everyone" (2:9–10), he has now entered into his kingly rest and is enthroned in the heavenly temple.

42. deSilva, *Perseverance*, 155.
43. Ibid.
44. Cf. Lane, *Hebrews 1–8*, 99.
45. Beale, *Temple*, 62.

Believers are encouraged to "approach" that throne with confidence in order to receive mercy and grace (4:16; cf. 7:19). The exhortation to draw near with confidence is not only linked with the throne but is elsewhere associated with the temple: "we have confidence to enter the sanctuary" (10:19). In 12:22, the recipients are said to "have come" (προσεληλύθατε) to the "heavenly Jerusalem," an image which resonates with the kingly and cultic language used throughout Hebrews. More specifically, believers are said to "have come" both "to God" (10:23) and "to Jesus" (10:24). The perfect indicative form of προσέρχομαι suggests a condition that is ongoing and reflects the already/not yet tension that runs through Hebrews. The recipients must persevere in faith and worship without turning away (10:25–29), but this does not mean that they have not already entered the place of Jesus' mediatorial presence. To the contrary, the pastor asserts that they have. If, as I have argued above, the place of Jesus' intercession and rule is also the place of his rest, and if believers have entered into the place of his intercession and rule in the present, then we must conclude that they have also begun to enter the place of rest. To put it another way: the heavenly temple is the place of divine rest, and if believers have access to Christ who is enthroned in that temple *in the present*, then they also have access to the place of divine rest *in the present*.

Reading Heb 3:7—4:11 through the lens of SIT invites us to consider entrance into rest in the present from the perspective of the recipients. How do they see themselves in relation to the divine rest? We have seen how the pastor's portrayal of the promise of entering rest can be described as a future possible social identity, and that it is positively evaluated by association with the divine rest in the creation narrative. Additionally, the pastor has portrayed the past in a way that stands in continuity with the future. Individuals tend to be drawn toward positively evaluated future possible social identities, and the draw is amplified if there is the perception of consistency over time. If the recipients find the pastor's account compelling and desirable, then they will be likely to behave in such a way as to achieve the future possible social identity, namely participation in the divine rest. If the condition is met, this will involve adopting characteristics like faith and obedience which are associated with the future possible identity. They will behave like people who are entering into the promised rest. If they perceive themselves in this way and behave accordingly, it could be suggested that they themselves embody the tension of the already/not yet. If they see themselves as those who will enter rest and as those whose experience of that rest is inaugurated in the present through faith, then they are likely to behave in a way that embodies that temporally consistent identity. This means resisting sin, disobedience, and faithlessness. It also means standing fast in the face of considerable pressure to commit apostasy, and the stronger their ingroup bond, the more likely they are to be faithful to Christ and one another instead of falling away under the pressure from the outgroup.

Thinking in terms of the group identity, Heb 3:7—4:11 functions to foster among the recipients the sense that they are a people entering presently into the divine rest. This sense of belonging stands in continuity both with the future consummation of that rest and earlier stories involving rest going back to the creation narrative. Their self-understanding as those entering into rest increases the likelihood that they will embody in the present the character associated with the future realization of rest. They have not yet entered the fullness of divine rest, and yet they already think and live as those who now inhabit that very rest because, as I have argued above, they have indeed begun to do so.[46] In this way, their experience could be said to embody the already/not yet eschatology of the NT in general and Hebrews in particular.

CONCLUSION

Throughout this essay I have attempted to interpret the language of "rest" in Heb 3:7—4:11 in light of its contribution to forming and maintaining a salient social identity among the recipients of the letter to the Hebrews. That the pastor uses the language of "rest" with regard to the past, present, and future indicates the fruitfulness of analyzing that language with a view to discerning its role in forming a temporally coherent social identity. As a tool for that analysis we looked primarily to the work of Marco Cinnirella in order to show that the language of rest in Heb 3 and 4 can be described as a future possible social identity. The pastor would have the recipients see themselves as members of the group that will enter into eschatological rest. The group's history is portrayed as standing in general continuity with that vision of the future. This is evident in the attention given to the creation narrative and God's rest on the seventh day. Additionally, the wilderness generation was, like the recipients, given the promise of rest. They, however, were disobedient and thus forfeited entrance into that rest. This might seem to detract from the overall continuity of the group identity. I have argued, however, that it does not. The promise of rest is portrayed as being held

46. Let me be clear that I am not suggesting social-psychological analysis should compete with or replace theological interpretation of this passage. I am simply offering as a fresh perspective a reading that takes into account the way the text might have been experienced and responded to by the first readers. It is my hope that my social-scientific reading can stand alongside a more theological reading allowing them to shed light upon one another.

forth to the people of God in each case, and therein lies the fundamental diachronic continuity. The wilderness generation functions as a negative example that heightens the positive distinctiveness of the recipients, increasing the likelihood that they will not themselves commit the same sin as the wilderness generation. Further, the recipients are encouraged by the pastor to enter this rest in the present. I have argued that the concept of the temple as a place of rest should be allowed to shed light on our reading of the rest motif in Hebrews. If believers now have access to Christ in the heavenly sanctuary, then they have present access to the place of his rest. The language of rest here functions in part to create a temporally coherent representation of group identity. Past, present, and future are characterized by the promise of participation in the divine Sabbath-rest. If this identity achieves salience among the recipients, they will begin to behave in a way that they believe will achieve the future desired social identity. They will begin to embody the norms of that identity, namely obedience and faithfulness, and be more likely to stand firm and resist the temptation to commit apostasy. They will embody the life that they aim to achieve, namely the life which embodies entrance into rest.

BIBLIOGRAPHY

Barrett, C. K. "The Eschatology of the Epistle to the Hebrews." In *The Background of the New Testament and its Eschatology*, edited by W. D. Davies and D. Daube, 363–93. Cambridge: Cambridge University Press, 1956.

Beale, G. K. *The Temple and the Church's Mission: A Biblical Theology of the Dwelling Place of God*. NSBT 17. Downer's Grove, IL: InterVarsity, 2004.

Bruce, F. F. *The Epistle to the Hebrews*. Rev. ed. NICNT. Grand Rapids: Eerdmans, 1990.

Cinnirella, Marco. "Exploring Temporal Aspects of Social Identity: The Concept of Possible Social Identities." *European Journal of Social Psychology* 28 (1998) 227–48.

Cockerill, Gareth L. *The Epistle to the Hebrews*. NICNT. Grand Rapids: Eerdmans, 2012.

Condor, Susan. "Social Identity and Time." In *Social Groups and Identities: Developing the Legacy of Henri Tajfel*, edited by P. Robinson, 285–315. Oxford: Butterworth Heinemann, 1996.

Condor, Susan. "Temporality and Collectivity: Diversity, History and the Rhetorical Construction of National Entitativity." *British Journal of Social Psychology* 45 (2006) 657–82.

deSilva, David A. *Perseverance in Gratitude: A Socio-Rhetorical Commentary on the Epistle "to the Hebrews."* Grand Rapids: Eerdmans, 2000.

Dumbrell, William J. *The Search for Order: Biblical Eschatology in Focus*. Grand Rapids: Baker, 1994.

Ellingworth, Paul. *The Epistle to the Hebrews: A Commentary on the Greek Text*. NIGTC. Grand Rapids: Eerdmans, 1993.

Gaffin, Richard B. "A Sabbath Rest Still Awaits the People of God." In *Pressing toward the Mark: Essays Commemorating Fifty Years of the Orthodox Presbyterian Church*, edited by Charles G. Dennison and Richard C. Gamble, 33–51. Philadelphia: Committee for the Historian of the Orthodox Presbyterian Church, 1986.

Hofius, Otfried. *Katapausis: Die Vorstellung vom endzeitlichen Ruheort im Hebräerbrief.* WUNT 11. Tübingen: Mohr, 1970.

Hogg, Michael A. and Dominic Abrams. *Social Identifications: A Social Psychology of Intergroup Relations and Group Processes.* New York: Routledge, 1988.

Käsemann, Ernst. *The Wandering People of God: An Investigation of the Letter to the Hebrews.* Translated by Roy A. Harrisville and Irving L. Sandberg. Eugene, OR: Wipf and Stock, 2002.

Lane, William L. *Hebrews 1–8.* WBC. Nashville: Nelson, 1991.

Lincoln, Andrew T. *Hebrews: A Guide.* London: T. & T. Clark, 2006.

———. "Sabbath, Rest, and Eschatology in the New Testament." In *From Sabbath to Lord's Day: A Biblical, Historical, and Theological Investigation*, edited by D. A. Carson, 197–220. 1982. Repr., Eugene, OR: Wipf and Stock, 1999.

Markus, Hazel, and Paula Nurius. "Possible Selves." *American Psychologist* 41 (1986) 954–69.

Muir, Steven. "Social Identity in the Epistle to the Hebrews." In *T&T Clark Handbook to Social Identity in the New Testament*, edited by J. Bryan Tucker and Coleman A. Baker, 423–39. London: Bloomsbury, 2014.

O'Brien, Peter T. *The Letter to the Hebrews.* PNTC. Grand Rapids: Eerdmans, 2010.

Walton, John H. *Ancient Near Eastern Thought and the Old Testament: Introducing the Conceptual World of the Hebrew Bible.* Grand Rapids: Baker, 2006.

———. *The Lost World of Genesis One: Ancient Cosmology and the Origins Debate.* Downers Grove, IL: InterVarsity, 2009.

Witherington, Ben, III. *Letters and Homilies for Jewish Christians: A Socio-Rhetorical Commentary on Hebrews, James, and Jude.* Downers Grove, IL: InterVarsity, 2007.

4

The Living and Active Word of God

A Theological Reading of Hebrews[1]

JON C. LAANSMA

HEBREWS FRONTS THE SPEAKING of God. This divine speaking is not merely the announcement and interpretation of God's deeds—his activity—but *is* his acting, and finally is he himself in the person of his Son. This acting has a definite historical form. Faith is a matter of falling in with that word, which necessarily means with that, and just that, history.[2]

    1. It is with affection and gratitude that I offer these reflections in honor of Gary Cockerill, and all the more as they bear on a part of the canon that has meant so much to both of us. Buen Camino, my friend.

    2. The overall unity of what follows should be evident from the introduction and conclusion but it comprises also a cluster of theses as if in passing. Key here is the conviction—already made operational in what follows—that Hebrews is to be received as it itself teaches us to receive divine speech rather than from some pretended and pretentious transcendent perspective. Again (and consistent with the first assumption), I assume that God acts in his speech and speaks in his act. The two main parts of what follows are therefore mutually dependent and are united by Christology, not as an idea but as the Son in his history. This christological understanding of divine speech requires us to honor the *history* of the divine promise, that is, its nature as Abrahamic and as already subsumed in the Son's history. The scope of our survey is selective so as to foreground what Hebrews itself foregrounds in 1:1–4; 4:12–13; and 12:25–29 with a view to the life situation of an audience that was required to accept all of this in a *preached word*. In the title I have opted for the word "theological" rather than "biblical theological" not because the latter is inappropriate for this exercise but because by some definitions "biblical theological" may be more limiting than my treatment has instantiated. Against that backdrop I have used broad strokes to cover as much as possible

This interest in the dual history of God's speech and activity shapes the substance and to some extent the structure of Hebrews. The writer expresses himself like a man who has before him a vision of the world and its history, a vision that finally supplies some of the discourse's mysterious coherence within an elusive structure. It is the story of the entrance of humanity (Jews and Gentiles) through God's Son into the ultimate sacred space in fulfillment of God's *promise* to Abraham; the correlative of promise is the enduring *faith* of the υἱός; the means of entrance into sacred space is cultic cleansing, and, ultimately, of bringing "perfection." The eternal (new) covenant is inaugurated by and mediates the consecrating sacrifice.

This is not to say that there are not other structuring principles beyond this underlying narrative, particularly stemming from the argumentative strategy of scriptural exposition. There are the questions, however, of why this expositional strategy is adopted, why the reading of these texts bends in the direction it does, and how these indicate the situation addressed by this rhetoric. In brief, the received *gospel* had rooted salvation in the promise to Abraham and his seed. The narrative of salvation was there, i.e., in the world of that inscripturated history, which is the story of the Son and thus *of necessity* the story of the Son's brothers and sisters, whatever their racial makeup. The writer's effort is less to apply the Scriptures to their lives than translate their lives into the drama of this great salvation, not by way of heavenly escapism but by way of inspiring perseverance in faith on the very real streets of their Italian home.

As for the logic of what follows, we will first develop the narratival aspect of our thesis (The God Who Acts) and then look at the same thing as divine speech (The God Who Speaks). Within the first part we will first illustrate the presence and importance of the narrative substructure in 2:5–18; 3:7—4:11; and 5:11—6:20, before expanding on key components of that narrative; this latter expansion further clarifies that these components are not merely theological topics in logical arrangement but features of an organically unfolding history. Within the second part we will reflect on the occasion and aims of what could be called Hebrews' "theology of the word," while also drawing out some implications for our own hearing of God's speech. This done, we will engage in a brief reading of the exordium (1:1–4) so as both to indicate (in part) the exegetical rootedness of all that we have said and to attempt to follow Hebrews' own witness. In all of this we are both suggesting this dual lens of act and speech as a fruitful approach to Hebrews (as if suggesting one of the better modes of transport from which to view

---

in descriptive fashion. Thanks are due to Caleb Friedeman, Daniel Treier, and Alexa Marquardt for their input.

a certain countryside), and utilizing this approach to survey Hebrews itself (shifting our attention from the mode of transport to the countryside itself, for its own sake).

THE GOD WHO ACTS

The storyline outlined above is detectable behind both isolated units and the whole of Hebrews, at times in overlapping fashion. Through the use of the traditional descent/ascent story of the Christ event as read through Ps 8, one can see almost the entire narrative in compressed form in 2:5–18. The mention of the σπέρμα Ἀβραάμ in 2:16 signals how completely the writer's thought revolves around the specifically Abrahamic promise from the very beginning of the letter. He indicates the same by mentioning the "world to come" (2:5), which he claims had been his topic all along in 1:5–14, and the meaning of which is bound up with the promise to Abraham. This promise is none other than the inheritance (1:14), the "city with foundations" promised to the patriarchs (11:9–10), for this is a writer who favors the notion of salvation as a locale, a future destination for the people of God traveling by the word of promise. In Paul's terms (as in wider Judaism), it is the world (κόσμος) that was promised as Abraham's inheritance (Rom 4:13). Hebrews 2:5–18 also portrays this promised locale as the "glory" into which many sons are being led, in terms that strongly invoke Jeremiah's new covenant promises. The passage from Jer 31 is not quoted until Heb 8 but it shapes the language and conception of Heb 2. Thus that new covenant, in which the singular promise given to Abraham comes to full flower, will not be like the old when God took them by the hand (ἐπιλαβομένου, 8:9) to lead them out of Egypt (ἐξαγαγεῖν, 8:9) but rather the leader of their salvation will take hold of Abraham's seed (ἐπιλαμβάνεται, 2:16) as his Father leads them into glory (εἰς δόξαν ἀγαγόντα). To a distinctive degree, for Hebrews that locale of the divine glory, the resting place (κατάπαυσις) at the end of the Abrahamic promise's arc, is the *holy* city of God (11:10; 12:22–24; 13:14), Ps 110's place of God's throne (already thematized by 1:3, 13), all of which are the *sacred* space of the tabernacle. The obstacle to entrance, which is the essence of so great a salvation as this (2:3), is accordingly the seed's disobedience and defilement, a human condition with roots in the history of the first covenant (9:15).[3] The need therefore is for cultic *cleansing, sanctification, perfecting, priestly mediation, ransom*—all categories that are activated in Heb 2:10–18—and precisely the cleansing of those who are the inheritance of

---

3. Hebrews is aware of Gen 3 (2:14; 5:14; 6:8; 9:27) but it finds the history of the world, including the history of sin, in the history of Israel and her tabernacle.

the Son and themselves heirs of the promise, namely the "blood and flesh" (2:14; cf. 2:11) seed of Abraham. It should be clarified that for this writer, the question of Jew and Gentile is not a pressing one; it is the "blood and flesh" nature of all of Abraham's seed, not genetic, racial seed, that concerns him. He already takes for granted the Gentiles' inclusion in Abraham's seed. His concern is with the *human* (vs. angelic) nature, of that seed, and thus the need of human (finally, God-man) priestly representation and mediation (2:10–11, 17–18) for the vision of 1:3 to be possible and effectual.

Advancing to 3:7—4:11, we observe that the theme of promise makes its *lexemic* entrance (ἐπαγγελία, ἐπαγγέλλομαι, εὐαγγελίζω) in Hebrews through the Ps 95/Gen 2 promise of humanity's entrance into the sacred locale of God's κατάπαυσις. The specifically *Abrahamic* and *cultic* aspects of the narrative are muted, but they are nevertheless integral to the very logic of 3:7—4:11, as a careful reading bears out. Indeed, word of promise, inheritance, sacred space, warning, faith—all these gather and mingle in 3:7—4:11. As well, we should note that the cosmic sweep of 4:1–11—pressing the story back to creation—recalls the universalistic, cosmic scope of Ps 8. The same underlying narrative we saw behind Ps 8 shapes the exposition of Ps 95/Gen 2 in 3:7—4:11.

Finally, for the moment we can glance ahead to 5:11—6:20. Abraham is not introduced there as a theme subservient to the Melchizedekian oath and priesthood, providing merely a kind of segue from the digression of the warning, via Gen 14, back to the exposition of Ps 110:4. It is closer to the mark to say that the real story arc that governs the Melchizedekian exposition is the Abrahamic promise. So important is Abraham to the whole of the warning and its surrounding context that we should summarize all of 5:11—6:20 as "the desperate need to fall in line with Abraham's faith in the promise" (that is, to subordinate the interpretive problems of 5:11—6:12 to the driving concern of 6:13–20), for it is precisely the fulfillment of *that* promise, the Abrahamic promise, that hangs on Christ's execution and humanity's appropriation of his Melchizedekian priestly and sacrificial role.

As to the components of this narrative: Salvation is a locale, the promised inheritance of the coming world (2:5) that is all "Most Holy Place." There is no longer a gradation of holiness working out in concentric circles from the Most Holy Place; in the achievement of this vision heaven has come to earth and enveloped it.[4] The need is therefore of *cleansing and ran-*

---

4. Salvation is the entrance into God's own glory and holiness; not merely to be in its presence, as if in closest, even the closest possible proximity. It is to be enveloped. God—Father, Son, Spirit—*is* salvation. To come at it from the side of his speech, this God's word is the word of creation, redemption, consecration, and blessing, which is all that faith receives.

som. The law-court imagery of *justification*, basic for Paul, is not utilized, though the law-court idea itself is included in the writer's very rich mix of theological categories and images (e.g., 4:12–13; 9:27; 10:27; 12:23; cf. 9:22; 10:18; 6:10; 12:25–29), and, as Marshall points out, "The Pauline concept of justification is in effect present in Hebrews but expressed with the aid of other categories."[5]

Closely related to cleansing is the language of *perfection*: Christ is "perfected" (2:9; 5:9; 7:28)—with respect to vocational fitness rather than moral development—and is the "perfecter" of faith (12:2) and of believers (10:14). The beneficiaries of a covenantal arrangement can also be said to have been or not been "perfected" (7:11, 19; 9:9; 10:1, 14; 11:40; 12:23). Ultimately perfection is everything involved in effecting arrival at the goal of creation's and salvation's history: the approach through Christ to God. Thus, rather than speaking of the "fulfillment" of the OT, Hebrews prefers to show how the imperfect anticipated that which alone brings us to the goal, the perfect.

Promise is the sign under which we live in continuity with the people of faith that preceded us from Abel on, though now from within the beginning of its coming-into-effect. Provocatively, the word of *promise* is first drawn by Hebrews from an oath that threatens the withholding of blessing (Ps 95:11), but just as music played through an equalizer can be adjusted so also the speech-act of promise can be brought to the fore as internal to the meaning of Ps 95 in its christological context. It is a primordial promise (4:3) consistent with the pre-creational appointment of the Son as heir (1:2) and the "eternal covenant" (13:20; 9:14). That it finds historical entrance with Abraham, though it predates him, is akin to the Son's being and becoming Son. It threaded through the history spanned by Heb 11 and was proclaimed through Moses (4:2, 6; 3:5) in the idiom of parables (9:9; 11:19), shadows, and copies (8:5; 10:1); it found relatively more direct expression in key texts such as Pss 2, 8, 95, and 110 (alongside Gen 14) along with Jer 31, among others. The promise is finally inseparable from the new covenant inaugurated by Christ's blood, which, like light refracted through a prism, disperses it into what can be called better promises.

The implications of this for the old covenant are total, if complex. The same God has spoken the same thing in old and new; those OT words still comprise the word that is living and active (4:12–13). The vision of Christ we are given in Hebrews is impossible without that Mosaic witness; Hebrews attests the truth of Matt 5:17–19 for the Levitical system. The description of the OT's idiom as copies, shadows, and parables applies not only to the cultic fabric of the Mosaic law (7:11–12; 8:10) but to its entirety and all

---

5. Marshall, "Soteriology in Hebrews," 253.

its surrounding Scriptures. A rejection of the Son is a rejection of the subject matter of the Scriptures and thus of the divine promise inscribed there; a rejection of those Scriptures is likewise a rejection of the Son. Moreover, until the time of the new order (9:10) it was the form of covenantal life and not merely the words that served as a figure of Christ. It is accordingly no entailment that by doing the law the Jews misunderstood it. Thus our continuing investigation of the "historical sense" of the OT Scriptures only stands to bring us closer to the figural meaning it carries, even if this is finally impossible without at the same time keeping our eyes on the full revelation of the Son. It is an entailment, however, that when the very form of old covenant life belonged to what was anticipatorily figural, it—the form of life—must give way to a new form of life (12:28; 13:9–16) in keeping with the "very image of the things" (10:1; cf. 9:23).

Also making its entrance with the exposition of Ps 95 is the theme of the community's *faith*, the response suited to a promise. There is no direct opposition of "faith and works of the law" in the Pauline style, though it might be quietly addressed when Moses' faith/fulness is emphasized (3:1–6; 11:23–29). It is in fact Abraham among the OT figures who most fully represents the fitting response to the promise (6:12–20; 7:1–10; 11:8–19, which culminates in a resurrection faith). Faith, however, is finally and exclusively defined as the faith/fulness of the Son (12:2; obviously implied in 5:7; both of these imply resurrection) who is high priest (2:17–18; 3:1–6).

The promise requires πίστις, a life response (3:18–19). Faith is a probing understanding of the present day—the "today" of history (3:12–15; 4:7; 13:8; 1:5; 5:5), these last days (1:2), the completion of the ages (9:26), during which "we do not see everything subject to [him]" but during which we do "see Jesus" (2:8–9). This has implications for the form of life that was formerly obedience but is no longer fitting; therefore, the opposition of faith and works is present also in this way, though not as in Paul. Faith is communal, resolute, and hopeful, carrying forward the Son's missional faithfulness in unshakeable confidence of forgiveness—accomplished once-for-all, applied along the way, and completed at his second coming. Doing this under the Son's leadership requires that we imitate his agonistic and cruciform life, going to him "outside the camp, bearing his reproach" for the same missional ends, for "here we do not have an enduring city, but we are looking for the city that is to come" (13:13–14). In so doing we learn obedience through suffering and so, as those once-for-all made perfect (10:14), undergo a process of perfection that is like (not the same as) the Son's experience; it is sanctification leading to perfection.

The writer has adopted the already/not yet scheme common to the NT with implications for all aspects of the argument, including the priestly work and sacrifice of Christ. That eschatological scheme did not arise from the writer's exegesis so much as shape it, with some aspects of the Mosaic system lending themselves to the idea of salvation accomplished once-for-all and other aspects to the provision of repeated cleansing and other resources for the difficult journey. In this, the tabernacle and its priesthood are genuine, not contrived "shadows" (etc.), so they can be relied on as guides. The Son himself in the event of his own appearance, however, is the surest guide, and he determines how the shadows are to be understood. Thus, how the tabernacle imagery relates to the unfolding eschatological event itself can only be discovered in the event. The result is not as tidy as some who make the OT patterns controlling might desire.

The locale of salvation—although it is "already" (e.g., 6:4–5; 10:19–39)—is finally a matter of the "not yet." One has not yet "been saved." One can leave the camino (the way, the pilgrimage), i.e., apostatize. Just as the moment of salvation undergoes an elongation, so the response of faith and the beginning moment of participation undergoes an elongation and can be cut off short of completion. As is true for Paul (1 Cor 10:1–13; 13:1–2; cf. Matt 7:15; Jude 5; 2 Pet 2:20–22), participation in the realities of grace is real for all who permeate the boundaries of the community in baptism (6:4–5). With 6:7–8 we are to think of the promised blessings of the new covenant (Jer 31; Ezek 34; 36; 11:18–19; cf. Deut 11:11; 28:1–14) so that even from within the fulfillment of those promises (cp. Isa 5:1–7!) the impossible is possible "as long as it is called 'Today'" (3:13–14).

A pressing issue for Hebrews' audience was the pathetic nature of Christian existence with its grinding wear on confidence. To this, too, Ps 110:1 spoke with its little word, "until." Ps 8, subsumed by the one "son of man," also spoke powerfully to the same reality for those grappling with the fear of death (2:15). That the divine word in the Son retained the speech form of *promise* would draw them into a fellowship of faith that stretched like one long line of pilgrims from Abel to the Son. The *Christus Victor* theme is announced (2:14–15) and the hope of resurrection is steadily affirmed (6:2; 11:11–12, 19, 35; 13:20). The teaching on discipline (12:4–11) gives meaning to suffering. But the question remains as to *why* the delay. There is no direct answer but the hints are in the direction of leaving space for the right response of creation to God's glory (12:28; 13:15–16), exemplified in the Son's faith and extended through the internalization of his gospel's missional logic and spirit. Moreover, in our very experience of continuing weakness as illuminated through this exposition we are more clearly to see that salvation had to be and is in fact heavenly and thus invisible but for just that reason more certainly *real* and *inevitable* for history. Where faith is active, that salvation is no longer merely invisible and future, but here and now precisely in our weakness (11:1; cf. 6:4–5).

Bringing ourselves back to the assumed Abrahamic plotline, we note the theme of household (2:13; 3:1–6) and other familial terms (not least 12:4–11). Attridge comments that God "is not simply a distant and aloof creator and judge, whose wrath awaits appeasement, but a Father intimately involved in the history of a family on earth, whose aim is to share with that family a festive heavenly homeland.... The whole short story of God in Hebrews revolves around that relationship between God and God's children."[6] Attridge associates this familial theme most directly with God's identity as creator, and there is no reason to reject his suggestion. What is actually said in 2:16, however, is that it is Abraham's seed that God helps and the promise of the inheritance, which roots in Abraham, includes the multiplication of his (Abraham's) seed (6:14; 11:11–12). The problem was how the promise of this *Abrahamic family* would come about. The answer came when the Son, by sharing in blood and flesh seed of Abraham, by his cleansing and through the resurrection that had been expressed parabolically in Isaac (11:18–19), brought forth a household "as numerous as the stars in the sky and as countless as the sand on the seashore" (11:12). It is the *Abrahamic household* and what it means to be the seed of Abraham that defines this overarching motif of family. This, too, defines the on-going mission of God.

Considered broadly, chapters 1–4 as a unit constitute a summons to listen to God's speech ἐν υἱῷ lest the readers should fail to arrive at the destination of their pilgrimage of faith—here designated as God's κατάπαυσις (resting place). Given both the background of the imagery he uses and the development of Hebrews' own argument, this κατάπαυσις is understood to be the cleansed cosmos as God's temple; it is thus *sacred space*. This entrance is the very content of the promise to Abraham (2:16), and since it is a matter of sacred space the entrance will require consecration, cleansing, perfection, ransom. That much is either expressed or anticipated in 1:1—4:13. Moreover, all this prepares the way for the fresh, theological development of Ps 110:4 and related passages in Heb 5:1—10:18, at which point the plot development slows and concentrates on the *means of entrance* into the sacred space of God's presence, that is, on how the Abrahamic promise is now fulfilled in the Son as priest and sacrifice. Finally, utilizing this theological vision of Christ's high priestly ministry, the discourse returns to a call for faithful endurance in response to the divine word of promise in 10:19—12:29.

---

6. Attridge, "God in Hebrews," 100, 102. This theme is developed at length by Peeler, *You Are My Son*.

To be sure, there is more to the story than we have related. There is the particular story of the Son from pre-incarnation eternity to resurrection and enthronement, which history is at once distinct from and comprehends the history of the promise, and thus comprehends the people and place of the promise. This man chooses his own creation (10:5–10) and we share in him, so that we no longer speak of ourselves as "thrown" into existence. We could further develop the idea that the *heavenly* drama into which the lives of the Christian readers are translated was a drama already etched in the *earthly* history, institutions, and hopes of Israel. History always proceeds from heaven to earth, first in the shadows and copies enacted in Israel, then in and as the Son in whom God has spoken. But time fails us . . .

In short, what is required for faith's endurance is the inhabiting of the history revealed with the promise, and, above all, a knowledge of the one who speaks and who *is* the content of the promise.

THE GOD WHO SPEAKS

Although Hebrews utilizes visual imagery (e.g., 2:8–9; 9:28; 11:1; 12:2), *auditory* imagery overarches the exhortation (1:1–4; 2:12–13; 12:25–29); seeing and hearing finally converge in the encounter with the Son in and as whom God speaks. By communication God gives a sign of his will for communion, in the face of which neutrality is impossible. Objectively speaking, all creation stands as already addressed, yet at present that powerful word is found only "under its opposite," under its weakness.

It is on that most ephemeral of things, a bare word, that believers must stake all. The preached word of the gospel has asked them to accept grinding hardship and tangible, material loss in exchange for an indefinitely postponed salvation, a merely promised salvation, and it has brought neither measurable support nor any hint as to how long they will have to endure.[7]

Considering the emphasis placed on a cleansed or perfected conscience (9:9, 14; 10:2, 22), it is possible that some of the original readers were tempted to (re)turn to tangible cultic rites for assurance. The overt applications in the letter itself, however, more strongly imply that, having already let go of tangible rites, the problem has become one of failing to take hold of what should replace them, with the result that their faith is collapsing into the void. At the deepest and likely unacknowledged level, the problem is in the disinclination of all humans to do what is essential,

---

7. It is not strictly true the gospel has not brought tangible support, but the support it does contain (6:10; 10:24, 33; 13:1–3, 16) is what the process of apostasy forfeits both in the giving and receiving (6:11; 10:25).

to draw near to God in faithfulness. Nearer the surface but at one with that refusal, the problem consists in an uncertainty over whether all of *this*—the preached gospel—does *in fact* constitute the truth of things; simultaneously it is the question of how one can be said to have entered into the promise when the commonplace suffering of life continues unabated—indeed, has worsened—since their allegiance was given to the gospel. The matter of a cleansed conscience is of practical consequence for it bears on the need for fortitude to endure resolutely the punishments meted out to those who resist Babylon's alternative version of history and reality, to borrow from the imagery of Revelation. Whether the readers were consciously and willfully *renouncing* their faith-life or only in effect doing so is unclear; it is possible that the answer differed among the church's members.

The theme of divine speech addresses all this right at its heart. Yes, it is a bare, invisible word on which they must hang everything, but this is a God *whose word has a history* and more; it is a word that *made* history, for it was his word that brought into existence tangible, visible reality (11:3), being, therefore, more certain than what can be touched. That same word bears up/along all history to its ultimate end (1:3), which means again that history is subject to the promise (with entailments for the nature and power of the promise giver!) rather than, as with human promises, the promise subject to history. It would be ironic for one to grasp the tangible effect rather than the causative word.

God *has* spoken anew (12:25–29). After so many years of silence, when this new announcement of his speaking inaugurated such a radical break with what went before, when it was so hidden by its meek and lowly form, and as it reached them only second hand (2:3), this claim of new speech would not have been obvious. It is underlined that this is a divine word that came "through the Lord" and was confirmed by those who had actually heard him (2:3). The event of this speaking is more than a conceptual tradition, however, for God himself had attested it through observable signs, including the giving of the Spirit (2:4; 3:7; 4:12–13; 6:4; 10:29). There is a realism about these passages that is all the more convincing for its understatement; in their own way they remind of Acts 2:22; 10:44–48; 15:8; Gal 3:2–5; 2 Cor 12:1–6 and the like. The writer is not summoning the readers to a merely theoretical commitment to this recent act of divine speech and to the identity of this Speaker with the God of Abraham but is taking for granted their *experience* of this as something that defies unbelief.

It is not the writer's interest, however, to emphasize the mystical or miraculous experience as such but to lodge that experience substantively in the covenantally differentiated and yet unified speech *in the Son*, which means with the *Spirit*. As to the character of this divine speech in the Son, it is evident that it is communicated through the very person and work of the Son—no dominical sayings are cited, though the gospel is traced back to Jesus' announcement (2:3)—in such a way that the Son himself, in *who* he is and what he *does*, himself *is* the speech of God. Yet he is the speech *of* (Abraham's) *God* and thus of one fabric with the earlier speech, the πολυμερῶς καὶ πολυτρόπως πάλαι speech which was τοῖς πατράσιν ἐν τοῖς προφήταις. The result is that when God, the Spirit (3:7; 9:8; 10:15),[8] or the Son (2:12-13; 10:5-10) actually speaks in Hebrews it is in the words of the Scriptures, albeit now manifestly for what those words always were, the gospel (4:2, 6) of Jesus Christ. What is also a given (1:1-2)—namely, that it is the *same* God who spoke in the prophets who speaks now in the Son—shows itself to be *demonstrable* for faith's edification. The successful and mutually illuminating dialogue of the Son with the OT Scriptures is its own demonstration of the fittingness of each to the other and their unity as the one God's act of speaking.

This is a christological reworking of the very understanding of divine speech, drawing in its wake its own understandings of Scripture and (incipiently, at least) canon. The result is a reading that is illuminating, coherent, compelling, and, we dare to say, *natural*. So far as the writer indicates his sources, this understanding came to the writer of Hebrews directly from God, which means through the Lord's proclamation, confirmed by those who heard him, and expressed in the confession learned and repeated in fellowship with the Holy Spirit (e.g., 2:1-4; 3:1). This understanding is through-and-through rational and reasonable, and yet it is irreducibly given, not discovered; it is received, not grasped. To push back further to the origin, it would be speculative but consistent with Hebrews' outlook to suggest that this theological-hermeneutical coherence came into existence with the Son's earthly life, i.e., his deeds, words, and person under the Spirit's shaping, including his post-resurrection ministry (Luke 24:45-47), and

---

8. Attridge's suggestion ("God in Hebrews," 109n23) that the Spirit is "a periphrasis for God, not yet a distinct 'person' within a Triune Deity" involves a false dilemma. If by "not yet a distinct 'person' within a Triune Deity" the standard is the precision of the later creeds, then it would be impossible to affirm or deny that the writer held such a conception, though most would consider it anachronistic to affirm that he did. But when the writer stands so generally in apostolic traditions and echoes them in speaking of "distributions of the Spirit" (2:4), it seems overly conservative to interpret his manner of speaking as a mere "periphrasis for God." Perhaps the way in which God can be presented as speaking *as* the Son, among other things, opened the way for thinking of the Spirit personally. As for OT background, it will be fruitful to think of the involvement of the Spirit in the history of the tabernacle (e.g., Exod 31:3; 35:31) and temple (e.g., 1 Chr 28:12; Ezra 6:14).

continued into the days of his heavenly session (Acts 1:1; John 14:25–27; 16:12–15).

The very Scriptures of Israel are now understood as the speaking of the God, *who is the Father of the Son*; not a merely conceptualized or anticipated "son" but *the* Son, Jesus of Nazareth, in all the concreteness and specificity of his epiphany. That these texts are divine speech at all cannot any longer be conceptualized apart from that divine identity encountered in the Son who is named Jesus. When he takes up the word of the triune God the Son will be faithful to himself, but the Son does not answer to the Scriptures so much as they answer to him, who in his very person *is* the speaking of God. The Son is not made like Melchizedek, but Melchizedek like the Son (7:3), and this very explicitly so; if this is not understood we cannot understand, much less find the warrant for, 7:1–3. This informs the whole of Hebrews, wherein we see what could otherwise only be called a shocking liberty of selective proof-texting in the interest of fashioning a collage-image of the Son as imagined, all assembled into a picture with an effect that is more artistically impressive than cognitively convincing if it is nothing more than a work of genius. Given that it is not in fact a product of human genius, no amount of exegesis will be able *finally* to retrace the exegetical path that led to this reading. It is ultimately the effect of the Big Bang of the epiphany of the Son who himself opened the Scriptures for his disciples. This is a given, the starting point which we cannot get past, though our exegesis may enable us to appreciate further the depths of its truth, coherence, and rationality—and that should define the very motives and aims of all our work as the appropriate response.

We are speaking, however, of ultimate explanations, of the truth that these things are what they are because the speaking God and the Son are who they are, for which finally we can give no account. As we have also insisted, this manner of reading is also finally rational with strong literary and historical rationales, warranting the identification of the methods and principles that seem to have been operative for Hebrews' author, including the interpretive principle of the OT's "self-confessed inadequacy." It has an immanent face to it, accessible to historical investigation, and seems to have the very intent of teaching us how to read by setting us on our feet, taking us far enough down the road, and pointing the way to continue. The writer of Hebrews appears to expect this of his readers (5:12). There is a hermeneutical practice to be followed. To arrogate to ourselves the authority that belongs within redemptive history uniquely to apostolicity, and thus to the once-for-all epiphany of the Son, is wrong. But we are everywhere and in all ways called to imitate the Son and his apostles; we, too, have the Spirit; our drama is a continuation of the day of the promise and the epiphany of the

Son. Not to do what they did hermeneutically would finally be disobedience to the gospel itself, to deny that it is the God *who is the Father* of the Son, who is known only in the Son, who speaks in these Scriptural texts. To refuse to read the Scriptures as this writer did—allowing for appropriate translation—would ultimately be to regard these texts as the words of a different god, an unknown god. We could not do so and remain robustly Christian. We must "do what they did," at the level of material principles without necessarily adopting their cultural methods.[9]

But is there a moment *within* that gospel reading that regards these OT words as a discrete canonical witness to the same God from a perspective that is historically *prior* to the epiphany of the Son? In certain respects an affirmative reply can be given respecting the entire canon, as we live between the advents and so remain in dramatic continuity with the "OT" saints of Heb 11, living, like them, under the sign of the promise. Although the first advent of the Son brings hermeneutical closure, that reality too is subject to the already/not yet dynamic; hermeneutical openness continues. Our question, however, is more sharply focused on a reading exercise that attempts to bracket out Christology and the NT broadly, so as to read the OT purely in its "original context."

This is not a reading that dominates Hebrews, but its way is opened by the first words of the sermon when it distinguishes the former speech from the speech in the Son in the last days (1:1). It is specifically this new speech, not the former speech, that is characterized as ἐν υἱῷ. We could then say that the former speech was not, or not yet, ἐν υἱῷ, without this making it any less God's speech. To be sure, reading the OT from within its incompleteness is not the interest of Hebrews, any more than it is the interest of the Synoptics to tell the story of the transfiguration from within the ignorance of the disciples prior to the resurrection, even as they remind us of their confusion. Yet that the OT word existed historically in a form of incompleteness—having as its meaning and coherence what was to be revealed in the gospel, but not yet known—makes that situation of the incompleteness of the word a part of true history and therefore worthy of being searched out. But even that incompleteness can be recognized *as such* and then understood only from the context of completeness, only from within the Son.[10]

Let OT scholars with all their historical tools freely attempt to trace out the *possible* trajectories along which these texts *might* run and in what directions they *might* lead, whether or not those obviously take us where

---

9. One must distinguish the false either/or of replication or replacement of what they did from *translation*.

10. Further, we cannot assume that for Hebrews that earlier speech represented the achievement of human understanding so much as the Spirit's own witness.

the NT seems to have gone. Because of the nature of the dialogue that exists between the members of the Trinity itself within Hebrews, we must always allow that we have not understood the Son without *first* hearing the word of the Father. Hebrews, distinctively within the NT, forces us to acknowledge that we would not know the Son apart from the prior revelation of the Scriptures, for only there do we meet him definitively as our high priest according to the order of Melchizedek.

This is a thought experiment only, however, for the sake of provisional conclusions. Ultimately to subordinate our understanding of the Son and his gospel to this historical exegetical work on the OT is to deny what the Son says of himself: "No one knows the Father except the Son and those to whom the Son chooses to reveal him" (Matt 11:27). He *is* the way, the truth, the light. We do not bring the Son into some other light so as to know him by means of that light, not even, that is, within the light of our historical exegetical results, but we know him and all things, including our exegetical work, only from within him, who is the light. I have used the words of the Gospels to make the point, but surely the same is contained in seminal form in the words of Heb 1:3 as those words form the premise of all that follows in Hebrews. Apart from the Son we do not know, then, even the Father whose prior speech, we might allow, was in some sense not yet ἐν υἱῷ. If this is so, then how can we claim to have understood that prior speech apart from the Son? To insist on the attempt might be tantamount to turning back to the shadows, against which this entire epistle warns, rather than holding fast to one's confession. Once the Son is revealed, the way back is firmly and irrevocably barred. The very covenantal conditions of the world within which the text was given and received prior to the Son—living prophets, anointed kings, etc.—no longer exist and cannot be recreated; they have been taken over by the new covenantal conditions. The *word* has moved on and the *world* with it.

Another question forces itself upon us by the characterization of the divine speech that cuts through this exhortation: "Today, if you hear his voice . . ." (3:7; cf. 12:25–27). Does the writer understand God's speech as having the radical character of an *event* that finally exists only as an event when and where God speaks in our present? The words of the psalm, "Today, if you hear his voice," are in fact best taken not in reference to a constant possibility that we await in each moment, as if there might be a new revelation in addition to what was said then ἐν υἱῷ, but in reference to the event of God's past speech ἐν υἱῷ. Surely, however, this writer understands that past event to be a still-unfolding act of speech, contemporaneous with what the Holy Spirit even now—decades if not centuries later—says to the community through the OT writings within this act of preaching (3:7; 10:15). In this sense, too, the word of God is "living and active." Yet it is less that the word is made contemporaneous with us (as if we are the center to which it must be adjusted) than that we are summoned to stand always before it (as made contemporaneous with it). Divine speech is in this sense certainly presented as being irreducibly of the nature of an event in time, but an event which has the quality of God's living speech (only) ἐν υἱῷ—which takes into itself the written Scriptures—and uttered in the words of Scripture by the Holy Spirit. It is an event that confronts us as we move ever forward in history but never out of the presence of that once-for-all, and irreducibly past, act of divine speech ἐν υἱῷ, who is the same yesterday, today, and forever. It would be impossible to find in this exposition a divine speech-event that was anything other than this one act of speaking ἐν υἱῷ. Any theology of revelation that involved even a slight re-centering of that speech away from this speaking in time ἐν υἱῷ would cease to have anything whatever to do with Hebrews' theology of the word. Likewise, to tear it away from the written Scriptures, as if they are not integral to this event, would also have us talking about something altogether different, and yet it is just as clear that these writings are not God's word *in themselves*, as if in a self-contained textual dynamic. It is the living speech of God, uttered as the Holy Spirit speaks, whose speech is always and exclusively God's speech ἐν υἱῷ.

To sum up and reiterate: What we have to do with is something on the order of an ultimate emergent, which in its complexity can be understood only in terms of itself and certainly not from the perspective of only one or two of its elements. That the God of Abraham has, in these last days, spoken ἐν υἱῷ is the assertion on which all else turns in this letter. This new act of speech has happened; it is a now a datum of history. That it is the *same* God now speaking who spoke in the prophets is both a given and for that reason demonstrable—he has not left himself without a witness. The demonstration of that identity consists for Hebrews in an exposition that establishes the coherence of the otherwise πολυμερῶς καὶ πολυτρόπως OT speech in the person of the Son and simultaneously in the finding of the Son in that OT speech, particularly in his identity as sacrifice and priest. That this God has spoken, and spoken ἐν υἱῷ, thus entails an understanding of the relationship between the former word and this new word, bearing implications for what is *now* being said, its relativizing impact on what was said earlier, the enduringly and normatively informing nature of what was said earlier, and the implications for belief and unbelief. Once the truth of this is drawn out one will recognize that this God's word has reached its end, with the offer of life for those who act in faith and death for those who act in unbelief.

It is the failure to grasp this—in its concreteness in the person of the Son as sacrifice and high priest—that has placed this community unwittingly in such peril. By treating this act of speech as either merely human speech or of the same quality as the earlier, figural speech and merely continuous with it, they are in the process of forfeiting the true promise—consisting in the Son and all in him. Within the argument of Hebrews this anticipatory nature applies directly to the Mosaic tabernacle and what came with it, but it carries implications for creation as such. As goes the tabernacle so goes the world. A search for security either in the rites of a temple or in the structures of a Roman city amounts to the same thing: a failure to stake all and order one's very life on the word of the promise which is the Son. These misplaced loyalties, whether Roman or Judaic, amount to the same thing, but saying so definitively requires a particular lens, to wit, that supplied by God's own earlier act of speaking in the form of the Mosaic law, for what is true there (in *Jerusalem*, we have no abiding city) is *a fortiori* true everywhere else (e.g., here, in *Rome*).

Against this backdrop we consider that he has spoken *in the Son*,

> ὃν ἔθηκεν κληρονόμον πάντων,
> δι' οὗ καὶ ἐποίησεν τοὺς αἰῶνας·
> ὃς
>   ὢν ἀπαύγασμα τῆς δόξης καὶ χαρακτὴρ τῆς ὑποστάσεως αὐτοῦ,
>   φέρων τε τὰ πάντα τῷ ῥήματι τῆς δυνάμεως αὐτοῦ,
>   καθαρισμὸν τῶν ἁμαρτιῶν ποιησάμενος
> ἐκάθισεν ἐν δεξιᾷ τῆς μεγαλωσύνης ἐν ὑψηλοῖς,
> τοσούτῳ κρείττων γενόμενος τῶν ἀγγέλων
>   ὅσῳ διαφορώτερον παρ' αὐτοὺς κεκληρονόμηκεν ὄνομα.

On the one side in these lines there are clear marks of wisdom reflection among the first theologians and on the other side there are strong anticipations of the exposition to come in this letter. Further behind (and in, and in front of) the wording is the larger image of this triune God that emerges from the Scriptures broadly and in post-first-century missional practices and theological probings of the church. A minimalist exegesis that tethers conclusions tightly to the "historical constraints" of what we convince ourselves would have been conceptually possible for an imagined Greco-Roman author and readership and in keeping with the immanent categories that gave rise to the linguistic components will not do. The result of such a reading is nothing more than linguistic idols forged out of immanent, inert linguistic material, of no value for revealing God. For a realist stance, the Greco-Roman words and images do not define or limit the writer's conception but help us *trace the direction of the writer's gaze* in ways that are faithful to his intent. We, like the witnesses themselves, approach the throne; our reading is a plea to receive mercy and find grace unto well-timed help. Exegesis will require the hard-won experiential training of ethical struggle in the movement of right worship as the writer indicates in 5:14, a struggle whose context is a community (from Abel to Jesus, and Jesus' siblings) within God's mission.[11]

The Son is the ἀπαύγασμα τῆς δόξης, the radiance of the divine glory. When the discourse goes on to call the Son God (1:8) and Lord (1:10, in a context [Ps 102] where the original refers unmistakably to the God of Israel), ascribe to him pre-existence and eternity (2:9, 14; 7:1–10; 10:5), place him above the angels, and give him a role in the creation and providence of the cosmos (1:2–3, 10–12; 3:4), we may be sure that the image of ἀπαύγασμα intends distinction within continuity of being but with the emphasis placed on visible manifestation. The leading claim, following 1:1–2, concerns the Son's role as revelator. It is *here* that the divine glory is seen, and it is precisely here that that glory is *seen*.

The reference to the "the glory" can be taken from the broad stream of OT and Jewish traditions, but the coming mention of Moses (3:1–6) will recall the revelation of the divine glory in Exod 33–34, the quintessential self-revelation of God to Moses. The featuring of Exod 34 (with Num 12:1–8 [cf. Heb 3:2]; Deut 34:10–12) elsewhere in apostolic traditions in which Hebrews shares (e.g., 2 Cor 3:7–18; John 1:1–18; 1 Cor 13:10), not least in the transfiguration, tends to confirm that these are the associations in mind both in 3:1–6 and here in 1:3. Not only uniquely but exclusively God is manifested here in the Son precisely because God is here, for the Son *is* God, as the Father (1:5) is God. Moses, as the OT prophet par excellence in whom God spoke to the fathers πολυμερῶς καὶ πολυτρόπως πάλαι, received no other revelation and spoke of no other God in his role as a "witness to what would be spoken" (3:5). "Jesus' glory is greater than Moses', for Moses' glory was the reflection, or remnant, of the glory that he saw, but the glory that he saw was the son, the glory of God."[12] Both in what he wrote and what he built with its rites (9:6–10), Moses projected the image of the Son in the form of shadows, copies, and antitypes (8:5; 9:24; 10:1), for the Son was the pattern, the τύπος, shown Moses (8:5).[13]

Complementary to and inseparable from this phrase is the claim that the Son is χαρακτὴρ τῆς ὑποστάσεως αὐτοῦ, a reproduction, a representation of God's real being. The emphasis remains on the Son as the one in whom God speaks, for in seeing him (2:9; 12:2) who is the χαρακτὴρ of the Father's

---

11. Cf. Torrance, *The Trinitarian Faith*, 13–46; Vanhoozer, "Trials of Truth," 120–56.
12. D'Angelo, *Moses in Hebrews*, 162.
13. Ibid., 248, 254.

being we see God and we see God fully. As Jesus claimed of himself in John's Gospel, "Anyone who has seen me has seen the Father" (John 14:9; cf. 1 John 2:23). As theologians would later put it, "There is no unknown God behind the back of Jesus."[14] Or, coming at it from a different angle, "When we have seen the face of Jesus, we have seen the face of God, and we will know that we have never seen that face elsewhere and will never see it elsehow."[15] Hebrews 1:3 is necessarily also a statement about ontology and implications along those lines are properly inferred; but when the trajectory launched in 1:1–4, like a stone twice skipped across a pond, "lands" in both 4:12–13 and 12:25–29, we do well to stay on the main line of thought, namely, divine *speech* in the Son with the corresponding need to listen in the obedience of faith.

The triad of participles into which these phrases are grouped extends through the Son's incarnation to his heavenly session. This, combined with the entire discourse to follow for which these phrases have their very *point*, would make it odd to insist that the imagery of radiance and representation applies to the pre-existent Son and *not* to the incarnate and ascended Son. The divine speaking in and working of the Son are finally one thing and are irreducibly of the Son's "blood and flesh" nature required to bring the Abrahamic promise to fulfillment.

If this is so, then it is appropriate to see in his φέρων τε τὰ πάντα τῷ ῥήματι τῆς δυνάμεως αὐτοῦ not only a further underscoring of his involvement in the divine activity and thus also divine identity but what the remainder of the discourse will unfold at length, his bearing of all creation *up* and *along* toward its goal in keeping with the divine word. The word and the rule are bound together. The divine speech-act of Ps 110:1—"Sit at my right hand!"—had placed the risen Son on the divine throne from whence God's rule proceeds, anticipating the rule of the Son projected through Ps 45 (Heb 1:8–9) and Ps 8 (Heb 2:5–9). Then, that the "powerful word" of 1:3 includes the inscripturated word is what we see, for example, in the exposition of Ps 8 in 2:5–9. The visible face of God's world-bearing speech finds its outer contours in the written Scriptures; in this case in the words of Ps 8. Yet the words of Ps 8 would have been mere human sentiments of dubious truthfulness had they not found their substance in the Son; in the Son the created purposes of humanity announced in that (Ps 8's) "word of his power" are borne up and along to their goal. The Son's atonement, inclusive of his incarnation, is *internal to* his "bearing all things." Moreover, as with the Son's identity as the radiance and representation of God's being, it is precisely

---

14. Torrance, *Preaching*, 55.
15. See Torrance, "Hugh Ross Mackintosh," 163–64.

divine *speech* that is in focus in this line, speech that not only brings about the cosmos (11:3) but carries it to its goal.

This Son—who is the revelatory radiance, the representation, the one who bears by means of his speech—worked cleansing from sins in being and doing all this. This cleansing is evidently of the "all things" that he bears, in keeping with the larger vision of Hebrews for the cosmos, which foresees not the discarding annihilation of the created, material realm, but rather its cleansing and reconstitution as the temple of God. The perfective (aorist) participle (ποιησάμενος) is suited to express the idea that the whole discourse to follow will drive home at length, namely, the once-for-all and perfect *accomplishment* of this cleansing, to which nothing more could be or will be added by the Son. Along with the clause to follow ("he sat . . ."), which the three participles modify, it anticipates 10:11–15, which in turn begins the conclusion of the extended expositional unit of 4:14—10:25. In other words, the same argument being made at length in 4:14—10:25 is made *in nuce* here. The God whose speech creates and cleanses has now spoken conclusively, definitively, finally. The discussion of this writer's multifaceted vision of the atonement is, however, one that we do not have space to pursue at present.

The three participial phrases we have just reviewed are of course embedded in the third of three relative clauses that describe the Son in whom God has spoken definitively in these last days. The first two of these relative clauses are stylized versions of the formula used elsewhere of God (2:10; Rom 11:36) and the Son (Col 1:16; cf. 1 Cor 8:6; John 1:3). For instance, in Col 1:15–18, which generally attests the conventional substance of Heb 1:1–4, God created all things through the Son and unto him (τὰ πάντα δι' αὐτοῦ καὶ εἰς αὐτὸν ἔκτισται). In Hebrews this formula places the Son in parallel with the Father who is described similarly in 2:10, while it is tailored to fit the driving narrative underlying the entire discourse by substituting for εἰς αὐτὸν the statement that the Son is "heir of all things" that were given Abraham in the promise; precisely because this theme is integral to the assumed narrative (outlined above) it is not only rephrased but fronted. The Son's inheritance is "the nations" and the "ends of the earth" of which Ps 2:8 spoke, "the world to come" concerning which the author is speaking throughout the following context (2:5). The Son is, quite exclusively, the heir of the promise, the seed of Abraham.

Thinking of this exclusivity, one has strong reservations against stating that the sons and daughters are made heirs by virtue of *participation* with the Son, being *in* the Son, since Hebrews, unlike Paul, nowhere expresses that idea verbally and seems otherwise to favor the idea of believers being companions of the Son, or the Son being instrumental to their reception of the inheritance. Yet some such idea as *participation*, if not also *substitution*, seems finally required for his argument throughout the discourse to work. What is patent through these first two relative clauses, and what the following argument will make explicit, is that this salvation bounds the cosmos spatially and historically, an emphasis that remains in the service of the overarching claim regarding divine *speech*. The one who is the end and goal of all things was their creator, which means that in him the ultimate speech of God is to be found (12:25–29). As for the resurrected Son's seat at the right hand of the Majesty, this indicates at once the full realization of the work of God in humanity, humanity's full reception of what was promised Abraham, and the full revelation of God in the Son, whose inheritance can be summed up in a name above all names (Phil 2:9). In the Son resides all the glory and bounty of God, whose speech does what it says and whose speech is the Son in his being and work.

CONCLUSION

This brings us back to the recognition of the grammatical structure of these verses, for all three relative clauses with the three[16] modifying participial phrases serve to explicate and underscore the leading assertion that it is in this Son that God has now spoken, with the result that one must be sure not to refuse the one who speaks (12:25) but rather be united in faith with those who listen (4:2). Hebrews is at bottom the promissory speech-act of *forgiveness* (10:18); it is a performative word effecting by its very pronouncement cleansing for the seed of Abraham, the seed that is now finally and actually made God's family, God's household, through the incarnation and priestly office of God's Son, himself the seed of Abraham, himself that Word; forgiveness once and for all, uttered and accomplished by God in and as the Son in accordance with what God had spoken by Moses and all the prophets. This brings to its concluding moment the long history of God and those who believed him through the years of waiting. Accordingly, it opens access in the present to the presence of God, formerly unapproachable in his holiness but now "the throne of grace" for the people. It inaugurates the achievement of the promise God made to all humanity in Ps 8, words whose truth was to be found exclusively in the Son and only thereby for his fellow children. The drama is not yet closed, however, as that closing moment undergoes elongation for the sake of God's mission. "These last days" are days of arrival but also of continued waiting while the Son waits for all

---

16. *Four* participial modifiers, of course, when we include the explicating and transitional v. 4.

his enemies to be made a footstool for his feet and while those who believe that the promise is the Son voice back their gratitude by rendering pleasing worship, learning what it means to be genuine sons and daughters of God, going outside the camp and bearing Jesus' reproach for the sake of his mission, because "here we have no enduring city, but we are looking for the city that is to come" (13:14). The destination is thus the holy city, the cosmos cleansed and reconstituted as God's dwelling. Meanwhile and forevermore, the Son has become their text, their Scripture, their God in whom they find themselves, their family, their history, and their inheritance. As such, Hebrews constitutes a uniquely successful canonical theology in its own right.

BIBLIOGRAPHY

Attridge, Harold A. "God in Hebrews." In *The Epistle to the Hebrews and Christian Theology*, edited by Richard Bauckham et al., 95–110. Grand Rapids: Eerdmans, 2009.

D'Angelo, Mary Rose. *Moses in the Letter to the Hebrews*. SBLDS 42. Missoula, MT: Scholars, 1979.

Marshall, I. Howard. "Soteriology in Hebrews." In *The Epistle to the Hebrews and Christian Theology*, edited by Richard Bauckham et al., 253–77. Grand Rapids: Eerdmans, 2009.

Peeler, Amy L. *You Are My Son: The Family of God in the Epistle to the Hebrews*. LNTS 486. London: T. & T. Clark, 2014.

Torrance, T. F. "Hugh Ross Mackintosh: Theologian of the Cross." *SBET* 5 (1987) 160–73.

———. *Preaching Christ Today: The Gospel and Scientific Thinking*. Grand Rapids: Eerdmans, 1994.

———. *The Trinitarian Faith*. Edinburgh: T. & T. Clark, 1991.

Vanhoozer, Kevin J. "The Trials of Truth. Mission, Martyrdom, and the Epistemology of the Cross." In *To Stake a Claim: Mission and the Western Crisis of Knowledge*, edited by J. Andrew Kirk and Kevin J. Vanhoozer, 120–56. Maryknoll, NY: Orbis, 1999.

5

"You are my Son"

Climactic Revelation in the Son of God in Mark and Hebrews

CALEB T. FRIEDEMAN

THE BOOK OF HEBREWS first captured my imagination under the tutelage of Gary Cockerill—initially through a project for a Septuagint seminar, and subsequently in a Greek exegesis of Hebrews. As I studied Hebrews' use of the OT, I was both captivated and vexed by how much the pastor's exegesis differed from my own.[1] What principles undergirded his interpretations? Where was the control in his method? How could he place words written by OT authors in the mouth of the Father, Son, or Spirit at will? In this essay, I hope to contribute something of an answer to these questions by exploring a topic that lies at the nexus of several interests I have inherited from Dr. Cockerill, namely Hebrews, the gospel of Mark, and a desire to hear Scripture as a whole (i.e., biblical theology).[2]

Hebrews scholarship has long recognized the pastor's indebtedness to prior traditions about Jesus. On a general level, Cockerill notes that, "The most significant aspect of the pastor's worldview is his fundamental dependence on common Christian tradition. The pastor is committed to the Son's eternal preexistence . . . incarnation . . . crucifixion . . . and exaltation . . .

---

1. In this essay I adopt Cockerill's practice of calling Hebrews' author the "pastor" and his work the "sermon" (*Hebrews*, 2).

2. Dr. Cockerill has taught an English Bible inductive study of Mark for many years at Wesley Biblical Seminary. I had the privilege of taking this course, as well as the Septuagint seminar mentioned above, at WBS during the fall of 2011. The Hebrews course noted above took place in the spring semester of 2012.

including belief in his resurrection."[3] Similarly, Attridge considers it "highly likely" that the pastor "has adopted and modified traditions" of the Christian community to which he writes.[4] In addition, Moffitt has argued that the resurrection is central to Hebrews' exposition of Jesus' role as High Priest.[5] It is therefore not surprising that some exegetes have made passing comments about resemblances between Hebrews and various passages in the gospels.[6] In particular, numerous interpreters have seen in Heb 5:7 a reference to Jesus' passion in general, or more narrowly his prayer in Gethsemane or cry of dereliction (unique to Mark and Matthew).[7] Furthermore, Cockerill has pointed out intriguing verbal parallels between Matt 26:28 (τὸ αἷμά ... ἐκχυννόμενον εἰς ἄφεσιν ἁμαρτιῶν) and Heb 9:19b–22 (χωρὶς αἱματεκχυσίας οὐ γίνεται ἄφεσις) that suggest that Hebrews "may echo" Matthew at this point.[8]

Although Hebrews' knowledge of Jesus traditions is well-noted and a few scholars have suggested specific parallels between Hebrews and concepts or pericopae in the gospels, the relationship between Hebrews and Jesus traditions remains undefined. Here I will attempt to make a modest contribution to the matter by exploring a theme that Hebrews and the Synoptics share uniquely: climactic revelation in the Son of God via Ps 2:7. In this essay, I will use "climactic revelation" to refer to *divine revelation that is in continuity with God's prior revelation yet is demonstrated to be superior to it by virtue of a greater revelatory agent*.[9] The Synoptic gospels and Hebrews each develop such a concept, portraying Jesus as God's climactic revelation by virtue of his identity as God's Son, with reference to Ps 2:7. I will begin

---

3. *Hebrews*, 24.

4. *Hebrews*, 30. However, Attridge is also skeptical about efforts to ground Hebrews' priestly Christology in a particular literary tradition (e.g., Synoptic, Johannine).

5. Moffitt, *Atonement*. See ibid., 299, for a summary of the argument.

6. E.g., Bruce, *Hebrews*, 30, 54; Cockerill, *Hebrews*, 140, 143–44, 431; Kistemaker, *Hebrews*, 60, 293, 295; etc.

7. For Gethsemane, see Spicq, *L'Épître*, 2:113; Hughes, *Hebrews*, 182–83, as well as Attridge's critique of this position (*Hebrews*, 148). For the cry of dereliction, see Vanhoye, *Old Testament*, 125.

8. Cockerill, *Hebrews*, 409, 409n34. Cockerill points out that "αἱματεκχυσία ('shedding of blood') is compounded from the words used in Matthew for αἷμα ('blood') and ἐκχέω/ἐκχύννω ('pour out')."

9. By "revelatory agent," I do not mean to imply that the agent merely conveys revelation external to himself. Both the Synoptics and Hebrews arguably portray Jesus as both revealer and revealed—he simultaneously *gives* and *is* God's climactic revelation. Here I use the less precise phrase "revelatory agent" to avoid prejudicing the exploration of Second Temple Jewish literature below by creating too tight of a definition at the outset.

by examining this theme in Mark (generally thought to be the earliest of the Synoptics[10]) and Hebrews individually, and then explore what these texts might say if heard in concert with one another. I will argue, among other things, that Hebrews ultimately seems to be indebted to Jesus traditions for its concept of the Son as God's ultimate revelation.[11]

MARK AND CLIMACTIC REVELATION IN THE SON OF GOD

Mark introduces his work as, "The beginning of the good news about Jesus the Messiah, the Son of God [υἱοῦ θεοῦ]." Although the phrase υἱοῦ θεοῦ is missing in several manuscripts, it has strong support from Vaticanus, Beza Cantabrigiensis, and Freerianus, and is also probable based on the internal evidence of Mark (see below). If original, then Mark places the concept of Jesus' divine Sonship on the table from the first, forming an inclusio with the centurion's revelation at the cross: "Surely this man was the Son of God!" (15:39). Such bracketing would suggest that for Mark the Son of God concept is central.

Mark follows this with a composite quotation from Exod 23:20, Mal 3:1, and Isa 40:3 that anticipates the messenger who will prepare the way of the Lord. The key point here is that within Mark's narrative world, the messenger predicted is clearly John the Baptist, who appears in the very next verse (Mark 1:4). This implies that "the Lord" of Isa 40:3/Mark 1:3 is Jesus, the one for whom John has prepared the people (1:7–8, 9). But who is the "I" who will send the messenger? Presumably it is none other than YHWH himself. In these opening verses and their narrative fulfillment, Mark gives a remarkably compact explication of Jesus' identity that the rest of his gospel will unpack: Jesus is the Son of God, who is identified with YHWH ("the Lord" of Isa 40:3) yet is distinct from the divine speaker of Exod 23:20/Mal 3:1.

Mark continues his exposition of Jesus' divine Sonship at his baptism. As Jesus comes up out of the water, a voice declares from heaven, "You are my Son, whom I love; with you I am well pleased" (σὺ εἶ ὁ υἱός μου ὁ ἀγαπητός, ἐν σοὶ εὐδόκησα, Mark 1:11). As with the divine speech in 1:2–3,

---

10. E.g., Carson and Moo, *Introduction*, 95–98; McKnight, "Source Criticism," 74–105; Watson, *Gospel Writing*, 121–31.

11. The phrase "son of God" had a number of possible connotations in the ancient world (for a survey, see Dunn, *Christology*, 13–22). My purpose in this essay is not to argue for a particular interpretation of "Son of God" in its own right, but rather to show how both Mark and Hebrews connect this title with the idea of climactic revelation, and to expound the significance of this observation.

these words recall OT Scripture, yet again Mark's discourse seems to defy a single OT reference.[12] The clearest allusion is to Ps 2:7 LXX: "The Lord said to me, 'You are my son [Υἱός μου εἶ σύ]; today I have begotten you.'"[13] Although Mark's σὺ εἶ ὁ υἱός μου exhibits a slightly different word order and adds a definite article, the resemblance is undeniable. The allusion to Ps 2 is especially apt because, as in Mark, it is the Lord who speaks the words of affirmation. In addition, Ps 2 contains both of the christological titles that Mark introduced in 1:1, Messiah (Ps 2:2) and Son (2:7).

Mark's ὁ ἀγαπητός, however, finds no equivalent in Ps 2:7 LXX. For this reason, some have suggested that here Mark alludes to Gen 22:2 LXX (τὸν υἱόν σου τὸν ἀγαπητόν; cf. 22:12, 16) in addition to Ps 2:7.[14] However, there is another explanation for the appearance of ὁ ἀγαπητός. The word "beloved" appears in the Targum of Ps 2:7: "You are as beloved [חביב] to me as a son to a father" (Tg. Ps. 2:7). Mark may reflect an earlier form of this targumic tradition.[15] In sum, Mark's ὁ ἀγαπητός may allude to both Ps 2:7 and Gen 22:2, or it may simply allude to Ps 2:7 via a textual tradition similar to that preserved in *Targum Psalms*. Given our limited knowledge, we may not be able to adjudicate between the two options. What *is* clear—and significant for this study—is that in Mark 1:11 God affirms Jesus as his Son using the language of Ps 2:7.[16]

Although Ps 2 can account for most or all of the first clause of the divine affirmation (σὺ εἶ ὁ υἱός μου ὁ ἀγαπητός), it does not explain the second (ἐν σοὶ εὐδόκησα). Two OT references seem possible here. In 2 Sam 22:20 LXX, David praises God for saving him from Saul: "He brought me out into a wide place and delivered me, because he was well pleased in me [εὐδόκησεν ἐν ἐμοί]." The use of εὐδοκέω fits well with Mark 1:11, and the passage shares the Davidic interest of Ps 2. On the other hand, Isa 42:1 LXX

---

12. For a summary of the OT passages proposed and their proponents, see Watts, "Mark," 122-23. Although Exod 4:22-23 has often occupied a position in the discussion, I omit it here because in my view it lacks sufficient verbal connections with Mark 1:11.

13. For the purposes of this study, "LXX" will refer to the text of the Göttingen edition where available, and the Rahlfs-Hanhart in books where the Göttingen edition has not yet been published (e.g., 2 Samuel below). All translations of LXX texts are my own.

14. Best, *Temptation*, 169-72; Daly, "Significance," 68-70; Wood, "Isaac," 586; Boring, *Mark*, 45; Rindge, "Akedah," 762-66; for Gen 22:22 in Matt 3:17, see Huizenga, *Isaac*, 153-87. Vermes (*Scripture*, 222-23) argues for Gen 22:2 *instead of* Ps 2:7, but the verbal and conceptual links with Ps 2:7 render this view untenable.

15. Watts, "Mark," 123; Evans, *Texts*, 213.

16. Although the allusion to Ps 2:7 has been challenged by a few (e.g., Zimmerli and Jeremias, *Servant*, 80-81; Fuller, *Foundations*, 169-70), it has widespread support, e.g., Lane, *Mark*, 57; Collins, *Mark*, 150; Black, *Mark*, 59.

is also possible: "Jacob is my servant; I will lay hold of him. Israel is my chosen one; my soul has accepted him [προσεδέξατο αὐτὸν ἡ ψυχή μου]." Clearly, the verb προσδέχομαι is not as close to Mark as the εὐδοκέω of 2 Sam 22:20. On the other hand, both Symmachus and Theodotion have "... my chosen one, in whom my soul is pleased [ον ευδοκησεν η ψυχη μου]" here, and it is at least possible that Mark may have had access to this textual tradition. If so, then 2 Sam 22:20 and Isa 42:1 could account for the use of εὐδοκέω equally well. As with Ps 2:7 and Gen 22:2 above, it is difficult to be dogmatic about whether 2 Sam 22:20 or Isaiah 42:1 has the better claim. However, in my view several contextual factors tip the scale in favor of Isaiah: First, in both Isaiah 42:1 and Mark 1:11 it is YHWH who is speaking. Second, Isaiah's promise that YHWH will put his Spirit on this chosen one with whom he is pleased (42:2) is also especially *apropos* to the Markan context, in which the Spirit descends on Jesus like a dove (1:10). Finally, Mark's earlier citation of Isaiah (1:2–3) give Isa 42:1 the benefit of recurrence. In Mark 1:11, then, God verbally affirms Jesus as his Son using the language of Ps 2:7 in concert with Isa 42:1 and possibly Gen 22:2. This affirmation confirms Jesus' divine Sonship that Mark has asserted earlier (1:1) and again places Jesus' identity as God's Son at the fore as a key theological motif for the rest of the gospel to develop.

Mark's next reference to Jesus' divine Sonship comes in 3:11: "Whenever the impure spirits saw him, they fell down before him and cried out, 'You are the Son of God [ὁ υἱὸς τοῦ θεοῦ].'" Here Jesus' identity as Son is linked with his authority over demons. Similarly, when the Gerasene demoniac approaches Jesus, he falls on his knees and cries out, "What do you want with me, Jesus, Son of the Most High God [υἱὲ τοῦ θεοῦ τοῦ ὑψίστου]? In God's name don't torture me!" (5:7). Mark goes on to note that the demoniac did this because Jesus was commanding the unclean spirit to come out of him (5:8). Therefore, both of these passages suggest that Jesus' divine Sonship entails his supreme authority over the powers of evil.

At the transfiguration (9:2–8), however, Mark highlights another aspect of Jesus' divine Sonship: As the Son of God, Jesus is God's ultimate revelation. The whole scene evokes the imagery of the Sinai revelation.[17] Six days after the events of Mark 8:31—9:1 (cf. Exod 24:16) Jesus takes Peter, James, and John with him up onto a high mountain (cf. Exod 24:1–9, 12–15). Jesus is transfigured there before them (cf. Exod 34:29–35) and Elijah and Moses appear, conversing with him. Peter, not knowing what to say because the Three are so frightened (cf. Exod 34:30), suggests that they build three shelters—one for Jesus, one for Moses, and one for Elijah. However, this is

---

17. See Watts, "Mark," 186, for a fuller account of the parallels.

not to be; a cloud covers them, and a voice comes from within it: "This is my Son, whom I love. Listen to him!" (οὗτός ἐστιν ὁ υἱός μου ὁ ἀγαπητός, ἀκούετε αὐτοῦ, 9:7) This scene clearly recalls the Father's earlier affirmation of Jesus as his Son at the baptism (1:9-11), but the saying has been reshaped to fit the new context. Instead of speaking directly to Jesus in the second person (σὺ εἶ), God now speaks primarily for the benefit of the disciples using the third person (οὗτός ἐστιν). In addition, whereas at the baptism the Father's second phrase expressed his pleasure in the Son (ἐν σοὶ εὐδόκησα), here the Father expounds the significance Jesus' Sonship for the Three: "Listen to him!" Thus, although the allusion to Ps 2:7 (and possibly Gen 22:2) remains, the reference to 2 Sam 22:20 and/or Isa 42:1 has now been replaced with an exhortation to listen. This likely recalls Deut 18:15 LXX, where Moses exhorts Israel to listen to the coming prophet like Moses (αὐτοῦ ἀκούσεσθε).[18]

Mark's scripturally-rich narrative underlines the significance of the transfiguration: Although Jesus stands in continuity with God's revelation through Elijah and Moses, the OT prophets *par excellence*, he is God's climactic revelation by virtue of his identity as the Son of God. Peter's mistake, then, is likely that he attempts to rank Jesus alongside Elijah and Moses as merely another prophet. The Father, however, affirms that Jesus is his Son and that the disciples are to hear his voice above all others. Mark's conclusion to the epiphany underscores the point: when the disciples looked up, they "no longer saw anyone with them except Jesus" (9:8). It is probably no coincidence that to this point in the gospel Jesus has constantly been disputing with various Jewish groups precisely over the correct interpretation of Torah.[19] Jesus nowhere jettisons his commitment to Israel's Scriptures, but he does interpret them differently than the scribes, Pharisees, etc. Similarly, the transfiguration shows Jesus to be in full continuity with Elijah and Moses, while making it clear that it is Jesus the Son of God that the disciples must hear.

It is also no accident that at the transfiguration God the Father reiterates the words he had spoken earlier at Jesus' baptism. Indeed, when read in context, Mark's account of the baptism makes a point similar to that of the transfiguration: In the verses immediately preceding the baptism, John the Baptist predicts that someone more powerful will come after him (1:7). Mark has already framed John in Elijah-like terms through his earlier quotation of Malachi, who portrayed the eschatological messenger of YHWH as Elijah (Mal 3:1; 4:5-6). Therefore, when Jesus arrives on the scene, the

---

18. Marcus, *Way*, 80-92.

19. See esp. Mark 2:24, 26; 3:4, where the question is precisely about what is lawful (ἔξεστιν). Cf. also 10:2; 12:14. More generally, see 2:1—3:12; 3:20-30; 7:1-23.

reader has been prepared to understand that this newcomer fulfills John's prophecy that one superior to John—and therefore superior to Elijah as well—would follow him, just as Malachi and Isaiah had predicted. At the baptism, then, the Father affirms Jesus' identity and implicitly explains why he is superior to John, the eschatological Elijah: whereas John is God's prophet, Jesus is God's Son. In fact, Jesus' words to the disciples after the transfiguration recapitulate this John-Elijah theme: "To be sure, Elijah does come first, and restores all things. Why then is it written that the Son of Man must suffer much and be rejected? But I tell you, Elijah has come, and they have done to him everything they wished, just as it is written about him" (Mark 9:12–13). In sum, in both Mark 1:11 and 9:7 we find the Father's verbal affirmation of Jesus as his Son connected with the concept of Jesus as God's ultimate revelation.

The parable of the tenants (Mark 12:1–12) further illustrates this connection between Jesus' as God's Son and climactic revelation. The story is well known: A man builds a vineyard and rents it to tenants, who refuse to give any of its fruit to the man's representatives. After sending many servants to no avail, the man finally sends his beloved son (υἱὸν ἀγαπητόν, 12:6), thinking that the tenants will respect him. The tenants, however, kill the son and throw him outside the vineyard. In his epilogue to the parable, Jesus tells of the judgment that will come on the tenants and how others will inherit the vineyard. Jesus' meaning is clear enough: the tenants are the leaders of Israel, the servants are YHWH's prophets, and he is the beloved son (cf. 12:12; Isa 5). Mark's parable of the tenants, then, gives a storied portrait of what the baptism and transfiguration have already said: God has sent many prophets, but his Son constitutes his ultimate revelation. Ironically, Israel's leaders will reject even God's ultimate act of communication.

Indeed, this rejection coincides with Mark's next mention of Jesus' Sonship. At Jesus' trial before the Sanhedrin, the high priest asks Jesus, "Are you the Messiah, the Son of the Blessed One [ὁ υἱὸς τοῦ εὐλογητοῦ]?" (14:61). Jesus answers in the affirmative and adds, "And you [pl.] will see the Son of Man sitting at the right hand of the Mighty One and coming on the clouds of heaven" (14:62). Jesus' answer seals his fate in the eyes of the Sanhedrin. The high priest's question about Jesus' Sonship and the Sanhedrin's response seem to both fulfill and build on Jesus' use of the son motif in the parable of the tenants—after all, it would be odd for the Jewish leadership to condemn a man for merely claiming to be a Davidic king. As Thielman notes, "The high priest . . . seems to understand the unusual connotations of Jesus' claim to divine sonship in the parable of the wicked tenants."[20]

---

20. Thielman, *Theology*, 63.

Mark's development of the Son of God theme comes to a climax at the cross. Mark tell us that "with a loud cry, Jesus breathed his last" (15:37) and when the centurion standing in front of him saw how he died, he declared, "Surely this man was the Son of God [υἱὸς θεοῦ ἦν]!" (15:39). We must consider this saying on two fronts: On the one hand, the centurion likely did not intend to convey the full Markan sense of the Son of God title. On the other hand, for Mark's readers, the phrase would inevitably evoke the earlier occurrences of the title in the gospel. Although υἱὸς θεοῦ ἦν might be interpreted as "a son of God," due to the lack of the definite article, this is both unnecessary and unlikely for two reasons: First, from a grammatical standpoint Colwell's rule would suggest that in general an anarthrous pre-verbal predicate nominative like the one here would be "*normally qualitative, sometimes definite, and only rarely indefinite*" (emphasis original).[21] So, the *most likely* interpretations here would be either (1) that Son of God describes the attributes and qualities of Jesus' identity (qualitative),[22] or (2) that Jesus simply is *the* Son of God (definite). Second, the indefinite interpretation becomes even less likely when we consider that Mark has already used the anarthrous υἱοῦ θεοῦ in 1:1, where it is surely either qualitative or definite.[23]

Mark 15:39 concludes our survey of the Son of God motif in Mark. Although much of what I have said about climactic revelation in the Son of God in Mark also applies to Matthew and Luke as well, Mark is unique in his exposition of this theme in two ways: First, Mark frontloads the Son of God concept as key through his inclusio at 1:1 and 15:39. In addition, although Matthew and Luke reiterate the three principal pericopae that emphasize the Son as God's climactic revelation (baptism, transfiguration, parable of the tenants), they do not develop the theme of the Son as climactic revelation beyond Mark's exposition, their greater length notwithstanding. Therefore, while all three Synoptics affirm the Son as God's climactic revelation, Mark seems to emphasize this point somewhat more strongly.

In sum, from the first verse of his gospel Mark emphasizes Son of God as a key theological motif. For Mark, a key element of Jesus' Sonship is his role as God's climactic revelation. Mark first draws attention to this at Jesus' baptism, when God affirms Jesus as his Son, implying his superiority to John—and by extension Elijah and the other prophets—by virtue of his identity. However, the Son's status as climactic revelation becomes

---

21. Wallace, *Greek Grammar*, 262; see also ibid., 256–66; Harner, "Predicate Nouns," 76.

22. Here I draw on Wallace's exposition of the qualitative sense in relation to John 1:1 (*Greek Grammar*, 269).

23. Cf. Stein, *Mark*, 718–19; France, *Mark*, 659–60.

most evident at the transfiguration, when the Father again affirms Jesus as his Son who is both in continuity with and superior to the preeminent OT prophets Moses and Elijah. The Son's superiority to the prophets comes to the fore again in Jesus' parable of the tenants, where the son of the vineyard's owner comes after a long line of servants as the ultimate manifestation of his father's will. The tenants' rejection and murder of the son foreshadow the Jewish religious leaders' similar treatment of Jesus at the trial and ultimately at the cross, where Jesus' death moves the centurion to acknowledge Jesus' identity as Son of God, forming an inclusio with Mark's mention of Jesus' Sonship in 1:1. With this survey of Mark in hand, we now turn to see how Hebrews develops the idea of the Son as climactic revelation.

HEBREWS AND CLIMACTIC REVELATION IN THE SON OF GOD

In the opening verses of Hebrews, the pastor enunciates the basic ideas that will undergird the rest of his sermon: "In the past God spoke to our ancestors through the prophets at many times and in various ways, but in these last days he has spoken to us by his Son" (Heb 1:1–2a). In these verses the pastor creates a rhetorically potent parallelism that emphasizes the climactic revelation that has taken place in God's Son:

1. In the past . . . at many times and in various ways	in these last days
2. God	he
3. spoke	has spoken
4. to our ancestors	to us
5. through the prophets	by his Son[24]

This parallelism highlights both the continuity and contrast between the two instances of God's speech in "the prophets" and in the Son. On the one hand, in each case it is *God* who has spoken (λαλέω).[25] In this way, the pastor affirms that the prophets are no spurious speech of God; they convey legitimate divine revelation. On the other hand, God's speech in his Son far surpasses the revelation of old. Whereas God's speech through the prophets took place long ago, in diverse places and ways, and was directed to the

---

24. Cockerill, *Hebrews*, 88; Kistemaker, *Hebrews*, 27; etc.

25. Hebrews' emphasis on divine revelation as God's speech is well noted and stands in contrast to Paul and other NT writers who introduce Scripture quotations with phrases like "as it is written" (καθὼς γέγραπται).

ancestors of the pastor's listeners, this speech in the Son has taken place in these last days and is pointed at the pastor and his listeners. However, the primary reason that this latter speech is superior is the one in whom it takes place: God's Son. After mentioning the Son in 1:2a, the pastor spends the remainder of his lengthy introductory sentence (1:2b–4)—and in a sense the rest of the chapter—expounding the virtues of the Son that qualify him as God's climactic revelation.

The pastor ends his introduction by claiming that the Son is superior to angels (1:4), and then goes on to provide Scriptural substantiation for this claim in 1:5–14. Interestingly, the first passage of Scripture that the pastor marshals to support his thesis is none other than Ps 2:7: "For to which of the angels did God ever say, 'You are my Son; today I have become your Father'?" (Heb 1:5). Although in the context of Ps 2 God speaks these words to the Davidic monarch, here in Hebrews he speaks them to the Son. As the catena of Scripture quotations unfolds, we find this pattern repeated—verses from such diverse contexts as 2 Samuel and Pss 45, 102, 110, and 8 are applied to Jesus to prove his superiority to the angels.

This peculiar comparison between the Son and angels has caused some to advance elaborate theories that paint Heb 1:4–14 as a corrective to an unorthodox angelology or an angelic Christology.[26] Although such theories may have some explanatory power, they are largely speculative and distract from the pastor's own logic as evidenced in 2:1–3a: "We must pay the most careful attention, therefore, to what we have heard, so that we do not drift away. For since the *message spoken through angels* was binding, and every violation and disobedience received its just punishment, how shall we escape if we ignore so great a salvation?" (emphasis added). Here the pastor applies his argument in chapter 1 to his listeners, suggesting that they are more accountable to respond because they have received a greater revelation than that spoken through angels. This makes it clear that 1:4–14 does not compare the Son to angels in some general sense, but rather to angels primarily *as mediators of a message*. This draws on the well-attested belief in Second Temple Judaism and early Christianity that angels mediated God's revelation at Mount Sinai.[27] The implied point of 1:5–14, then, is that God's revelation in the Son is superior even to the momentous Sinai revelation by virtue of the Son's superior identity. Incidentally, this is a particularization of the point made in 1:1–4. Hebrews 1:1–14, therefore, forms a tight argument

---

26. E.g., Attridge, *Hebrews*, 50–53; Hughes, *Hebrews*, 51–53. However, neither is dogmatic about the matter. For a more thorough treatment of angel veneration in early Judaism and Christianity, see Stuckenbruck, *Angel Veneration*, esp. 119–39, on Heb 1:5—2:18.

27. Acts 7:38, 53; Gal 3:19; *Jub.* 1.27, 29; 2.1; Josephus, *Ant.* 15.136.

for God's climactic revelation in his Son. This initial exposition of the Son as God's climactic revelation in Heb 1 is foundational to the whole book, since it is the basis of the lesser-to-greater argument that runs throughout: The pastor consistently operates with the assumption that although God spoke truly in the prophets, he has now spoken his ultimate word in his Son, and that this new speech demands an appropriate response from the pastor and his listeners.

Hebrews further develops this idea of climactic revelation in the Son in 3:1–6, where the pastor directs his hearers' attention toward Jesus. Here, the pastor invites his audience to consider Jesus, whom he shows to be like Moses, yet superior to him. Although Jesus was faithful to God as Moses was, he is not to be equated with Moses. On the contrary, Jesus "has been counted worthy of more glory than Moses" (Heb 3:3) on the basis of his superior identity. Whereas Moses *was* faithful *in* all God's house as a *servant*, Jesus *is* faithful *over* God's house as a *Son* (Heb 3:5–6). Although the pastor does not explicitly raise the issue of revelation here, since Moses was remembered primarily in terms of his role as a prophet and lawgiver, it stands to reason that the force of the comparison is to emphasize that Jesus is a superior revelatory agent by virtue of his identity as God's Son.

These two passages, Heb 1:1–14 and 3:1–6, develop the idea that as God's revelation, Jesus is both in continuity with and yet superior to the prophets—even Moses—because of his identity. Although it would be incorrect to say that for Hebrews the Son is merely climactic revelation, this theme is near to the heart of the book. The Son in Hebrews may be more than God's ultimate revelation, but he is certainly not less.

PSALM 2 IN EARLY JUDAISM AND THE NEW TESTAMENT

In both the Synoptic tradition and Hebrews, we have noted a convergence of two elements: (1) divine sonship via Ps 2:7, (2) emphasizing God's climactic revelation in the Son—i.e., the idea that as Son, Jesus reveals God in a way superior to yet in continuity with the prophets. In order to further define the relationship between these expositions and hear them together, we first need to recognize how unique this combination truly is. In order to discern how unusual it is for two texts to combine the elements sketched above, we will pursue one of the elements, namely the use of Ps 2, in the thought-world of Mark and Hebrews—i.e., Second Temple Judaism and the NT (after all, non-Christian Greeks and Romans were not likely to cite the Psalter). If Ps 2 occurs regularly with the idea of climactic revelation, then

Mark and Hebrews will not be especially unique at this point. On the other hand, if Ps 2 occurs in conjunction with these other themes never or only rarely, then we will have grounds to hear a unity between the distinct voices of Mark and Hebrews, and may also have resources to suggest a plausible relationship between them. The survey below will explore uses of Ps 2 in Second Temple and early Christian texts, with a focus on Ps 2:7.[28]

Psalm 2 appears in quotation three times in the Dead Sea Scrolls, and all instances seem to follow the Masoretic text. Unfortunately, 3Q2 and 11Q7 only preserve fragments of the Psalm with no comment, so they are of little help. 4Q174 quotes Ps 2:1 and connects it with the eschatological persecution that will come upon Judah to perfect it (1.18–2.1). Although it identifies this time with Dan 12:10, where the wicked go on acting wickedly and do not understand but the righteous purify themselves and understand (4Q174 2.4–6), there is no mention of any new revelation that surpasses the law or the prophets. Earlier, the document quotes 2 Sam 7:12–13 (4Q174 1.10–12), which Ps 2 may itself assume. However, the interpretation merely identifies the son of God as a Davidic descendant who will arise with the Interpreter of the Law to rule in Zion at the end. The mention of the Interpreter may imply some eschatological revelation. However, this is distinct from the concept of climactic revelation in the Son in Mark and Hebrews, since (1) the Interpreter is a different person from the Messiah, (2) in 4Q174 the revelation is merely an interpretation of the law, with no hint of new revelation that surpasses it, and (3) there is no comparison to previous revelatory agents.[29] One possible allusion to Ps 2:7 occurs in 4Q246 2.1. Here, however, it is debated whether the son of God is a messianic figure or a pagan king. In any case, no revelatory status is ascribed to him.

The Pseudepigrapha allude to Ps 2 a number of times. Typically, Ps 2 appears in connection with the son of God's triumph over his enemies. For instance, in *1 Enoch* the kings of the earth and mighty land owners are humiliated and submit, never to rise again, since they have denied "the Lord of the Spirits and his Messiah" (cf. Ps 2:2).[30] Similarly, *Pss. Sol.* 2.32 proclaims the Lord's judgment to the officials of the earth (cf. Ps 2:2). *Psalms*

---

28. See Janse, "*You are My Son*," for a more extended survey of early Jewish and Christian interpretation of Ps 2:7; and Davies, *Torah*, for early Jewish perspectives on the Law and its relationship to the Messiah.

29. One might, of course, argue in this passage and others that the eschatological setting implies that the revelation is by definition superior or climactic. Even if this is so, Mark and Hebrews portray Jesus (the Son of Ps 2:7) as superior precisely by comparing him to the prophets, and this sort of clarity does not seem to appear in 4Q174 or the other Second Temple sources.

30. *1 En.* 48.8–10, trans. E. Isaac (*OTP* 1:35–36). Cf. Ps 2:2.

of Solomon 17 also trades on this theme of Messianic triumph using the language of Ps 2. Here the psalmist exhorts the Lord to raise up a Davidic king, and to "undergird him with the strength to destroy the unrighteous rulers, to purge Jerusalem from gentiles."[31] A few lines later, the psalmist envisions the Messiah smashing the arrogance of sinners like a potter's jar and shattering their confidence with an iron rod (*Pss. Sol.* 17.23–24; cf. Ps 2:9). Although a number of passages in *Pss. Sol.* 17 portray the Messiah as wise, taught by God, and judging righteously (e.g., 17.29, 32, 37), Davies rightly notes that, "There is nothing in the context to suggest . . . that he will will bring a new Law but merely that he will establish a condition when the life of righteousness in accordance with the Torah will prevail."[32] Similarly, *Pss. Sol.* 18.7 anticipates the Messiah's rod, but this time the rod is for the discipline of Israel rather than the Gentiles. The *Sibylline Oracles* also allude to Ps 2 in connection with judgment. In *Sib. Or.* 3.663–71, the kings of the nations launch an attack against the land of Israel to destroy the temple, but God intervenes on behalf of his people (cf. Ps 2:1–6). *Sibylline Oracles* 8 predicts that at the final judgment, all people will come to God's tribunal, and "an iron shepherd's rod will prevail."[33] Of the Pseudepigrapha, *4 Ezra* (which, we must recall, was written around AD 100, after both Mark and Hebrews) comes closest to envisioning the son of Ps 2 in terms of revelation: In *4 Ezra* 7.28, God's son the Messiah is revealed and rejoicing ensues for four hundred years, at which time God's son dies along with all humanity before being resurrected after seven days of primeval silence. Similarly, in the interpretation of Ezra's seventh vision, the son-Messiah is said to be revealed (13.32). However, this revelation serves to incite the nations to battle against God's son, who promptly destroys them by the law (13.38). Therefore, although *4 Ezra* brings together the son of Ps 2 with the concept of revelation, this revelation is quite different from what one finds in Mark and Hebrews. Whereas Mark and Hebrews expound Jesus' Sonship explicitly in terms of his continuity with and superiority to the prophets, *4 Ezra* sees the revelation of God's son as a goad to draw the nations out to receive judgment. Thus, in the Pseudepigrapha, we find a fairly uniform emphasis on the militaristic triumph of God and his Messiah in Ps 2 that is distinct from the concept of the Son as climactic revelation that we have noted in Mark and Hebrews.

As translations (and therefore interpretations) of Ps 2, the LXX and Targum are also important witnesses to Jewish exegesis of Ps 2. As a whole,

---

31. *Pss. Sol.* 17.22, trans. R. B. Wright (*OTP* 2:667).
32. Davies, *Torah*, 43.
33. *Sib. Or.* 8.248, trans. J. J. Collins (*OTP* 1:424). Cf. Ps 2:9.

Ps 2 LXX is quite close to the MT. However, a major difference occurs in vv. 6–7: Whereas the MT has YHWH declaring, "I have set my king on Zion, my holy hill" (2:6), and the king intervening with, "I will proclaim the Lord's decree" (2:7a), the LXX puts both in the mouth of the king: "*But I was established king by him*, on Zion, his holy mountain, *proclaiming* [διαγγέλλων] the Lord's decree" (emphasis added). Another major difference comes in 2:12: Instead of the MT's, "Kiss his son," the LXX has "accept instruction [δράξασθε παιδείας]," possibly interpreting נשקו as a form of a different lexeme with the same triconsonantal root and בר as the Torah.³⁴ *Targum Psalms* 2 is also reasonably close to the MT, with occasional embellishments. Besides the more fulsome version of 2:7b noted above, the only significant variation is in 2:12, where similar to the LXX the Targum exhorts the kings and rulers to "accept instruction" rather than to kiss the son. As a whole, these departures from MT in the LXX and Targum interpretations of Ps 2 both place a greater emphasis on the king's didactic role, although this is present in Ps 2:7a, 10–11 MT as well and may not be connected solely with the king.³⁵ Although this emphasis (especially in the LXX) could have possibly facilitated a concept of the Son as climactic revelation such as we find in Mark and Hebrews, it is distinct from it—to say that the son of Ps 2 has a didactic role is different than declaring him to be God's ultimate revelation over and above the prophets.

In rabbinic literature, Ps 2 appears quite frequently and in a variety of contexts. In keeping with the trend noted above, rabbinic literature connects Ps 2 most often with YHWH's and Israel's conflict with (and ultimately triumph over) the nations. Many passages speak of this conflict generally;³⁶ however, there are a number of variations on the theme. At times, the conflict with the nations is explicitly eschatological.³⁷ In a number of places, Ps 2 is applied to humanity's rebellion against YHWH at the Tower of Babel.³⁸

---

34. Rabbinic interpreters were well aware of this issue and developed a number of explanations (see below for specific references).

35. Rabbinic interpreters seem to have considered Pss 1 and 2 as a single unit (see references below). If this is indicative of early Jewish exegesis, then the exhortation to accept instruction may have been seen as referring not only to Ps 2 (particularly the king's words in Ps 2:7–9), but also to the wisdom of Ps 1.

36. *y. 'Abod. Zar.* 2.1.1; *Exod. Rab.* 51.5 (on Exod 38:21); *Midr. Pss.* 83.2 (on Ps 83:5); *Midr. Pss.* 149.6 (on Ps 2:2); *Midr. Tanḥ.* (B) on Gen 11:3 (*Noah* 28). *Exodus Rabbah* 51.5 (on Exod 38:21) emphasizes that the nations attack Israel because they are unable to attack YHWH. Similarly, *Midr. Pss.* 83.2 (on Ps 83:5) asserts that the nations attack Israel because of YHWH.

37. *Midr. Pss.* 92.10 (on Ps 92:11); *Midr. Tanḥ.* (B) on Gen 14 (*Lek-Leka* 12); *Pesiq. Rab Kah.* S 2.2; *Pirqe R. El.* §18; *Pirqe R. El.* §28.

38. *Midr. Tanḥ.* (B) on Gen 11:3 (*Noah* 28); *Midr. Tanḥ.* (B) on Gen 20:1 (*Wayyera*

Elsewhere, it is mentioned in connection to Pharaoh and the Exodus.[39] However, by far the most common biblical scene that the rabbis connect with Ps 2 is the eschatological battle with Gog and Magog.[40] Occasionally, the Babel and Gog-Magog associations are combined,[41] and one passage connects Ps 2 to Daniel's confrontations with Gentile officials.[42] Another stream of rabbinic exegesis interprets Ps 2:11 as an instruction to Israel about how to worship appropriately.[43] The rabbis also discuss the unity of Pss 1 and 2,[44] the translation issue in Ps 2:12 noted above,[45] and use Ps 2 as a proof-text in a number of peripheral matters.[46] Psalm 2:7 appears infrequently, and the focus falls not on the affirmation of sonship, but on God's promise of the nations in 2:8.[47] In sum, although Ps 2 appears frequently in rabbinic literature with a variety of associations, nowhere do the rabbis connect the son of Ps 2 with the idea of God's climactic revelation.

Indeed, the idea of climactic revelation in God's Son via Ps 2 is unique not only within early Judaism but within the NT itself. Psalm 2 is quoted four times in the NT: In Acts 4:25–26, the believers apply Ps 2:1–2 to Jesus' passion at the hands of Gentiles and Jews. In Acts 13:33, Paul relates Ps 2:7 to Jesus' resurrection. As noted above, Heb 1:5 quotes Ps 2:7 to substantiate his superiority to the angels who mediated God's revelation at Mount Sinai.

---

24); *Midr. Tanḥ.* (B) on Gen 11:7 (*Noah* 28).

39. *Mekilta* on Exod 15:9–10 (*Šir.* 7.64).

40. *b. ʿAbod. Zar.* 3a–b; *b. Ber.* 7b; *Exod. Rab.* 1.1 (on Exod 1:1); *Midr. Pss.* 118.12 (on Ps 118:11); *Midr. Tanḥ.* (B) on Gen 11:1 (*Noah* 24). In this vein, some passages explicitly mention that whereas others have foolishly attacked Israel not realizing that Israel had a divine protector, Gog and Magog plot to attack YHWH directly, and connect this with Ps 2:2: *Lev. Rab.* 27.2 (on Lev 22:28); *Esth. Rab.* 7.23 (on Esth 3:12); *Midr. Tanḥ.* (B) on Lev 22:28 (*Emor* 18); *Pesiq. Rab Kah.* 9.11.

41. *Midr. Pss.* 2.2 (on Ps 2:1).

42. *Midr. Pss.* 64.1 (on Ps 64:1–2).

43. *y. Ber.* 5.1.6; *b. Ber.* 30b; *Midr. Mish.* on Prov 1:3; *Midr. Pss.* 100.3 (on Ps 100:2); *Midr. Tanḥ.* (B) on Gen 11:7 (*Noah* 28); *Midr. Tanḥ.* (B) on Gen 18:17 (*Wayyera* 9). See also *b. Yoma* 4b and *Sop.* 1.16b, which connect Ps 2:11 to Moses' awed worship when receiving the Torah on Sinai. *Midrash Tanḥuma* (B) on Gen 11:7 (*Noah* 28) interprets the first part of Ps 2 as judgment on the nations, but applies 2:11 to Israel's worship.

44. *y. Taʿan.* 2.2.2; *b. Ber.* 9b–10a; *Sop.* 16.41a (references the shorter Psalter); *Midr. Pss.* 20.2 (on Ps 20:1–2).

45. *b. Sanh.* 92a; *Lev. Rab.* 12.5 (on Lev 10:8); *Midr. Mish.* on Prov 11:25; *Num. Rab.* 10.4 (on Num 6:2); *Song Rab.* 7:3 §3.

46. *Sop.* 4.37a; *Gen. Rab.* 44.8 (on Gen 15:2); *Gen. Rab.* 14.7 (on Gen 2:7); *Midr. Pss.* 120.7 (on Ps 120:7); *Num. Rab.* 9.9 (on Num 5:12).

47. This promise is applied to the Messiah in *b. Sukkah* 52a, and to the Sages' Torah-declaring disciples in *S. Eli. Rab.* 18 (107). *Soperim* 4.37a makes a passing comment on the אל preposition in Ps 2:7.

Finally, Heb 5:5 mentions Ps 2:7 with respect to Jesus' appointment as High Priest. The NT also alludes to Ps 2 a number of times in addition to those noted above. Although John omits God's affirmation of Jesus' Sonship at the baptism, John the Baptist testifies that Jesus is the Son of God directly after baptizing Jesus (1:34). Paul's phrase "with fear and trembling" (μετὰ φόβου καὶ τρόμου) in 2 Cor 7:15 and Phil 2:12 may allude to Ps 2:11 LXX (δουλεύσατε τῷ κυρίῳ ἐν φόβῳ καὶ ἀγαλλιᾶσθε αὐτῷ ἐν τρόμῳ). However, the connection is loose. 2 Peter 1:17 alludes to Ps 2:7 somewhat obliquely by mentioning the Father's words to Jesus at the transfiguration. However, although Jesus' superiority to prior revelation may stand in the background of this passage, the author's primary point is to underscore his status as an eyewitness of Jesus' majesty and thereby vindicate his testimony over and against that of false teachers (see 2 Pet 2:1–22). Finally, Revelation regularly uses the language of Ps 2 to describe Jesus' triumph over the nations and eschatological reign.[48] In short, although all of of the NT writers would likely affirm Jesus as God's climactic revelation, the Synoptics and Hebrews are unique in emphasizing that Jesus *as Son* is God's climactic revelation in connection with Ps 2:7.

This survey of the use of Ps 2 in early (and some later) Jewish literature and the NT demonstrates that the elements noted above (divine sonship via Ps 2:7, climactic revelation) converge only in the Synoptic tradition (Mark 1:11; 9:7; 12:6 par.) and in Hebrews (1:1–4; 3:1–6).[49] Psalm 2 was quite prominent in early Judaism, but its emphasis on YHWH's and the Messiah's (and therefore Israel's) triumph over the nations took center stage. Although 4 Ezra and the LXX and Targum interpretations of Ps 2 provide some distant analogies to Hebrews and the Synoptics, there seems to have been no concept of climactic revelation in God's son directly comparable to what we find in the Synoptics and Hebrews. Although the NT writings frequently portray Jesus as God's climactic revelation (e.g., Matt 5; John 1:1–18; Gal 6:2; etc.), the collocation of this concept with Ps 2:7 occurs only in the Synoptics and Hebrews. Therefore, we may conclude that the concept we have traced above constitutes a synthesis that is unique to Hebrews and the Synoptic tradition.

---

48. Rev 2:26–27; 11:15, 18; 12:5; 19:15, 19. The "kings of the earth" (τῶν βασιλέων τῆς γῆς) over whom the great prostitute has authority in Rev 17:18 may allude to the "kings of the earth" (οἱ βασιλεῖς τῆς γῆς) in Ps 2:2 LXX.

49. The observant reader will have noticed that Philo and Josephus are conspicuously absent from this survey. To my knowledge, neither writer quotes or alludes to Ps 2.

HEARING MARK AND HEBREWS TOGETHER

Now that we have seen how Mark (representative of the Synoptics) and Hebrews each develop this concept of God's climactic revelation in the Son, and how unique this concept is against the backdrop of early Judaism and the NT, we are in a position to examine what these two texts might say on this topic if heard together. Just as in a complex piece of music it can be hard to discern the unity that makes sense of the various instruments, as hearers of Scripture it can likewise be difficult to hear diverse voices speaking in harmony—perhaps this is why more has not been said about Hebrews' relationship to the gospels. However, when we listen carefully, a rich harmony emerges from these two texts.

One of the striking differences between Mark and Hebrews is the temporal frame in which each book places the affirmation of Jesus' Sonship. Whereas in Mark the Father affirms Jesus as his Son during during Jesus' earthly life, Hebrews locates the "Today" (σήμερον) of this declaration at Jesus' exaltation and enthronement.[50] Although at first blush these two claims may seem contradictory, this need not be so. As Cockerill notes, Heb 1:5 does not deny that the Son existed as such before being exalted, but rather affirms that "at his exaltation and session the Son entered his inheritance as Son and the fruition of a sonship that had always been his."[51] If we allow ourselves to hear the voices of Mark and Hebrews in harmony rather than in competition, we find Hebrews declaring that what was true about Jesus during his earthly existence is true, and (in classic Hebrews fashion) *even more so* in light of his resurrection, exaltation, and enthronement. Further, while Mark's narrative exposition of the Son as climactic revelation is somewhat understated and rhetorically remote for the reader, Hebrews brings the point to the σήμερον of its hearers with urgency:[52] "*In these last days* [God] has spoken to *us* by his Son" (Heb 1:2, emphasis added). In concert, Mark and Hebrews proclaim God's climactic speech *both* in the Son's earthly mission *and* in his current position at the Father's right hand—a revelation grounded in redemptive history yet speaking powerfully to the present.

Furthermore, the similarities charted here between Mark and Hebrews provide one more data point in plotting Hebrews' relationship to the Synoptics. To the numerous points of contact noted above between Hebrews and Jesus traditions, we may now add that Hebrews shares with the Synoptic

---

50. So Bruce, *Hebrews*, 54; Cockerill, *Hebrews*, 103–4; Ellingworth, *Hebrews*, 113–14; Koester, *Hebrews*, 191; Mitchell, *Hebrews*, 47; Hagner, *Hebrews*, 32; Hughes, *Hebrews*, 54

51. Cockerill, *Hebrews*, 104. See also Bruce, *Hebrews*, 54.

52. Cf. Heb 3:13; 13:8; see also 3:7, 15; 4:7.

tradition a unique interest in the Son (via Ps 2:7) as God's climactic revelation. Hebrews and the Synoptics may converge on this point because they draw on a common stream of tradition, or Hebrews may depend directly on the Synoptic tradition for this concept (the converse seems highly unlikely). To define the relationship with precision is likely beyond our reach, and is also unnecessary to the broader point: Hebrews has an impressive knowledge of Jesus' life, and this knowledge is formative for its theology at key points.

Hebrews' indebtedness to Jesus traditions may also shed some light on the perennial question of Hebrews' hermeneutics. Many an exegete (not least myself) has been perplexed by Hebrews' use of the OT. The freedom with which the pastor places OT passages in the mouth of the Father, Son, or Holy Spirit can seem quite, well, arbitrary. Cockerill has helpfully pointed out that Hebrews considers the whole OT to be God's speech,[53] and indeed, grasping this underlying conviction is of great use in understanding Hebrews' hermeneutics. However, this principle alone cannot explain why, for example, the pastor places Ps 2:7 in the mouth of the Father and Ps 40:6–8 in the mouth of the Son—it is not as if one could simply switch the speakers and all would be well because for Hebrews all Scripture is divine speech. The similarities sketched here between Mark and Hebrews suggest that the events of Jesus' life provide the interpretive matrix that allows Hebrews to interpret the OT as it does. This is true in a specific sense for Heb 1:5—the pastor has the Father speak Ps 2:7 because he had already spoken these words to Jesus before. However, it may also true in a more general sense for the rest of Hebrews—Jesus can speak Ps 40:6–8 to the Father because the events of his life make these words uniquely appropriate for him. In sum, it is the OT understood as divine speech *and interpreted in light of the specific, known events of Jesus' life* that provides the foundation for the pastor's hermeneutics. Thus, in the light of Jesus traditions in general, and Mark and the Synoptic tradition in particular, Hebrews' seemingly arbitrary appropriation of the OT emerges as an authentic and coherent interpretation of the OT flowing from the early church's witness to Jesus' life.

CONCLUSION

In this essay, I have explored how the Synoptic tradition (via Mark) and Hebrews each develop a concept of climactic revelation in the Son of God and have demonstrated that these concepts are in fact quite similar to each other and are also unique against the backdrop of early Judaism and the NT, to the

---

53. Cockerill, *Hebrews*, 41–45.

extent that Hebrews is likely indebted to Jesus traditions on this point. As I have attempted to show, this way of hearing Mark and Hebrews together yields satisfaction on both theological and hermeneutical fronts. To bring a gospel and an epistle together in this way is somewhat unusual in the guild of NT studies, but it demonstrates the need for exegetes to listen carefully to the distinct voices of Scripture and to hear the rich harmony that emerges. It is to this task that Gary Cockerill has devoted much of his life, and it is my honor to dedicate this essay to him.

BIBLIOGRAPHY

Attridge, Harold W. *The Epistle to the Hebrews*. Philadelphia: Fortress, 1989.
Best, Ernest. *The Temptation and the Passion: The Markan Soteriology*. SNTSMS 2. Cambridge: Cambridge University Press, 1965.
Black, C. Clifton. *Mark*. ANTC. Nashville: Abingdon, 2011.
Boring, M. Eugene. *Mark*. NTL. Louisville: Westminster John Knox, 2006.
Bruce, F. F. *The Epistle to the Hebrews*. Rev. ed. NICNT. Grand Rapids: Eerdmans, 1990.
Carson, D. A., and Douglas J. Moo. *An Introduction to the New Testament*. 2nd ed. Grand Rapids: Zondervan, 2005.
Charlesworth, James H. *The Old Testament Pseudepigrapha*. 2 vols. Peabody, MA: Hendrickson, 1983.
Cockerill, Gareth L. *The Epistle to the Hebrews*. NICNT. Grand Rapids: Eerdmans, 2012.
Collins, Adela Y. *Mark: A Commentary*. Hermeneia. Minneapolis: Fortress, 2007.
Daly, Robert J. "The Soteriological Significance of the Sacrifice of Isaac." *CBQ* 39 (1977) 45–75.
Davies, W. D. *Torah in the Messianic Age and/or the Age to Come*. JBLMS 7. Philadelphia: SBL, 1952.
Dunn, James D. G. *Christology in the Making: A New Testament Inquiry into the Origins of the Doctrine of the Incarnation*. 2nd ed. Grand Rapids: Eerdmans, 1989.
Ellingworth, Paul. *The Epistle to the Hebrews: A Commentary on the Greek Text*. NIGTC. Grand Rapids: Eerdmans, 1993.
Evans, Craig A. *Ancient Texts for New Testament Studies: A Guide to the Background Literature*. Grand Rapids: Baker Academic, 2005.
France, R. T. *The Gospel of Mark: A Commentary on the Greek Text*. NIGTC. Grand Rapids: Eerdmans, 2002.
Fuller, Reginald H. *The Foundations of New Testament Christology*. New York: Scribner's, 1965.
Hagner, Donald A. *Hebrews*. NIBC 14. Peabody, MA: Hendrickson, 1990.
Harner, Philip B. "Qualitative Anarthrous Predicate Nouns: Mark 15:39 and John 1:1." *JBL* 92 (1973) 75–87.
Hughes, Philip E. *A Commentary on the Epistle to the Hebrews*. Grand Rapids: Eerdmans, 1977.
Huizenga, Leroy A. *The New Isaac: Tradition and Intertextuality in the Gospel of Matthew*. NovTSup 131. Leiden: Brill, 2009.
Janse, Sam. *"You are My Son": The Reception History of Psalm 2 in Early Judaism and the Early Church*. CBET. Leuven: Peeters, 2009.

Kistemaker, Simon J. *Exposition of the Epistle to the Hebrews*. NTC. Grand Rapids: Baker, 1984.
Koester, Craig R. *Hebrews: A New Translation with Introduction and Commentary*. AB 36. New York: Doubleday, 2001.
Lane, William L. *The Gospel according to Mark*. NICNT. Grand Rapids: Eerdmans, 1974.
Marcus, Joel. *The Way of the Lord: Christological Exegesis of the Old Testament in the Gospel of Mark*. Louisville: Westminster John Knox, 1992.
McKnight, Scot. "Source Criticism." In *Interpreting the New Testament: Essays on Methods and Issues*, edited by David A. Black and David S. Dockery, 74–105. Nashville: Broadman & Holman, 2001.
Mitchell, Alan C. *Hebrews*. SPS 13. Collegeville, MN: Liturgical, 2007.
Moffitt, David M. *Atonement and the Logic of Resurrection in the Epistle to the Hebrews*. Leiden: Brill, 2011.
Rahlfs, Alfred, and Robert Hanhart, eds. *Septuaginta: Id est Vetus Testamentum graece iuxta LXX interpretes*. Stuttgart: Deutsche Bibelgesellschaft, 2006.
Rindge, Matthew S. "Reconfiguring the Akedah and Recasting God: Lament and Divine Abandonment in Mark." *JBL* 130 (2011) 755–74.
Septuaginta: Vetus Testamentum Graecum. Auctoritate Academiae Scientiarum Göttingensis editum. 16 vols. Göttingen: Vandenhoeck & Ruprecht, 1931–.
Spicq, Ceslas. *L'Épître aux Hébreux*. 3rd ed. EBib. Paris: Gabalda, 1953.
Stein, Robert H. *Mark*. BECNT. Grand Rapids: Baker Academic, 2008.
Stuckenbruck, Loren T. *Angel Veneration and Christology: A Study in Early Judaism and in the Christology of the Apocalypse of John*. WUNT 2/70. Tübingen: Mohr, 1995.
Thielman, Frank. *Theology of the New Testament: A Canonical and Synthetic Approach*. Grand Rapids: Zondervan, 2005.
Vanhoye, Albert. *Old Testament Priests and the New Testament Priest according to the New Testament*. Petersham, MA: St. Bede's, 1986.
Vermes, Geza. *Scripture and Tradition in Judaism*. StPB 4. Leiden: Brill, 1961.
Wallace, Daniel B. *Greek Grammar beyond the Basics: An Exegetical Syntax of the New Testament*. Grand Rapids: Zondervan, 1996.
Watson, Francis. *Gospel Writing: A Canonical Perspective*. Grand Rapids: Eerdmans, 2013.
Watts, Rikk E. "Mark." In *Commentary on the New Testament Use of the Old Testament*, edited by G. K. Beale and D. A. Carson, 111–249. Grand Rapids: Baker Academic, 2007.
Wood, J. Edwin. "Isaac Typology in the New Testament." *NTS* 14 (1968) 583–89.
Zimmerli, Walther, and Joachim Jeremias. *The Servant of God*. SBT 20. Naperville, IL: Allenson, 1952.

6

If Son, Then Priest

The Filial Foundation of Ordination in Hebrews and Other New Testament Texts

AMY L. PEELER

IN MY NEW TESTAMENT class, as we were learning about Hebrews, a student posed this question: "If Jesus is truly our high priest, should anyone else play the role of priest on earth?" It is a question, admittedly, that I had asked myself before. If Jesus is our only savior, mediator, and advocate, as Hebrews so vigorously argues, then is it right to have earthly spiritual leaders or does that run the risk of elevating humans to a place of competition with Jesus? The question became even more pressing when I joined the Anglican Communion, a group that explicitly used the language of priesthood.

I knew, however, that without compromising the supremacy of Jesus, Hebrews also envisioned its readers doing priestly acts, most shockingly in its invitation to go into the holy place, through the veil (10:19–20). The invitation to contribute to this volume seemed the perfect opportunity to wrestle further[1] with this question: what should human priesthood look like in light of Jesus' sole, sufficient, and eternal priestly ministry? Since Gareth Cockerill has contributed powerfully to the understanding of priesthood

---

1. I presented an earlier version of this paper at the annual session of the Analytic Theology Consultation at the Evangelical Theological Society in Atlanta, November, 2015. I am grateful for that invitation and the stimulating dialogue that followed my paper. This version is much improved because of the conversation in that group.

through his work in Hebrews[2] and since he is himself a faithful minister of the church, I hope the investigations here will constitute a fitting honor to his academic and ministerial work.

In the Epistle to the Hebrews, Jesus is both "Son" and "Priest." On that, most interpreters agree.[3] Defining the relationship between those identities results in a variety of interpretations. In previous work, I have taken the position that the logic of Hebrews works in this way: Jesus is Son and therefore he is Priest. His priestly call comes to him from his Father (Heb 5). The pedagogical training he receives from his Father—suffering that leads to perfection—results in his offering of himself as a sacrifice, the inaugural event of his priesthood. Because of his participation in this training, he becomes a sympathetic High Priest (Heb 2:17). Then, finally, his acts as eternal High Priest—including the presentation of the final atoning sacrifice and living intercession—serve his filial right to inherit all things in that these actions garner the human contingent of his inheritance.[4] It seems plausible, then, that the sharers of Christ, who also relate to God in filial[5] and cultic[6] ways, would follow a similar pattern. Believers serve God as priests because they are first and foremost all sons.[7]

In good Hebrews fashion, this investigation of Hebrews led me to think about its concepts of priestly ministry *and much more*. I discovered that Hebrews *and* other authors of the canon, including the writings of Peter, Paul, and John, also affirm a relationship between sonship and priesthood, and do so in that particular ordering: If sons, then priests. Reflections on Jesus as Priest in Hebrews, then, resulted in insights about the ministry of all the priests in God's holy nation (1 Pet 2:9).

Such a comprehensive statement necessitates the second stream of investigation in this paper: If all are priests then what is the biblical justification

---

2. Cockerill's comments on Melchizedek as one who foreshadows but does not compete with the eternal being of the Son were incredibly helpful in the development of my own understanding of Melchizedek's role in Hebrews (*Hebrews*, 298–306). See also his article, "High Priest Title."

3. Cockerill himself states, "[H]igh priesthood is intrinsic to the Son's identity as both all-sufficient Savior and Revealer" (*Hebrews*, 77). Similar confirmations appear in Bruce's commentary, which Cockerill's edition replaces (*Hebrews*, 29), Attridge's commentary (*Hebrews*, 25), and O'Brien's commentary (*Hebrews*, 35), to name a few.

4. Peeler, *You Are My Son*.

5. Heb 1:14; 2:10, 13–14; 3:1, 6; 6:12; 9:15; 11:8; 12:5–11, 23.

6. See discussion that follows for presentation and analysis of cultic texts.

7. I choose the gender exclusive language intentionally here. I believe that Hebrews speaks of all in its congregation—men and women—as the sons of God (2:11; 12:5) to ground their identity in *the Son* of God. This language actually serves to invite women into the realms normally prohibited to them: education, inheritance, and priesthood.

for the ordination of some? Texts from these same authors also affirm that since all believers are sons of God, all are called to priesthood, but only some to leadership. A filial perspective of ordination then heightens the great privilege and power of ordination for all believers, yet also strengthens the graced vocational identity of those who are set apart to care for the other priests. In whatever particular way one might be gifted and called, it is a filial relationship with God that grants and sustains the priestly vocation.

SONS THEN PRIESTS: FOUR CANONICAL VOICES

1 Peter

Peter's first letter is one of two NT texts in which the author explicitly declares the followers of Christ as members of the priesthood, and so it seems a fitting place to begin an investigation of Christian priesthood. Twice in the second chapter, Peter declares that his readers are a priesthood (ἱεράτευμα, 2:5, 9). Such language is fitting for his readers as he calls on them to offer spiritual sacrifices that are pleasing to God (2:9).

Peter says many powerful things about these communities of believers in this section of his letter, but it is striking for the present investigation to notice how he entwines statements concerning priesthood with familial language. They are, he says at the beginning of the chapter, newborns (ἀρτιγέννητα), who should long for the pure milk of the word so that they might grow up into salvation (2:2). Moreover, they should see themselves as living stones being built up into a spiritual house (2:5). It is likely that οἶκος here denotes both the temple and a household, capturing both cultic and familial connotations.[8]

Peter's extensive appeals to Israel's Scriptures also affirm the idea of his readers' status as children of God. Peter declares that they have been chosen as God's people (1 Pet 2:9–10), whom God calls his child (Exod 4:22–23; Deut 1:31; 8:5; 14:1; 32:6; Isa 63:16; 64:8; Jer 3:4, 19, 22; 31:9, 20; Mal 1:6 ; 2:10; 3:17; Ps 103:13; Hos 11:1–4). When Peter calls them "elect people" in

8. 2 Samuel 7 provides an excellent co-text in which David and Nathan articulate both meanings of οἶκος. David desires to build a structure for God (2 Sam 7:2), but God says the structure will come through his household (7:11, 13). Concerning 1 Peter, Calvin highlights the cultic meaning: "[B]y calling us living stones and a spiritual house, just as he had already said that Christ is a living stone, he implies a comparison between us and the ancient temple" (*Epistle*, 259). Jobes's comments leave room for the multiplicity for which I am arguing: "they too, said Peter, are like living stones, build into a spiritual temple, taking their places to serve God through Jesus (2:5). The placement of the Living Stone with living stones in the temple implied the close relationship of Christ with believers and their common nature as human beings" (*Letters to the Church*, 285).

v. 9, his words echo the prophecy in Isa 43 where the hope of restoration is the hope of the return of God's sons and daughters (43:6). When Peter refers to them as God's special possession he recalls Malachi's vision in which the people will be God's possession. In the same verse, God says, "I will choose them as a person chooses his son who is subject to him" (3:17 LXX).[9] Hosea's proclamation of the reversal of the status of the people of God, which Peter quotes in 2:10, is a change from being "not my people" to "sons of a living god" (Hos 1:10 LXX).

This double assertion of sonship and priesthood runs throughout 1 Peter. Initially, Peter says that their calling has priestly entailments including sanctification and being sprinkled with blood (1:2). As he continues to talk about their salvation, he employs a familial statement in the following verse: they have been born again into the hope they now carry, a hope that will come to fruition in a lasting inheritance. In light of this reality, they should conduct themselves as obedient children who resemble their Father's holiness, for he is both their Judge and Father (1:17). Again, in 1:22-23, their holy sacred life arises out of their new birth. Later he states that they look forward both to their great inheritance (3:9) as they also anticipate the fatherly training and accountability from God (4:17). God will first judge his own household, echoing sentiments in Israel's literature about the more intense discipline God brings to his children.[10] Being a child of God captures how Peter describes their entry into faith (1:3), their future hope (1:4) and the present maintenance of their faith (1:14-17). If they had not been brought into his family, they could not make up the members of his house where sacrifices are offered (2:5). If they weren't being obedient children, in other words, if they were not becoming holy as their Father is holy, (1:14-15), they could not be a part of the holy priesthood (2:5) for which they have been set aside. For Peter, these believers in Christ call God their Father, and because they do so, they have been set aside by him to serve as priests.

Revelation

Near the beginning of John's letter to the seven churches of Asia Minor, he declares that the Son of God has made them to be a kingdom and priests to his God and Father (Rev 1:6). At the outset, then, John grants his readers a sense of the powerful role they possess in service to God and also begins to describe how they relate to the One they serve. Because they have been

---

9. All translations from the Septuagint taken from *NETS*.

10. Deut 8:5; Prov 3:11-12; *Pss. Sol.* 13.9.

transformed by Jesus, his God has become their God (Rev 3:12; 7:3; 21:3) which also suggests that his Father has become theirs.[11]

This suggestion finds confirmation when twice more John records the similar proclamation. When the Lamb of God opens the sealed book in Rev 5, the elders praise him by singing: "with your blood you purchased for God persons from every tribe and language and people and nation. You have made them to be a kingdom and priests to serve our God, and they will reign on the earth" (5:9–10). What is striking in this instance is that the priesthood is so expansive: open not only to the correct tribe in Israel but to all Israelites[12] and all peoples.[13] Finally, concerning the martyrs who are raised to reign with Christ during the millennium, John reveals that they also serve God and Christ as priests (20:6).

Because John so freely draws from the Scriptures of Israel throughout his book, most commentators also believe that Exod 19:6 ("you will be for me a kingdom of priests") and Isa 61:6 ("And you will be called priests of the Lord, you will be named ministers of our God") echo in the background of these proclamations. In Exodus, God tells Moses to share with Pharaoh that Israel is the firstborn son of God (Exod 4:22). In these chapters of Isaiah, the prophet looks forward to the restoration and coming victory of God's people. In the sixty-third chapter, Isaiah also reminds God that he is their Father (63:16). This relationship should motivate the restoration and priestly vocation, which the prophet anticipates. If these passages exert influence on John, he puts forth the vision of a future reality in which God enacts his compassionate paternity by calling his people—all the faithful no matter their ethnicity or nationality that make up the body politic of God the Father—to serve Him and his Son as priests.

Paul

On six different occasions in his letters, Paul uses cultic terminology to describe the acts of the believers to whom he is writing. To the Romans, he issues the general instruction that they should present their bodies to God as

---

11. As affirmed in the gospel and letters of John (John 14:20; 20:17; 1 John 3:1), and other authors in the NT (Matt 6:9; Mark 11:25; Luke 6:36; Rom 1:7; 8:15–16; Gal 4:6–7), they constitute the priestly servants of God, who, as the Father of Jesus Christ, is also their Father by virtue of their relationship with Jesus.

12. Keener notes, "For John's audience such an application is no small matter: Many are probably Jewish believers expelled from their synagogues for faith in Jesus" (*Revelation*, 71).

13 Beale states that this redemption includes "all without distinction (people from *all* races)" (*Revelation*, 359). See also Ford, *Revelation*, 95.

a holy and pleasing sacrifice (θυσία, 12:1). The paradox is that they will not die but live as a sacrifice, and this will be their act of worship. Paul describes this worship as λατρεία, a word utilized for cultic priestly service.[14] This sets the context for Paul's discussion of the body and although it is common for Paul to use familial terminology, we should not miss that Paul addresses these statements to those he considers brothers and sisters, members of the family of God.[15] He saw them all, no matter their ethnic background, united in the same household under God the Father.[16] This language of fictive kinship carried powerful theological and social implications.[17]

Later in Romans, Paul speaks of the offering of the Gentiles, which could be the praise or obedience of the Gentiles, or even the Gentiles themselves,[18] as that which is pleasing to God and sanctified by the Holy Spirit (15:16). Offering, προσφορά, in Israel's Scriptures can refer to the cultic sacrifice (1 Kgs 7:34; Ps 39:7) and to sanctify, ἁγιάζω, frequently denotes the necessary sanctification of the sacrifices.[19]

While these texts seem to speak of the general Christian life, Paul also applies similar cultic language in more specific situations. The churches in Macedonia and Achaia who give tangibly (ἐν τοῖς σαρκικοῖς, "material blessings") to the saints in Jerusalem do so as an act of service (λειτουργέω, Rom 15:27). The term Paul uses for service appears in Israel's scripture most often for the ministry of the priests.[20] Similarly in 2 Corinthians, he speaks of the collection as a ministry (λειτουργία, 9:12) that meets the needs of the saints and overflows in thanksgiving to God. Through this offering, they are worshiping God and showing the unity of the followers of Christ. For the Corinthians to give to these Christian believers, who are separated by geography and ethnicity, demonstrates the intimate unity of the church. Paul is calling the Gentile Christians in Corinth to provide for the Jewish believers in Jerusalem as they would be expected to respond to members of their own family.[21]

---

14. Rom 9:4; Heb 9:1, 6; Josh 22:27; 1 Chr 28:13.
15. Rom 8:15–16; 9:26; Gal 4:6–7; Eph 1:5.
16. O'Brien, "Church," 128.
17. Aasgaard, *My Beloved*.
18. Moo, *Romans*, 890; Byrne, *Romans*, 436.
19. Exod 28:38; 29:36; 40:9–10; Lev 8:11; Num 5:9.
20. Exod 28:31, 39; 29:30; 30:20; 35:18; 36:34; 38:27; 39:11–12; Num 1:50; 3:6, 31; 4:3, 9, 12, 14, 23–24, 26, 30, 35, 37, 39, 41, 43; 8:22, 26; 16:9; 18:2, 6–7, 21, 23; Deut 10:8; 17:12; 18:5, 7; 1 Kgs 8:11; 1 Chr 6:17; 15:2; 16:4, 37; 23:13, 28, 32; 26:12; 2 Chr 5:14; 8:14; 11:14; 13:10; 23:6; 29:11; 31:2; Neh 10:36; Jdt 4:14; 1 Macc 10:42; Sir 45:15; Joel 1:9, 13; 2:17; Jer 52:18; Ezek 40:46; 42:14; 43:19; 44:11, 15–17, 19, 27; 45:4–5.
21. Matt 15:4–5; Mark 7:10–11. Plummer moves in this direction, "Thanks be to

In Philippians, Paul speaks of the congregation's expressions of faith as a sacrifice (θυσία), ministry (λειτουργία), and sweet smell (ὀσμή εὐωδίας), like that of an offering[22] (Phil 2:17; 4:18). Just before this statement, he declares that this sacrifice comes from those are who are children of God (2:15).[23] Here too, an intimate, even familial, context envelops a sacrificial call. This new family is to offer themselves to God and to each other just as the people and the priests would offer gifts and sacrifices. Paul's call to the congregations is not strictly priestly, for all the people of Israel are called to bring offerings,[24] but it is cultic. In this way, Paul cultivates among his congregations, made up of brothers and sisters in the family of God, an attitude of sacrifice to their Lord. Although Paul does not develop it explicitly, it is plausible that Paul would expect these pleasing sacrifices to come from those who are acceptable because they are no longer slaves, but sons and daughters (Gal 4:1–7), having been made holy like their holy Father, God (1 Cor 3:17; 6:19; Eph 4:30).

Hebrews

As previously stated, it comes as little surprise that in a book that so vigorously argues for the Christ as the sole, effective, and eternal High Priest, the author never grants the audience a priestly title. That being said, it is worth asking why he describes Jesus as the *High* Priest (Heb 2:17; 3:1; 4:14–15; 5:5, 10; 6:20; 7:26–8:1; 8:3; 9:7, 11). Could it be that he imagines in some way that the human followers of Jesus serve as priests under him in his new order? And that they do so precisely for the same reason that Jesus does so because they too are sons of God? It seems that a positive answer is correct, since the author of Hebrews ascribes priestly attributes to the audience in close connection with his affirmations that they are children and heirs of God. These sons of God are holy, have access to God, and offer ministry to God.

Following the prologue in which the author describes humanity as the recipients of God's speech, he declares them to be the heirs who will inherit salvation (1:14) and then, with his first vocative, addresses them as holy

---

God for effecting such brotherly love between Jew and Gentile" (*2 Corinthians*, 257), but Hellerman explicitly advances the ideas that Paul is calling the Corinthians to respond to the Jews based on accepted sibling values (*Ancient Church*, 110–13).

22. Gen 8:21; Exod 29:18, 25; Lev 1:9, 13, 17; 2:2, 9, 12; 3:5, 11, 16; 4:31; 6:15, 21; 8:21, 28; 17:4, 6; 23:13, 18.

23. Most commentators see this as a reference to the offering of the Philippians not of Paul. Hellerman, *Philippians*, 140.

24 Exod 29; Lev 1–5; Deut 18:3; Ps 20:3.

brothers and sisters (3:1). His insistence that they are pure continues into the center section of the letter. Their consciences have been purified (9:14) and sprinkled clean (10:22), by God's will they are sanctified (10:10), and he states just a few verses later that by Christ's offering they have been sanctified for all time (10:14). As all the Israelites were purified by the blood of the covenant (Exod 24),[25] a story to which he alludes in Heb 9:20, all the people to whom he is writing are made holy by God's will enacted in Christ. All of them have been given the quality, then, necessary for priests to do their ministry. Holiness, in the Scriptures of Israel, describes God's space (Exod 15:17; 26:33), God's time (Exod 16:23), God's instruments (Exod 28:3), and God's servants, the priests (Exod 19:22; 28:41).

What distinguished priests from laity was their purity and, consequently, their proximity—they could be nearer to the presence of God. This is true in the inaugural giving of the law,[26] the tabernacle,[27] and the temple.[28] Therefore, when the author calls his readers to draw near to the presence of God, the heavenly holy temple, he is inviting them into priestly space. Cultic terminology first appears after presenting the negative example of the wilderness generation; the author reminds the audience, in chapter 4, that they have a great and sympathetic High Priest. They are, in fact, full of weakness, possibly in other words they are imperfect, but even so he allows them to draw near to the throne room (4:16), the session of God and his Son, not with trepidation but with boldness, confident that they will find mercy and grace. Similarly in chapter 7 he reiterates the same idea with the word employed in chapter 4, προσέρχομαι. Those who are approaching God through Jesus are the ones he is able to save (7:25). By his leadership and redemption, he purifies them so that they can come near to God (Heb 4:16; 7:19, 25; 10:22; 11:6; 12:22). Shifting terminology in chapter 7, the author juxtaposes the ineffective and temporary nature of the law with a better hope that allows him and his audience to draw near (ἐγγίζω, 7:19). In chapter 10, the author affirms the reality of approach and the attending demeanor. He and his audience as members of Christ have confidence to enter the holy place, best understood as God's heavenly throne,[29] because of the blood of Jesus (10:19). They can come into this inner part of the sanctuary past the veil with full assurance because both their hearts and bodies have been

---

25. See Dozeman, *God on the Mountain*, and my argument about purity as one of the meanings of the Exodus 24 narrative ("Desiring God").

26. Exod 19:22; 24:1, 9–10.

27. Exod 28–30.

28. Sanders, *Judaism: Practice and Belief*, 79–118.

29. Cockerill states, "the very presence of God" (*Hebrews*, 466); Lane, *Hebrews 9–13*, 283.

cleansed with blood and water. The sprinkled blood features again in the Mount Zion section in chapter 12. When they arrive through Jesus' blood they also arrive at the presence of God. On Mount Zion, they join in with the celebrating angels and the righteous who have been perfected and with the assembly of the firstborn. Whether or not the author imagines them as part of this festal gathering in the present time,[30] he certainly is hopeful for their ultimate arrival there.

In Israel's Scriptures, this terminology of approach applied to the first high priest, Aaron, who is commanded to come near to the altar to perform his duties (Lev 9:7, 8). The same term appears in Leviticus, but in a prohibitive sense. Those who have any blemish, the outsiders, and finally all Israel except the priests are *not* allowed to approach (Lev 21:21, 23). Hebrews' other term for approach, ἐγγίζω is the same term used in the covenant narrative in Exodus, first for the priests who must be consecrated to draw near (Exod 19:22), and then for Moses who alone can come closest of all (Exod 24:2).

The prohibitions in the first covenant contrast with Hebrews in a rather striking fashion. Even though all of them are weak, they can still approach the very throne of God boldly. To some degree, the audience has access or will have access to the presence of God in a way that was in Israel's written laws reserved for the priestly class and even the high priest.

Other Jews of the time articulate worship and prayer in priestly terms. Philo believes a special class exists that can approach God. He calls them priests and prophets and talks of them throwing off the veil (*Gig.* 53–60) to come to God. He affirms the importance of the functional priests in Israel (*Migr.* 92), but also imagines a larger group of Israelites carrying out priestly functions, like being representatives for the nations (*Abr.* 98), following the law (*Spec.* 1.243), especially in the practices of Passover (*Mos.* 2.224).[31] The Qumran documents as well describe prayer as a replacement for the sacrifices they cannot offer in the temple. Prayer was "a sacrifice offered in righteousness" (CD 11.20–21)[32] or in the Songs of Sabbath Sacrifice a

---

30. Cockerill adeptly captures the already/not yet tone of this scene: "[T]his passage assumes both the present privileges available in Christ and the ultimate goal to which he gives access, as described throughout Hebrews" (*Hebrews*, 653n51).

31. Seland concludes, "Law. There is no real spiritualization in this view. The priesthood is not abolished nor deprived of its value; it coexists with the 'common priesthood'. Nor is there much psychologizing in Philo's views here. The Jewish nation is a priesthood to the world at large because of its sacred institution of Jerusalem, and by its special allegiance to the Law, the Torah, as displayed by their obedience and the Passover rites (prayers and sacrifices) that are carried out on behalf of all" ("Common Priesthood," 98).

32. Nitzan, *Qumran Prayer*, 48.

"burnt offering."[33] These early Jewish believers in Jesus, then, are making a move similar to what other Jews are doing, imagining prayer and worship as a priestly act open to more than just the official priests.[34]

When they approach God's presence, they can also perform the ministry of priests. Λατρεύω, to worship, appears twenty-one times in the NT,[35] and can indicate worship in general or more specifically temple service. In Hebrews, it appears a total of six times with the latter connotation, namely temple service four times when discussing ministry of priests differentiated from the priestly ministry of Jesus (Heb 8:5; 9:9; 10:2; 13:10). That makes it more likely that the two other occurrences (Heb 9:14 and 12:28) also bear a sacrificial meaning, but in these instances it is the audience who does the ministry. Having been cleansed by the blood of Christ and having obtained pure consciences, they can turn from dead works to serve/worship/minister to the living God (9:14). Interestingly, after proclaiming this service the author in the next verse discusses the inheritance granted to those who are called because of a death. Jesus' death then, gives them both the identity of heirs and the vocational function of priests. The author calls them to worship again after he proclaims that they are receiving a kingdom (12:28). While not explicitly an inheritance idea, it would certainly be the case that a kingdom would ideally pass from a Father to his children. The possession of this kingdom should result in the giving of thanks, which is the worship to which they are called. This worship should be conducted with both reverence and awe because the God whom they serve is a consuming fire, which evokes both God's judgment (Deut 4:24; 9:3) and the whole burnt offering sacrifice (Lev 6:10; 1 Chron 21:26).

Finally, in his closing instructions, he proclaims again that they should continually offer a sacrifice of praise to God, that is, the fruit of lips that confess his name: Do not neglect to do good and to share what you have, for such sacrifices are pleasing to God (13:16). It is clear that he follows a tradition in which sacrificial language applies to moral acts,[36] which are open to all people. Nevertheless, it is still an appeal to cultic language for all of those who are invited into God's kingdom.

---

33. Ibid., 285.

34. Gender remains a legitimate question here. It seems that if Christians are writing to mixed audiences, they might be saying something about priestly prayers more inclusive to women than probably would have been imagined by Philo or the DSS community.

35. Matt 4:10; Luke 1:74; 2:37; 4:8; Acts 7:7, 42; 24:14; 26:7; 27:23; Rom 1:9, 25; Phil 3:3; 2 Tim 1:3; Heb 8:5; 9:9, 14; 10:2; 12:28; 13:10; Rev 7:15; 22:3.

36. Pss 50:14; 51:17; 141:2; Prov 21:3.

It might be appropriate to include Heb 13:10 here in the list of passages in which the members of the congregation are called to make priestly offerings. There the author states, "We have an altar from which those who minister at the tabernacle have no right to eat." He is proclaiming that they possess an altar that those who are not followers of Jesus cannot access. Whether this altar refers to the sacrifice of Christ,[37] an altar located in the Christian gathering, one in heaven, or something ambiguously comprehensive in "a symbolic fashion typical of the early church to refer to the sacrifice of Christ in all of the complexity with which that is understood in Hebrews,"[38] it again applies priestly service language to the congregation.

This author was well aware that the priests in Israel had to be the right person's son as he states in ch. 7 (7:14). Sacramental ministry was a birthright. I would argue that he would say this principle still holds. It is true for Jesus, and true for his people. There might now be a different priestly order, but the necessity of familial connections has not changed.

Summary

If these authors grant the audience priestly rights and responsibilities because they are sons and daughters of God—brothers and sisters of the Son—a more precise articulation of the genesis of that relationship is needed. In other words, if they can be priests only because they stand in the right family line, how did they become the sons of God? How did humans become related to God in the same relationship as Jesus is related to God? John in his Revelation gives Jesus the power. He is the one who made them to be a Kingdom and priests (Rev 1:6), a statement the elders echo (Rev 5:10). Paul articulates the cause for the transformation clearly. When God bought back his people, he sent the Spirit of his Son into their hearts, a Spirit that cried out with the cry of a child to a father, voiced as the call "Abba" (Gal 4:5–6). If, Paul says to his congregation, you are being led by the Spirit of God, then you are a son of God. This Spirit allows you to cry out to God as Abba and in so doing communicates the reality to God's people that they are his children (Rom 8:14–16). Peter resonates with the Spirit theme as well. Those believers to whom he is writing are chosen according to the foreknowledge of God

---

37. Cockerill argues that this phrase "recalls the high-priestly ministry of Christ that 'we have' (4:14–16; 10:19–25), and reminds the hearers that his once-for-all sacrifice on the cross is the continuous source of this heart-confirming grace" (*Hebrews*, 697); Lane, *Hebrews 9–13*, 538.

38. Attridge, *Hebrews*, 396.

by the sanctifying of the Spirit (1 Pet 1:1–2), and this is how they are born again into the living hope of the resurrection of Christ (1 Pet 1:3).

Hebrews shows its relationship with the others on this point as well. Explicitly, the Holy Spirit is the medium of God's speech.[39] The author can alternate between describing Scripture as the speech of God and the speech of the Holy Spirit.[40] If the Spirit of God is present in God's speech, then when God speaks in the Son (1:2) to humanity to proclaim his identity as Father (1:5), the Spirit is the vehicle of that relational speech. We could see the Spirit present in the vocalization of God's relationship with the Son (1:5), and so similarly the Spirit is present when God speaks paternally to humanity to affirm the same type of relationship (12:5). As in Paul, there is also a move from slavery to sonship, when Christ rescues them from the fearful power of the devil (2:14–15). After this rescue and this Spirit-articulated relationship, the readers are then proclaimed to be holy brothers, sharing in God's Holy Spirit (3:1) because it is God's Spirit who allowed Christ to make the offering that brings about the sanctification (9:14). They have experienced the gifts of the Holy Spirit (2:4) and have shared in the Holy Spirit (6:4). For Hebrews, in agreement with Paul, it is the Spirit that creates the relationship of sonship by speech and sanctification that allows them to serve as priests. They resemble the Son because they have the same Spirit; this is the family mark of holiness that allows them to approach and serve the Holy God.

ORDINATION OF SOME

The literature on ordination, although its purpose is to focus on the specific call of some, seems to unanimously support the idea that all believers are called to serve, and even that all believers are called to serve as priests to God. In light of texts like 1 Pet 2:9, Anglican divine Claude Beufort Moss makes just this claim: "The Christian Church, of which He is the Head, is 'a royal priesthood' (1 Peter ii.9), sharing in the priesthood of its Head, and His heavenly work of Offering. This the church does by the whole of her life, which is, ideally, one long self-offering, united with the self-offering of our Lord in Heaven."[41] Similarly, Robert Terwilliger states, "The language of priesthood is actually used of Christ and of the church, but not of the

---

39. Heb 3:7; 10:15.

40. This multivocality occurs in the Ps 95 quotation cited in Heb 3 and 4, and the Jer 31 citation recounted in Heb 8 and 10. For a discussion of the Spirit as speaker in Hebrews, see Schenck, "God Has Spoken."

41. Moss, *Christian Faith*, 370.

ministry." In this priesthood, "all Christians are members together."[42] Orthodox theologian John Zizioulas claims even more strongly, "There is no such thing as a 'non-ordained' person in the Church."[43]

If everyone is ordained and if everyone is a priest as these texts and theologians seem to agree, then why do most churches have a ceremony or ritual of ordination and call forth some in a different way? As one who seeks to base practice on Scripture, I ask, is there textual warrant for doing so? Immediately, we might think of the call of the disciples (Mark 1:16–20; Matt 4:18–22; John 1:35–51), the appointing of those who waited tables (Acts 6:1–6), the instructions for overseers and deacons (1 Tim 3; 5; Titus 1). Could we also find, in these texts that affirm the filial priestly call of all believers, a specific call for some to take the lead as priestly mediators of the knowledge and worship of God?

1 Peter

The vast majority of Peter's first letter concerns all those aliens scattered across the region of Asia Minor: their calling (1:2), their suffering (4:12–19), their comfort in Christ and his Spirit (5:6; 1:11), and, as I have highlighted, their familial relationship with God and the subsequent priestly vocation. Yet even here Peter acknowledges a diversity of gifts. If he is influenced in his statement about priesthood by the Exodus narrative, he affirms what that text does, that there are different types of priesthood, likely the priesthood of all Israel (Exod 19:6)[44] and the priesthood of the line of Aaron called by God (Exod 28–29). Each one has received a χάρισμα that they should minister for the sake of one another, just as a good steward of a household should do (1 Pet 4:10). Many different kinds of χαρίσματα exist, as he demonstrates in the next verse. Some speak, and they should do so with the mindset that they are speaking the words of God. Some serve, and should do so out of the strength provided by God (4:10–11). Does he mean to portray different gifts here, or even more specifically, the two different ministries of word and service, of presbyters and deacons? If he does have in mind different gifts, he has chosen two ends of the spectrum of prominence, namely the one seen

42. Terwilliger and Holmes, *To Be a Priest*, 6.
43. Zizioulas, *Being as Communion*, 215–16.
44. A minority interpretation exists that says Exod 19 speaks not of the priesthood of all Israel but the royal status of Israel's priests, still a limited group (Caspari, "Das priestliche Königreich"; Moran, "Kingdom of Priests"; Scott, "Kingdom of Priests"; Bauer, "Könige und Priester"; Fohrer, "'Priestliches Königtum." Even if this interpretation for Exodus is legitimate, Peter clearly applies priesthood to the group of Christians to whom he is writing.

and heard and the one in the background. Whatever specific gifts he might have in mind, these gifts are unified in several vital respects. First and foremost, as he says in v. 10, everyone is *serving* no matter what they are doing. All should follow Christ in his humble servant-like attitude (Mark 10:45; 1 Pet 2:21–25). Moreover, all of the gifts are exercised in the household, as members of the family of God. As people are serving others with their gifts, they should remember they are serving their siblings united to them in the family of God under Christ by the Spirit. Finally, all the gifts work toward the end of bringing glory to God through Christ.

Secondly, in chapter 5, Peter has a word for the elders. In comparison with the young men of v. 5, these could possibly be those advanced in age, but their seniority is not simply chronological. They are also charged with oversight.[45] Peter likewise positions himself as an elder who knows the bitterness and the blessing of following Christ. He encourages this group to shepherd the flock of God by looking over them, not because they have to do so but because they want to do so; not because they will receive some kind of monetary or honorific gain, but because they desire to care for these people. Their oversight should not be grounds for domineering, for they are all—old or young, sheep or shepherd—meant to interact with one another in humility. The grace of God, even the gifting of God comes to those who are humble. They lead by providing a type, an example, of the way of following the chief shepherd. If they are able to lead with this pure motivation, they will in fact at the end be granted an unfading reward (1 Pet 5:4). As will be true for other NT authors including Hebrews, Peter encourages a comprehensive priesthood along with an apportioned leadership, all taking place humbly within the household of God.

Paul

Peter's statements affirm the good of pastoral leadership, but Paul's vision specifies *sacerdotal* kind of actions for those who minister. As Paul urged his congregation to offer sacrifices to God, he envisions his own ministry

---

45. Jobes (*1 Peter*, 302) summarizes the relationship between chronological and authorial eldership: "Following the Jewish tradition, the Christian church from its earliest days adopted the term *presbuteroi* to refer to leaders of a local group of believers (e.g., Acts 14:23; 15:2) who were probably heads of households where house churches met (R. Campbell 1994). At the earliest stage of the church in any given locale, elders probably were not office holders in the formal sense of later ecclesiology but men who, by virtue of their age and the prestige of their families, exercised 'an authority that is informal, representative and collective,' based on their seniority in relationships that already existed (R. Campbell 1994:4, 64)."

in a priestly way. In Rom 15, he describes his apostolic call to evangelize and disciple the Gentiles with cultic terminology. He describes himself as a minister (λειτουργός) of Christ Jesus unto the Gentiles and then again as one who serves as a priest (ἱερουργέω) on behalf of the Gospel of God (Rom 16:16). He serves in this way so that the offering of the Gentiles might be pleasing, as it is sanctified by the Holy Spirit (Rom 15:16). Paul portrays himself as a priestly mediator who prepares the sacrifice of the Gentiles so that it is ready to be presented to God.[46] His particular call to be an apostle to the Gentiles, to tirelessly spread the gospel where it has not been spread and then to encourage their growth in the faith, the God-given call to evangelize and disciple, Paul envisions as a priestly call.

In some of his other letters, Paul shifts the metaphor a bit to describe himself not as priest but as sacrifice. In 2 Corinthians, he portrays the ministry of himself and his compatriots as a pleasing sacrifice to God. He uses both the term εὐωδία (2 Cor 2:15) and ὀσμή (2 Cor 2:14, 16), terms used for the sacrifices burned to God.[47] Paul is not the priest here, but the sacrifice, which emphasizes the personal cost that comes to him in ministry. This act that pleases God also testifies to others of the power of God. He draws a similar picture of himself and his ministry in Philippians, a letter addressed to the Philippian believers including the overseers and deacons (1:1). He states, "Even if I am being poured out as a drink offering on the sacrifice and service coming from your faith, I am glad and rejoice with all of you" (Phil 2:17). Again he pictures his congregations as an offering to God, but it is not clear here who is the priest, for he is the drink offering (Exod 25:28) added to bring glory to God. Finally, at the end of his life, as he can see his death drawing close, he again asserts that he is being poured out as a drink offering (2 Tim 4:6). Paul describes his own ministry cultically in the same two ways that Hebrews describes the work of Christ, as priest and sacrifice.

Revelation

In his vision that portrays the priestly ministry of God's people, John also has a place for a variety of gifts. He has the particular role of a messenger and teacher. God gave him this vision (1:1) and Jesus instructed him to

---

46 Moo states, "Paul therefore pictures himself as a priest, using the gospel as the means by which he offers his Gentile converts as a sacrifice acceptable to God" (*Romans*, 890).

47. Gen 8:21; Exod 29:18, 25, 41; Lev 1:9, 13, 17; 2:2, 9, 12; 3:5, 11, 16; 4:31; 6:15, 21; 8:21, 28; 17:4, 6; 23:13, 18; Num 15:3, 5, 7, 10, 13–14, 24; 18:17; 28:2, 6, 8, 13, 24, 27; 29:2, 6, 8, 11, 13, 36; Jdt 16:16; Sir 24:15; 50:15; Ezek 16:19; 20:28.

record it (1:11, 19) so that others could read it and be blessed by it. Robert Mulholland suggests that the angels of the churches (Rev 1:20; 2:1, 8, 12, 18; 3:1, 7, 14) could be the human messengers and based on the model of the synagogue represented the congregation in prayer.[48] Even more interesting is the role John describes for the twenty-four elders. They sit around the proximity of God's throne (4:4) and take a leading role in the worship of God in which all participate (5:9, 11–14; 11:16; 19:4). They, like John, also serve as teachers giving him insight and instruction into the visions that he is seeing (5:5; 7:13–14).

Most striking for this investigation is the role they play in worship that this text describes in priestly terms. When the Lamb takes the book that only he is worthy to open, the four living creatures and the elders fall down in worship of him. As previously discussed, it is in their song of worship that they proclaim that the Lamb has purchased people from every tribe and tongue to be priests to God (5:10). As they worship God and make this proclamation, they present bowls of incense that are the prayers of all the saints (5:8).[49] This again is a mediatorial priestly role played by the elders, priests among priests who facilitate the offering to God.

Hebrews

If any NT book might reject the concept of human priests, it would be the Epistle to the Hebrews. Whether it be the case that the author is trying to persuade his readers not to go back to Judaism or rather comfort them after the temple's dissolution in 70 AD,[50] he leaves no space for any other salvific mediator in the congregation other than Christ. That being said, I have also endeavored to show that as followers of Christ he invites his readers to view themselves and their worship in priestly ways.

The author of Hebrews also allows and even encourages human leaders in the congregation. Throughout the long encomium of chapter 11, he

---

48. Mulholland, *Revelation*, 91–92.

49. This is the one truly priestly action of the twenty-four elders (Smalley, *Revelation*, 116). Interpreters offer several options for the identity of the elders, including angelic and human (ibid.). It is better support for my argument if they are humans performing priestly actions on behalf of others, but even if John intended them to be angelic, they could function as representatives of the church's future heavenly existence. Beale states, "[T]he church is pictured in angelic guise to remind its members that already a dimension of their existence is heavenly" (*Revelation*, 323).

50 Cockerill arrives, safely in my opinion, only at a range of dates: "The evidence is insufficient, however, to narrow the time of Hebrews' composition with certainty beyond a range of A.D. 50 to 90" (*Hebrews*, 41).

directs the attention of his audience to the faithful in Israel's history and asks that they follow their example (6:12; 10:39; 12:1). That kind of leadership by example, however, could be and should be exercised by all members of the congregation. It is also the case that he recognizes some who are set apart for particular roles of leadership. Christ leads, but some of those who follow him are better prepared to strengthen the weak bodies and straighten the rough paths of the rest of the followers (Heb 12:12–13).

The clearest example of one set apart to lead might be the author himself. Through his rhetorically adept letter, he functions as a leader primarily through the office of teaching them about the Scriptures and Christ, but also by inspiring them, through encouragement or exhortation, to hold fast their faith as they run toward Zion.[51] It is his great desire that they heed his exegetical insights and consequently respond to his exhortations to hold fast, to keep running, to stay free from sin (13:22). He displays and affirms the necessity of the authority of teaching and exhortation.

Outside of his own witness, he appeals to several prominent leaders in the life, historically and presently, of the community. In the catalogue of the faithful, a good number of those whose stories he recounts including Noah (11:7), Joseph (11:22), Moses (11:23–29), Gideon, Barak, Sampson, Jephthah, David, and Samuel (11:32) were set apart for particular leadership. More immediately to their situation, he says that the previous generation of leaders should be remembered (13:7). They spoke the word to the congregation—maybe they are apostles or witnesses of Christ mentioned in 2:3—and they lived faithfully until the end of their natural lives. Their faith, presumably in believing in God's actions in Christ, speaking of them, and living in response to them makes them a worthy model of emulation. While Jesus is their ultimate example, the author is comfortable with having other (helpful yet imperfect) human examples to follow as well.

Most explicitly, in the second mention of leaders in the closing set of instructions, he refers to a group of leaders currently in the congregation. Everyone else should trust and submit to these current leaders (13:17). For their part, the leaders are called to watch over the souls of the congregation; for this, they will have to give an account to God. Their spiritual oversight should be done with joy and not groaning, for a disgruntled leader will offer no benefit. While they all confess Christ as High Priest, while they all should live as faithful examples, it is necessary and good in his opinion that some in the congregation serve in roles of the leadership of spiritual oversight. They are called to be accountable for the souls of the others. He asserts that

---

51. Cockerill rightly highlights the idea that this author is a pastor (*Hebrews*, 2), and therefore causes readers to think about his pastoral leadership.

someone must be on spiritual watch, to remain alert (ἀγρυπνέω), and that weighty task falls to this group. To continue the metaphor, it would not be beneficial for everyone to take the night watch, so only some are called to this duty.

The leaders' role may not immediately appear as strictly cultic. They are not offering sacrifices on behalf of others (though one does wonder about the nature of the altar they have, 13:10),[52] yet it does show that this author imagines some priestly children of God chosen to care for others, and in his vision of the priesthood, that is precisely the ministry Jesus employs currently. Jesus is merciful (2:17). He offers help to those who are being tested (2:18). He is sympathetic (4:15), allows them to get timely help (4:16), provides a firm hope (6:18–19), lives to intercede (7:25), and gives bold access to God (10:18–22). He inaugurated his priestly ministry through offering himself to God, but he lives now to understand sympathetically, to encourage, empower, and intercede. These are the aspects of eternal priestly ministry that human leaders can now employ as well. In their caring oversight of the members of the congregation, they are following after the great High Priest.

CONCLUSION

In the ancient world, especially in Jewish contexts, priesthood and sonship were closely related arenas.[53] One could serve as priest because and only because that man stood in the right family line.[54] I would argue that this holds true for Jesus as well. As one who stands in the line of David, the promises of Ps 110, including God's promise that he would be a priest in the order of Melchizedek, come to him. Moreover, as the Son of God, he can be the eternal and effective High Priest this promise anticipates.[55] Therefore, the priestly position of believers who serve in worship and ministry and service, who present offerings to God, who can approach his holy presence do so because they now stand in the right line having been declared as children of God by virtue of being members of Jesus Christ. Their identity has changed and so has their vocation. If they are non-Levitical Jews, if they are Gentiles, if they are women, if they are imperfect in any way, this language now gives them access to the presence of God that the practices of the cult would have

---

52 "'For we have an altar' recalls the high-priestly ministry of Christ that 'we have' (4:14–16; 10:19–25)," argues Cockerill (*Hebrews*, 697).

53. See the discussion of priestly patriline in Eisenbaum, "Father and Son."

54 Cohen, *Maccabees to the Mishnah*, 106–7.

55. Peeler, *You Are My Son*, 104–39.

denied to them. From every nation and tongue, gender and ability, they are priests of God.

For those who sense a call to the ministry of teaching, preaching, leadership, and/or sacraments, this filial identity gives them a firm foundation as well. They have not taken this honor for themselves, as the author of Hebrews asserts (5:4–5), but they have been called, not simply because of their particular giftedness but primarily because of their identity in Christ. This acts as a check against pride for some, and adds confidence for others. For all, it creates a sense of gratitude. If the ministerial call comes not from ability, but filial identity, then no place remains for either self-doubt or pride.

Moreover, knowledge of this identity creates a sense of boldness. A priest is approaching the God of the universe as a representative leader of the people in the congregation. This should never be taken flippantly, yet the power—especially pronounced in Hebrews—is that this approach can be a bold one because the members of Christ have an advocate in the One who has opened the way. That boldness only increases when those priests realize that the heavenly advocate is at the same time their brother and that Holy God they are approaching is their Father. Every believer has such a relationship, each one has such access, but it is the call of some to facilitate that worship through proclamation of the word and administration of leadership, sacraments, and pastoral care so that all—sons and daughters—might forever reign as priests of the most high God.

BIBLIOGRAPHY

Aasgaard, Reidar. *My Beloved Brothers and Sisters: Christian Siblingship in Paul*. JSNTSup 265. London: T. & T. Clark, 2004.
Attridge, Harold W. *The Epistle to the Hebrews: A Commentary on the Epistle to the Hebrews*. Hermeneia. Philadelphia: Fortress, 1989.
Bauer, J. B. "Könige und Priester." *BZ* 2 (1958) 284–86.
Beale, G. K. *The Book of Revelation: A Commentary on the Greek Text*. NIGTC. Grand Rapids: Eerdmans, 1999.
Bradshaw, Paul F. *Rites of Ordination: Their History and Theology*. Collegeville, MN: Liturgical, 2013.
Bruce, F. F. *The Epistle to the Hebrews*. Rev. ed. NICNT. Grand Rapids: Eerdmans, 1990.
Byrne, Brendan. *Romans*. SPS. Collegeville, MN: Liturgical, 1996.
Calvin, John. *The Epistle of Paul the Apostle to the Hebrews and the First and Second Epistles of St Peter*. Edited by David W. Torrance and Thomas F. Torrance. Translated by William B. Johnston. Calvin's Commentaries. 1963. Repr., Grand Rapids: Eerdmans, 1980.
Caspari, Wilhelm. "Das priesterliche Königreich." *TBl* 8 (1929) 105–10.
Cockerill, Gareth L. *Christian Faith in the Old Testament: The Bible of the Apostles*. Nashville: Nelson, 2014.

———. *The Epistle to the Hebrews*. NICNT. Grand Rapids: Eerdmans, 2012.
Cohen, Shaye J. D. *From the Maccabees to the Mishnah*. LEC 7. Philadelphia: Westminster, 1987.
———. "Heb 1:1–14, 1 Clem. 36:1–6 and the High Priest Title." *JBL* 97 (1978) 437–40.
Dozeman, Thomas B. *God on the Mountain: A Study of Redaction, Theology, and Canon in Exodus 19–24*. SBLMS 37. Atlanta: Scholars, 1989.
Eisenbaum, Pamela. "Father and Son: The Christology of Hebrews in Patrilineal Perspective." In *A Feminist Companion to the Catholic Epistles and Hebrews*, edited by Amy-Jill Levine and Maria Mayo Robbins, 127–46. FCNTECW 8. New York: T. & T. Clark, 2004.
Fohrer, Georg. "'Priestliches Königtum,' Ex. 19:6." *TZ* 19 (1963) 359–62.
Ford, J. Massyngberde. *Revelation*. Garden City, NY: Doubleday, 1975.
Hellerman, Joseph H. *The Ancient Church As Family*. Minneapolis, Minnesota: Fortress, 2001.
———. *Philippians*. EGGNT. Nashville: B&H Academic, 2015.
Jobes, Karen H. *1 Peter*. BECNT. Grand Rapids: Baker Academic, 2005.
———. *Letters to the Church: A Survey of Hebrews and the General Epistles*. Grand Rapids: Zondervan, 2011.
Keener, Craig S. *Revelation*. NIVAC. Grand Rapids: Zondervan, 2000.
Lane, William. *Hebrews 9–13*. WBC. Dallas: Word, 1991.
Macquarrie, John. *A Guide to the Sacraments*. New York: Continuum, 1997.
Moo, Douglas J. *The Epistle to the Romans*. NICNT. Grand Rapids: Eerdmans, 1996.
Moran, William L. "A Kingdom of Priests." In *The Bible in Current Catholic Thought*, edited by J. L. McKenzie, 7–20. SMTS 1. New York: Herder and Herder, 1962.
Moss, Claude B. *The Christian Faith: An Introduction to Dogmatic Theology*. New York: SPCK, 1943.
Mulholland, M. Robert, Jr. *Revelation: Holy Living in an Unholy World*. FAPC. Grand Rapids: Asbury, 1990.
Nitzan, Bilha. *Qumran Prayer and Religious Poetry*. Leiden: Brill, 1994.
O'Brien, Peter Thomas. *The Letter to the Hebrews*. PNTC. Grand Rapids: Eerdmans, 2010.
———. "Church." In *The Dictionary of Paul and His Letters*, edited by Gerald F. Hawthorne and Ralph P. Martin, 123–31. Downers Grove, IL: InterVarsity, 1993.
Peeler, Amy L. "Desiring God: The Blood of the Covenant in Exodus 24." *BBR* 23 (2013) 187–206.
———. *You Are My Son: The Family of God in the Epistle to the Hebrews*. LNTS 486. London: T. & T. Clark, 2014.
Plummer, Alfred. *A Critical and Exegetical Commentary on the Second Epistle of St. Paul to the Corinthians*. ICC. New York: Scribner's Sons, 1915.
Ramsey, Arthur M. *The Gospel and the Catholic Church*. London: Longmans, Green, 1937.
Sanders, E. P. *Judaism: Practice and Belief, 63 BCE–66 CE*. Philadelphia: Trinity, 1992.
Schenck, Ken. "God Has Spoken: Hebrews' Theology of the Scriptures." In *The Epistle to the Hebrews and Christian Theology*, edited by Richard Bauckham, 321–36. Grand Rapids: Eerdmans, 2009.
Scott, R. B. Y. "A Kingdom of Priests (Exodus 19:6)." In *Oudtestamentische Studiën* 8, edited by P. A. H. de Boer, 212–19. Leiden: Brill, 1950.

Seland, Torrey. "The 'Common Priesthood' of Philo and 1 Peter: A Philonic Reading of 1 Peter 2.5, 9." *JSNT* 57 (1995) 87–119.

———. *Strangers in the Light: Philonic Perspectives on Christian Identity in 1 Peter.* Leiden: Brill, 2005.

Smalley, Stephen S. *The Revelation to John: A Commentary on the Greek Text of the Apocalypse.* Downers Grove, IL: InterVarsity, 2005.

Terwilliger, Robert E., and Urban T. Holmes. *To Be a Priest: Perspectives on Vocation and Ordination.* New York: Seabury, 1975.

Zizioulas, John D. *Being as Communion: Studies in Personhood and the Church.* CGC 4. Crestwood, NY: St. Vladimir's Seminary Press, 1993.

7

Preexistence, Kenosis, and Exaltation in Hebrews, John, and Paul

Distinctive Explications of a Common Underlying Narrative

CAREY B. VINZANT

GARY COCKERILL IS PROBABLY best known in scholarly circles for his work with the Epistle to the Hebrews, and Hebrews had certainly been the primary focus of his scholarly work until the publication of his *Christian Faith in the Old Testament*. At the same time, however, his work with Hebrews has been an expression of his particular perspective regarding hermeneutics and biblical theology. It is his clear conviction that the exegete will only properly understand Scripture insofar as he or she is committed to let God's word speak on its own terms. This essay, then, proposes to reflect on a particular set of themes in Hebrews by considering how those same themes emerge in the NT books traditionally associated with John and Paul. We will consider the origins and nature of biblical theology, interact with Hebrews, John, and Paul, and draw implications for the practice of biblical theology.

ORIGINS AND NATURE OF BIBLICAL THEOLOGY

Biblical theology as a movement emerged in response to two problematic approaches to the Bible. The first problem this movement sought to address was a confessional approach to exegesis which tended to read doctrine into Scripture, to harmonize Scripture with doctrine, or both. In response to this the biblical theology movement sought to reestablish a proper distinction between revelation and doctrine. The second problem, and the one with which this essay is primarily concerned, was a consequence of Protestant Liberalism's approach to the Bible. The liberal project, it is important to remember, arose from Schleiermacher's conviction that Christianity could be shown to be reasonable at every turn. The shift, then, was from viewing the Bible as truth because it was revelation given by a transcendent God to viewing the Bible as containing truth that could be verified rationally. As a consequence of this change in viewpoint, biblical statements that could not be shown to be reasonable were treated as not being revelatory. Hans Frei notes:

> As the realistic narrative reading of the biblical stories broke down, literal or verbal and historical meaning were severed and literal and figural interpretation, hitherto naturally affiliated procedures, also came apart. Figural reading had been literalism extended to the whole story or the unitary canon containing it. But now figural sense came to be something like the opposite of literal sense.[1]

The phrase "unitary canon" is of particular importance to the discussion with which this essay is concerned. A natural consequence of the liberal emphasis upon the human authorship of Scripture was the tendency to view the Bible as many books rather than as one canon. Bright summarizes the emergent problem of liberalism: "That such an approach had an atomizing effect on the Bible cannot be doubted."[2] To say it another way, that conviction concerning the unity of Scripture which had so long been the starting point of Christian exegesis had at this point eroded largely away. Childs observes: "Critical scholars were faulted for having lost themselves in the minutiae of literary, philological, and historical problems. As a result the Bible had been hopelessly fragmented and the essential unity of the gospel was distorted and forgotten."[3] The implications of this were profoundly disturbing both theologically, as Christians struggled to think meaningfully and substantively about a gospel that had seemingly become a fast-moving target, and pastorally, as ministers sought to cast a compelling vision of what had become a decidedly hazy and disjointed picture. It became needful to find ways of speaking about the Bible in which clarity and coherence were driving concerns. Bright observes: "The question of the unity of Scripture must be taken seriously if the Bible is to be saved from disuse and misuse.

1. Frei, *Eclipse*, 6.
2. Bright, *Kingdom*, 9.
3. Childs, *Crisis*, 15.

But it is not a question that can be brushed aside with an easy answer. In one sense the Bible exhibits more diversity than unity. It is a very variegated book; rather, it is not a book at all, but a whole literature."[4]

At the same time, however, Marshall has cogently argued that, "... we can proceed through a recognition of the diversity in the documents to a recognition that there is a fundamental unity between them."[5] The Bible is indeed a sort of anthology, a related collection of texts written over several centuries by various authors. How then, can it be understood as a *canon*, an essentially unified work? One promising line of thought in response to this question arose within the movement that has variously been called Narrative Theology or Literary Theology. Where prior exegesis had often taken an approach that focused primarily on particulars of grammar or history, the literary approach sought to understand God's revelation by giving special attention to the medium of that revelation; it asked what significance it might have that the Bible is a *written document*. The idea that the Bible was God's written word was hardly new, but this movement emphasized in a new way the literary nature, the *written-ness*, of Scripture. Considering the Bible with due attention to how literature works helps the reader to understand how the Bible works, and thus to better get at what it is saying to its audience.

One stream of thought in this area which is of particular interest in this connection is the application of archetypal criticism to study of the Bible. Archetypal criticism focuses on the power of recurrent imagery in a text. Tate explains the concept of archetypes succinctly by saying that they are "master images around which meaning is organized."[6] Ryken further fleshes out this idea by adding that "Archetypes are recurrent images and motifs that keep appearing in literature and in life and that touch us powerfully, both consciously and unconsciously."[7] Indeed, for Ryken, archetypes are "the basic building blocks of the literary imagination. When we read literature we are constantly in touch with them."[8] This attention to biblical archetypes offers a way forward in understanding the unity of the canon in that recurring images, by their very recurrence, represent a kind of unity. The power of these images must necessarily arise from their richness of reference. In other words, the archetypal elements in the Bible are powerful precisely because they evoke so much of the Bible. One outstanding example of this phenomenon is the image of the lamb. Anyone who has

---

4. Bright, *Kingdom*, 9.
5. Marshall, *Theology*, 707.
6. Tate, *Interpretation*, 71.
7. Ryken, *Literature*, 143.
8. Ibid., 187.

read the Bible deeply will immediately recognize how profoundly this image resonates throughout the canon. It evokes, among other things, Abraham's words to Isaac on Mount Moriah, the Passover, John's portrayal of Christ as the paschal lamb in his gospel, and the reprising of this image in the Revelation. As such, the biblical archetype of the lamb is a sign of thematic unity within the Bible.[9] In this light, then, the recognition of common images and thematic elements across the canon (biblical archetypes) helps the reader to recognize its fundamental unity. A particular motif in Hebrews, John, and Paul offers both a sort of case study in this approach and a further way to conceive the unity of the NT.

In examining the Christology of Hebrews in comparison to those of John and Paul, it becomes clear that, while Hebrews has its own distinctive set of metaphors for describing how Christ saves, it also bases its account in a particular narrative arc that is common to the clusters of books traditionally attributed to all three authors: Christ's preexistence, kenosis, and exaltation. Recognizing that Hebrews, John, and Paul[10] (as a shorthand for the corpus broadly associated with each) are each speaking in their own distinctive voices about a single grand narrative that they have in common makes it necessary to consider that narrative to be a major theme in the theology of the NT. As such, this narrative becomes not just a theme in Hebrews, John, or Paul, but a larger canonical theme. In other words, this narrative is not merely a trope common to Hebrews, John and Paul; on the contrary, it is a NT theology in the purest sense—a clear indicator of what is considered by the earliest Christians to be at the heart of the apostolic message.

This commonality has been recognized and/or debated in relation to John and Paul, but Hebrews seems not to have been a significant part of this discussion. There are at least two possible reasons why this has been the case. First, scholars have tended to accept the higher critical premise that common narratives must arise from literary dependence. In other words, if two authors say the same thing one must have known the other's work. This ignores the very real possibility that both authors see the same significance in the events of Christ's life because those events simply do signify what they both see. Second, the authorship of Hebrews has never been definitively

---

9. At this point it is worth noting that archetypal analysis, while it does encompass typology, is not limited to it. Typology demands a foreshadowing sign and a later fulfillment, while the concept of biblical archetypes is less strictly defined.

10. It is not the intent of this essay to debate the specific authorship of the Revelation or the so-called deutero-Pauline epistles. Rather, these clusters of books are taken as groups due to (1) a recognizable thematic and stylistic affinity within each that warrants their being thought of as a sort of sub-unit within the NT, and (2) traditional attribution.

established, so discussing it in relation to John or Paul has been problematic. It is precisely at this point, however, that Gary Cockerill's work with Hebrews is salutary for the discussion. His *The Epistle to the Hebrews*, by setting aside assumptions about the authorship of the work and focusing on the text itself, has shed light on the distinctive character of Hebrews while still showing its deep solidarity with other voices within the NT canon.

A CHRISTOLOGY OF PREEXISTENCE, KENOSIS, AND EXALTATION

Jaroslav Pelikan notes in his *The Emergence of the Catholic Tradition* that the divinity and humanity of Christ was the subject of much discussion in the patristic period. This doctrine, while it was held to be central to the apostolic faith, was articulated from various perspectives. At least three of these perspectives, those historically associated with the churches of Alexandria, Antioch, and Rome, have all been recognized as viable expressions of orthodox Christianity. The Roman Christology in particular is important to understanding the common narrative that underlies Hebrews, John, and Paul. Pelikan describes this Roman perspective as "a theology of preexistence, kenosis, and exaltation."[11]

In the time immediately leading up to the Council of Chalcedon in 451, the Church was facing two opposite and equally problematic heresies. On the one hand, Eutycheanism, while it spoke robustly of Christ as one person, failed to properly distinguish between his divine and human natures. The remedy for this heresy was the Antiochene Christology, which focused on what Pelikan calls "the indwelling Logos."[12] At the other extreme, Nestorianism, while it dealt well with the distinction of natures in Christ, failed to speak adequately about the unity of his person. The remedy for this was the Alexandrian Christology, which focused on what Pelikan calls "the hypostatic union."[13]

A further twist comes when the student of Church history realizes that Eutycheanism arose around Alexandria and Nestorianism arose around Antioch. In other words, either of these perspectives left unbalanced by the other could easily be carried to a heretical extreme. The logic of Chalcedon, then, set these two views in a sort of dialectical relationship to one another, a dynamic tension for which both were the better. The Chalcedonian confession of Christ as one person in two natures and the four famous qualifiers

---

11. Pelikan, *Emergence*, 256.
12. Ibid., 247.
13. Ibid.

of this confession (without confusion, without change, without division, without separation) clearly reflect this dialectic.

At this point, however, it becomes clear that the dialectical relationship between the Alexandrian and Antiochene perspectives, while it effectively rules out the heretical accounts of the Incarnation with which it is concerned, does not provide a satisfactory positive account. It states very clearly what Christ is not, but little or nothing to clarify what he is. It was precisely this void that the Roman Christology filled, and it did so by articulating what can very justly be described as a biblical theology of Christ's person.

It is worth taking a moment to define and explicate these three terms. The concept of preexistence functions as proof of Christ's divinity. To say that Christ is preexistent is to say that he has always been, something that can only be said of God. Only God is uncreated. The concept of kenosis, or self-emptying, is a profession that in Christ God has radically entered creation and become the Man who suffers and dies in order to deliver all humanity from suffering and death. Kenosis signifies and demonstrates God's radical love for and commitment to humanity; it is God "going the distance" to bring humanity back to himself. The self-emptying of Christ is vicarious—it is not for his own sake but for that of humanity that Jesus takes suffering and death into himself. The exaltation of Christ vindicates his claims to divinity and grounds the eschatological hope of the believer. Christ is exalted in his resurrection, his ascension, and in his final triumphant coming again as King and Judge. Because Christ has been exalted, the believer recognizes that he is the God-Man and that the salvation he has accomplished is finished and sure. Christ's exaltation entails both divinity and humanity in that his exaltation comes in the aftermath of his suffering. Christ's suffering is patently and necessarily human, but his exaltation is only understandable as the aftermath of his suffering. The lifting up of the God-Man only makes sense in light of his having been brought low. Because he is truly God Jesus has been lifted up, but only as true Man could he be struck down for the salvation of humanity.

This Roman Christology considers the divinity and the humanity of Christ from a narratival perspective, i.e., by recognizing that Christ is presented as a single character in the gospel accounts. The uniqueness of Christ consists in the fact that the gospels portray him as a single person who does things that only God can do, but also does things that are unmistakably human. He heals the sick, forgives sin, commands the storm, walks on the sea, and casts out demons. This Jesus is more than a miracle-worker, as he demonstrates by forgiving the sins of the paralytic; such a one is God. This same Jesus is born, grows, gets hungry and thirsty, weeps, sweats, bleeds, and dies. Perhaps the most paradoxical moment of all is the resurrection; mere God would not die, but a mere man would not rise again. This confrontation with the paradox of Christ is central to the Gospels, and it drives the Roman Christology with which this essay is concerned. Probably the definitive expression of this perspective is the *Tome of Leo*, which eloquently says: "There enters then these lower parts of the world the Son of God descending from His heavenly home ... the LORD of all things, He obscured His immeasurable majesty and took on Him the form of a servant: being God that cannot suffer, He did not disdain to be man that can, and, immortal as He is, to subject Himself to the laws of death."[14]

These themes of preexistence, kenosis, and exaltation each emerge in John, Paul, and Hebrews. Each writer has his own way of presenting these themes, but in all three this story-arc fundamentally shapes the account. The reader begins to sense that this overarching narrative of preexistence, kenosis, and exaltation suggests an underlying confessional or liturgical tradition which provides parameters within which the story of salvation is told. From this basis, each writer then develops a distinctive account with its own central metaphors and ways of describing the problem of sin and the salvation accomplished by Christ.

PREEXISTENCE, KENOSIS AND EXALTATION IN JOHN

John offers perhaps the clearest account of Christ's preexistence. The immediate Johannine example of this theme comes in the prologue to the fourth gospel. John communicates the preexistence (and hence the divinity) of the λόγος in at least four ways.

First, John says, "In the beginning was the Word [λόγος], and the Word was with God, and the Word was God" (1:1) asserting outright that the Word was unequivocally God. Second, John says that the λόγος "was with God in the beginning" (1:2). John's use of "in the beginning" here clearly echoes the creation account of Genesis and John makes this clear when in 1:3 he describes the λόγος's full cooperation in creation. Only God was present in the beginning. Third, John consistently uses the verb "was" (ἦν) with reference to the λόγος and in deliberate contrast to the verb "came to be" (various forms of γίνομαι), which he always uses to refer to created things. John makes this clear when he says "Through him all things were made [came to be]; without him nothing was made that has been made" (1:3). John follows this pattern unswervingly until 1:14, when he shifts the focus to Christ's kenosis by saying "the Word became [came to be] flesh ..." Fourth, the full cooperation of the λόγος in the creation of all things

---

14. Leo the Great, *Ep.* 28.4 (*NPNF*[2] 12:40).

underscores His preexistence and divinity. By saying that λόγος existed "in the beginning," by saying the λόγος "was God," by consistently using "was" in reference to the λόγος, and by pointing to the λόγος as co-Creator of all things, John provides a clear, full picture of preexistence and its significance.

John presents the kenosis of Christ in both existential and theological terms. John says that the divine λόγος "became flesh" (1:14). John's clear message is that the divine λόγος took on createdness. The Nicene Creed's turn of phrase perhaps says it best: "and was *made* man."[15] At the same time John depicts the suffering of Christ in specific terms, such as His weeping at the tomb of Lazarus. Of course, John depicts Christ's most important self-emptying at the Cross.

The exaltation of Christ in John is primarily depicted in terms of his resurrection and his giving authority to the Eleven in chapter 20. Jesus does tell His disciples after eating the Passover with them that he will be exalted by the Father. This is expressed repeatedly and in various ways over the course of chapters 13–17.

All of these partial depictions, however, snap into focus in light of chapter 13. The foot-washing scene is essentially a dramatization of the preexistence-kenosis-exaltation arc. John dramatically shows Jesus' authority (and hence his divinity and preexistence) in that Jesus presides at supper. John shows us Jesus' self-emptying as Christ lays aside his robe and washes the feet of the disciples. John finally depicts Jesus exaltation in the moment when he finally resumes his robe and place at the table before saying to his disciples, "You call me 'Teacher' and 'Lord,' and rightly so, for that is what I am."[16] In sum, the foot-washing scene in John functions as a sort of icon for the whole of the fourth gospel. John presents the reader with a dramatic visual representation that summarizes the whole story the Evangelist is telling, and the preexistence-kenosis-exaltation arc clearly underlies the scene as John describes it.

PREEXISTENCE, KENOSIS AND EXALTATION IN PAUL

Certainly the obvious example of this narrative arc in Paul is the hymn which comprises Phil 2:5–11:

> In your relationships with one another, have the same mindset as Christ Jesus: Who, being in very nature God, did not consider equality with God something to be used to his own advantage;

---

15. *Book of Common Prayer*, 358; emphasis added.
16. John 13:13.

> rather, he made himself nothing by taking the very nature of a servant, being made in human likeness. And being found in appearance as a man, he humbled himself by becoming obedient to death—even death on a cross! Therefore God exalted him to the highest place and gave him the name that is above every name, that at the name of Jesus every knee should bow, in heaven and on earth and under the earth, and every tongue acknowledge that Jesus Christ is Lord, to the glory of God the Father.

This passage clearly shows the merciful descent of Christ into human existence.[17] It then shows Christ's obedience and suffering on behalf of humanity. It concludes by presenting the exalted Christ, before whom all must bow. The passage would probably be the undisputed example *par excellence* of the preexistence-kenosis-exaltation narrative arc, were it not for the fact that Paul is more explicit about Christ's preexistence elsewhere:

> The Son is the image of the invisible God, the firstborn over all creation. For in him all things were created: things in heaven and on earth, visible and invisible, whether thrones or powers or rulers or authorities; all things have been created through him and for him. He is before all things, and in him all things hold together. And he is the head of the body, the church; he is the beginning and the firstborn from among the dead, so that in everything he might have the supremacy. For God was pleased to have all his fullness dwell in him, and through him to reconcile to himself all things, whether things on earth or things in heaven, by making peace through his blood, shed on the cross. (Col 1:15–20)

It is noteworthy here that Paul alludes to Christ as "the beginning" and says that "all things were created through him"—both statements that are strongly reminiscent of John's words. This might be taken as evidence of John's literary dependence upon Paul, but this need not be the case. It is entirely plausible that John and Paul either inherited these phrases from an existing oral/liturgical tradition or that both simply saw and recognized this narrative arc in the life of Jesus.

---

17. The question might be raised at this point whether "being in very nature God" necessarily implies preexistence. Marshall cogently answers this objection, arguing that a robust view of Christ's preexistence is present even before Paul (*Christology*, 121). He goes on to connect this with "Jewish speculation about the figure of wisdom as the preexistent agent of God in creation who comes and dwells among men" (122).

PREEXISTENCE, KENOSIS AND EXALTATION IN HEBREWS

Hebrews also has a key passage that outlines this preexistence-kenosis-exaltation arc. The introduction to Hebrews, its very first words, reads as follows:

> In the past God spoke to our ancestors through the prophets at many times and in various ways, but in these last days he has spoken to us by his Son, whom he appointed heir of all things, and through whom also he made the universe. The Son is the radiance of God's glory and the exact representation of his being, sustaining all things by his powerful word. After he had provided purification for sins, he sat down at the right hand of the Majesty in heaven. (Heb 1:1–3)

Hebrews, like John and Paul, relates the preexistence of the Son to his role as co-Creator of all things. Cockerill expresses it nicely when he says, "Through the Son God created the temporal ages of the world and all they contain ..."[18] Hebrews then alludes to Christ's self-emptying (which will be later developed in terms of obedience and sacrifice) in its mention of "purification for sins." Finally, Hebrews describes the exaltation of Christ in terms of his being seated "at the right hand of the majesty in Heaven." Each of these ideas is expanded through the course of the epistle.

The eternity (and thus preexistence) of Christ is fleshed out in the discussion of Melchizedek in chapter 7. Because what is needed is an eternal sacrifice, only an eternal priest can make the offering needed. Christ, as a priest in the order of Melchizedek, is such a one. Christ can, because of his eternal priesthood, make the eternal sacrifice needed to provide purification from sin.

The kenosis of Christ is discussed in at least five major ways in Hebrews. First, Christ has been "made lower than the angels for a little while, now crowned with glory and honor ..." (2:9).[19] To say it simply, Christ's coming as a human being was in itself a kind of kenosis. Second, Christ has emptied himself by suffering temptation: "we do not have a high priest who is unable to empathize with our weaknesses, but we have one who has been tempted in every way, just as we are—yet he did not sin" (4:15). Christ emptied himself by enduring human weakness and suffering, by struggling as humans do. Third, Christ has offered his own blood as the perfect sacrifice on behalf

---

18. Cockerill, *Hebrews*, 93.

19. See Rick Boyd's essay in this volume for more in-depth treatment of this verse and its significance.

of God's people (9:11–14). Fourth, Christ emptied himself by living a life of obedience: "... he was heard because of his reverent submission. Son though he was, he learned obedience from what he suffered ..." (5:7b–8). Finally, Hebrews describes Christ as taking upon himself the consequences of human uncleanness in his suffering "outside the city gate" (13:12). This means in the simplest terms that Jesus, who was without sin, took upon himself the condition of separation from fellowship with God that the sinner has earned.[20]

The exaltation of Christ is revisited in Heb 8, which describes Christ as "a high priest, who sat down at the right hand of the throne of the Majesty in heaven, and who serves in the sanctuary, the true tabernacle set up by the Lord, not by a mere human being" (8:1–2). Hebrews 10 further develops the significance of Christ sitting down: "Day after day every priest stands and performs his religious duties; again and again he offers the same sacrifices, which can never take away sins. But when this priest had offered for all time one sacrifice for sins, he sat down at the right hand of God ..." (10:11–12). In other words, the sacrifice Christ has offered is perfect and eternal; no further work remains for him to do. Therefore, Christ "sat down" (as one who has perfectly completed his work) "at the right hand of the throne" (the place of highest favor) "of the Majesty in heaven" (because he is God's Son and heir).

Having examined the common narrative arc in Hebrews, John, and Paul, it now remains to consider how each of these develops his account. Paul, John, and Hebrews, as will be seen, each have distinctive metaphors for sin and salvation. Taken together, these various metaphors offer a rich and balanced picture of the human problem and also of how God provides the solution in Jesus Christ.

Sin and Salvation in John

John describes the problem of sin in three major ways: darkness, blindness, and death. The fourth gospel and John's first epistle both speak emphatically of fallen humanity in term of darkness. "God is light; in him there is no darkness at all. If we claim to have fellowship with him and yet walk in the darkness, we lie and do not live out the truth" (1 John 1:5–6). This darkness is actually in conflict with God's light: "The light shines in the darkness, and the darkness has not overcome it" (John 1:5). Of course, the problem of

---

20. Of course, this parallels the Pauline statement that "God made him who had no sin to be sin for us, so that in him we might become the righteousness of God" (2 Cor 5:21).

death comes to the fore in, among other places, John 3:16. Along with the problems of darkness and death, John also frames the human problem in terms of blindness. This becomes particularly clear in his references to Jesus' miracles as signs to be seen. The unbelief of the Jews in the fourth gospel is framed precisely in terms of an unwillingness to see the signs or, rather, to see what they signify—that Jesus is the Son of God.

John's ways of speaking about salvation in Christ are solutions precisely commensurate with the problems he has described. To the problem of darkness, John presents Christ as the shining light the darkness cannot overcome (John 1:5). To the problem of human sightlessness, John calls his reader to see the signs. The conclusion of Jesus' appearance to Thomas and the following verses spell it out: ". . . then Jesus told him, "Because you have seen me, you have believed; blessed are those who have not seen and yet have believed." Jesus performed many other signs in the presence of his disciples, which are not recorded in this book. But these are written that you may believe that Jesus is the Messiah, the Son of God, and that by believing you may have life in his name" (John 20:29–31). This of course brings to mind the third of John's metaphors: life. In the passage cited above, in John 3:16, and in the prologue to his gospel John says that Jesus brings eternal life to those who believe in him. The solution to the problem of death is the resurrection promised by God to those who believe in Christ.

Sin and Salvation in Paul

Paul, like John, also deals with the problem of sin in terms of death (Rom 6:23). To be in sin is to be dying. At the same time, however, Paul also uses the metaphors of guilt and debt to describe the human problem. His discussion of Abraham in Rom 4 uses the language of debt by speaking about "wages" (v. 4) and speaking of righteousness as being "credited" (v. 3) to the believer. Furthermore, Paul also describes the human problem in terms of guilt. To say that someone is sinful is to say that he or she has broken God's Law and is thus guilty.

The problems Paul mentions he deals with by speaking of Christ as offering life, pardon, and freedom. He deals with the problem of death by presenting Christ's death on behalf of humanity: "While we were still sinners, Christ died for us" (Rom 5:8). Paul later elaborates on this, presenting the death of Christ on behalf of humanity as a reality into which the believer is drawn:

> . . . don't you know that all of us who were baptized into Christ Jesus were baptized into his death? We were therefore buried

> with him through baptism into death in order that, just as Christ was raised from the dead through the glory of the Father, we too may live a new life. For if we have been united with him in a death like his, we will certainly also be united with him in a resurrection like his. For we know that our old self was crucified with him so that the body ruled by sin might be done away with, that we should no longer be slaves to sin—because anyone who has died has been set free from sin. Now if we died with Christ, we believe that we will also live with him. (Rom 6:2–8)

Because the believer has been baptized into the death of Christ, the consequences of guilt and debt are rendered null and void because the Law is no longer binding after death (Rom 7:4). Because Christ has already died, the one baptized into his death is effectively dead in the eyes of the Law and set free from the consequences it brings to bear.

The death which comes with sin as its wages is a death Christ has already died. Paul underscores this by pointing to the uniting of the believer with Christ's death and of Christ's life with the believer. Paul thus portrays Christ as uniting himself to the sinner and assuming the consequences set in place by God's Law. At the same time, Christ unites the sinner to himself and draws the believer into his own resurrection.

Sin and Salvation in Hebrews

The author of Hebrews, like John and Paul, does speak to the human problem in terms of death, but it deals with death primarily as God's judgment upon those who do not believe his promises.[21] The author of Hebrews warns the listeners of the consequences for those who do not believe God's promises and live accordingly: "Was it not with those who sinned, whose bodies perished in the wilderness?" (3:17). Unbelief leads to disobedience, which comes under God's judgment.

Having said this, however, the primary metaphors for the human problem in Hebrews are uncleanness and separation from God. The need for the priestly ministry of Christ arises from the problem of the uncleanness of humanity brought about by sin. Humanity has not believed God's promises and has thus not lived according to God's design. Out of this uncleanness arises the separation from God represented by the temple veil. The suffering

---

21. This motif does appear in a different way in John, who treats death as the absence of the eternal life afforded the believer through Christ. The Pauline perspective is closer to that of Hebrews in that Paul does present death as "the wages of sin," i.e., as the judgment of God upon transgressors of his Law.

of Christ "outside the city gate" signifies the condition of human life alienated from God by the uncleanness of sin.

The solution to the human problem in Hebrews, then, is presented in terms of the ministry of Jesus as the great High Priest. Jesus is presented as the fulfillment and perfection of the priestly ministry that was foreshadowed in the Aaronic priesthood. The limitations of the Aaronic priesthood (the sinfulness of the priests, the temporary nature of their ministry, and the imperfect, repetitive nature of their sacrifices) are transcended and overcome by the eternal, once-for-all, sacrifice of Christ the perfect and sinless High Priest. That the redemption accomplished by Christ is perfect is shown in his being seated at the right hand of the throne in heaven. Christ, having offered the perfect high priestly sacrifice, sits down at God's right hand because no further offerings are needed. The sacrifice offered by Christ has made God's people clean so that they may enter into the presence of God. The blood of Christ has parted the veil and opened the way into fellowship with God.

Conclusion

A few final observations are in order at this point. First, the presence of the common narrative arc of preexistence-kenosis-exaltation in Hebrews, John, and Paul makes it clear that this is not an idiosyncratic interpretation. On the contrary, this understanding of Christ's life and ministry seems to lie at the heart of the apostolic witness. As such, it offers a useful rubric for thinking about the basic theology of the NT. Of course, there are hints of this in the OT as well, one striking example being the figure of the Suffering Servant in Isaiah.

This suggests a second point. John, Paul, and Hebrews all draw upon the common heritage of Christianity. All appropriate the language of sin, death, and divine judgment that Christianity inherited from the OT and the Judaism of the first century out of which Christianity arose. What is striking, however, is the fact that in the effort to understand Christ's fulfillment of the OT each seems to have seized upon different images from the OT. John sees Christ as the perfect paschal lamb, while Paul describes Christ as the second Adam, and Hebrews describes Christ as the great High Priest.

To go further, historic Christianity has also done theology along various lines which echo these different biblical perspectives. Ignatius of Antioch seems to have the picture of Christ as paschal lamb in mind in his eucharistically-centered account of salvation. Irenaeus is clearly thinking of Christ as the second Adam in setting forth his theory of recapitulation.

Luther is of course thinking of the Pauline theme of pardon as he sets forth his account of justification by faith. In this vein, it may be Gary Cockerill's signal contribution to Christian scholarship that he has so clearly brought out the theme of cleansing that is central to Hebrews, while also showing that epistle's fundamental solidarity with the rest of the NT.

Finally, this diversity of metaphors brings to mind a point Cockerill has made on more than one occasion in conversation: the Atonement is a unique reality. It is both compatible with and larger than the various depictions in Hebrews, John, and Paul. It would be fitting to add that this should serve as a reminder to theologians and students of the Bible that the metaphors in the NT are just that: metaphors. In speaking of the Atonement these metaphors each portray a portion of what Christ accomplished, but no one of them is all-sufficient, and it would be a mistake to reify any of them. The best theologians are those who go about their work with reverence, diligence, and humility, who pursue their craft as a labor of love and an act of worship. Gary Cockerill is just such a one.

BIBLIOGRAPHY

The Book of Common Prayer. New York: Oxford University Press, 1979.
Bright, John. *The Kingdom of God.* Nashville: Abingdon, 1953.
Childs, Brevard S. *Biblical Theology in Crisis.* Philadelphia: Westminster, 1970.
Cockerill, Gareth L. *The Epistle to the Hebrews.* NICNT. Grand Rapids: Eerdmans, 2012.
Leo the Great. "Letter XXVIII To Flavian, Commonly Called 'The Tome.'" In *The Nicene and Post-Nicene Fathers,* second series, edited by Philip Schaff and Henry Wace, translated by Charles Lett Feltoe, 12:38–43. New York: Scribner's, 1908.
Frei, Hans W. *The Eclipse of Biblical Narrative.* New Haven: Yale University Press, 1974.
Marshall, I. Howard. *New Testament Theology: Many Witnesses, One Gospel.* Downers Grove, IL: InterVarsity, 2004.
———. *The Origins of New Testament Christology.* Downers Grove, IL: InterVarsity, 1990.
Pelikan, Jaroslav. *The Emergence of the Catholic Tradition (100–600).* Vol. 1 of *The Christian Tradition: A History of the Development of Doctrine.* Chicago: University of Chicago Press, 1971.
Ryken, Leland. *How to Read the Bible as Literature.* Grand Rapids: Zondervan, 1984.
Tate, W. Randolph. *Biblical Interpretation: An Integrated Approach.* Peabody, MA: Hendrickson, 1991.

8

"Son though he was, he learned obedience"
The Submission of Christ in Theological Perspective (in Dialogue with Thomas Aquinas and Karl Barth)

THOMAS H. MCCALL

THE AUTHOR OF HEBREWS tells us that Jesus Christ did not exalt himself (5:5). Instead, we are told that

> During the days of Jesus' life on earth, he offered up prayers and petitions with fervent cries and tears to the one who could save him from death, and he was heard because of his reverent submission. Son though he was, he learned obedience from what he suffered and, once made perfect, he became the source of eternal salvation for all who obey him and was designated by God to be high priest in the order of Melchizedek. (Heb 5:7–10)

This fascinating passage is both rich in insight and intriguing. It raises many interesting interpretive and theological questions. Central to this passage is the statement that Jesus Christ was obedient. The obedient subordination of the Son is an issue that is the subject of intense debate in contemporary Trinitarian theology and Christology. Surprisingly, however, Heb 5 has not figured significantly in those debates.

In what follows, I offer a brief exercise in the theological interpretation of Scripture. This means different things in different contexts, so let me be clear about what I mean: theological interpretation of Scripture seeks to interpret the Bible theologically; it looks, that is, to see what the Bible teaches about God (and all else as it is related to God). It does so in respectful dialogue with the insights of modern and contemporary biblical studies, and it also seeks to learn from the deep and broad Christian tradition of exegetes and theologians. Accordingly, in this study we look closely for a proper understanding of the biblical witness to the submission and subordination of the Son. We do so in close conversation with two important theologians: Thomas Aquinas and Karl Barth. While both theologians seek to understand the subordination of the Son in accordance with creedal orthodoxy, their positions are importantly different. In what follows, I will offer a summary of their views, outline some important criticisms, and then ask what Heb 5 contributes directly to these discussions. But first, however, it will be helpful to make a few preliminary observations about the text.

HEBREWS 5:7-10: SOME INITIAL OBSERVATIONS

This fascinating passage raises many interesting questions: what are we to make of the reference to "the days of his flesh" (ταῖς ἡμέραις τῆς σαρκὸς αὐτοῦ),[1] especially in light of the orthodox Christian commitment to the continuing incarnation (and thus humanity) of the Son?[2] To what do the "fervent cries and tears" refer; is this a reference to the prayer in Gethsemane (Mark 14:32-42),[3] is it a reference to the cry of dereliction of the Son from

---

1. My translation. Barth holds that these "days" refer to his passion and especially to his death (*Church Dogmatics* III/2:562. He also thinks that these extend into the present (*Church Dogmatics* IV/3:395). Aquinas puts the emphasis on the "flesh" here; he says that "flesh is taken for the entire human nature [*tota natura humana*]" (*Hebraeos*, 113).

2. I take these "days" to be a reference to his incarnate earthly career; his life on earth. See the discussion in Vanhoye, *Structure*, 158. At any rate, the use of σάρξ in Hebrews does not carry the negative connotations that it sometimes does in Pauline theology.

3. Barth is convinced that this is a reference to Gethsemane. Indeed, he says that it is an "insufficiently noticed" commentary on Gethsamane (*Church Dogmatics* III/2:337; cf. *Church Dogmatics* IV/2:95, 250). Aquinas is likewise certain that Gethsemane is in view here, e.g., *Hebraeos*, 114. Commentators as diverse as Bruce, Hughes, and Wiley are certain that Gethsemane is in view (Bruce, *Hebrews*, 98–100; Hughes, *Hebrews*, 182; Wiley, *Hebrews*, 181–83). On the other hand, scholars such as deSilva (who thinks that passages from 2 and 3 Maccabees are more likely), Attridge, and Lane deny that this is so obvious (deSilva, *Perseverance*, 190–91; Attridge, *Hebrews*, 148; Lane, *Hebrews 1-8*, 120). Cockerill says that the "reference to Gethsemane is suggestive without being definitive," and while noting that "the pastor could have made such a reference unmistakable had he so desired," he concludes that "it is better to see this entire verse as a depiction of the utter dependence upon God that characterized the Son's earthly life and came to its climax in Gethsemane and on the cross" (*Hebrews*, 244).

the cross (Matt 27:43; Mark 15:34),[4] or just what?[5] What are we to make of the statement that he was heard "because of his reverent submission" (5:7)? What is it to be a "high priest in the order of Melchizedek" (5:10)? And so on; there is no shortage of compelling questions here.

Along with the intriguing questions that arise in reading this text, however, we can also see that the passage makes some important affirmations. Several of these stand out as especially important for our discussion. First, we know that the Son was obedient. Jesus Christ "learned obedience from what he suffered" (v. 8). This theme is powerful in Hebrews (especially 10:7, 9). Of course this teaching is by no means unique to Hebrews. Philippians 2:5–11 tells us that the Son was "in very nature God" but did not count equality with God as something to be grasped or held (v. 6). Instead, the Son became human and took upon himself "the very nature of a servant" (v. 7). He "made himself nothing" and "humbled himself," and in so doing became obedient "to death, even death on a cross" (v. 8). Moving beyond Paul, Jesus himself says that "I seek not to please myself but him who sent me" (John 5:30), that "I do nothing on my own but speak just what the Father has taught me" (John 8:28), and that "the Father is greater than I" (John 14:28). So this is not a point that is unique to Hebrews, but it is important to see that it is very clear here. The Son really was obedient.

Second, the Son *learned* (ἔμαθεν) obedience (v. 8). This does not mean that he was ever *disobedient*. We should not assume that the options here are limited to merely *obedience* and *disobedience*, for someone could be *nonobedient* without being either obedient or disobedient. One person may stand in relation to another in which the options are either obedience or disobedience. So a soldier who enlists in the military and serves under a commanding officer must either be obedient or disobedient. But before he comes into this relationship—before, that is, he enlists—he is neither disobedient nor obedient. Before his enlistment he is merely non-obedient, and what makes the difference is the change that occurs. So, we should not over-interpret this passage. The text does not tell us that the Son was ever disobedient, nor should we assume that he was. In fact, Hebrews tells us explicitly that the Son was "without sin" (ESV)—even though he was truly tempted (4:15). But neither does it tell us that he was always obedient. It simply does not say that. So we should not draw the wrong conclusions from this passage or import assumptions into it, but neither should we fail

---

4. Barth connects this closely to the cry of dereliction, e.g., *Church Dogmatics* I/1:386; *Church Dogmatics* I/2:158. Calvin and Hughes are among those who opt for both Gethsemane and the cry of dereliction. See Calvin, *Hebrews*, 64.

5. Aquinas (*Hebraeos*, 114) connects this to another of Christ's statements from the cross: "Father, into your hands I commit my spirit" (Luke 23:46).

to see this salient point. What the text does say is clear enough, and it is important: the Son *learned* obedience.

Third, the Son learned obedience *through suffering* (v. 8). The learning (ἔμαθεν) comes via suffering (ἔπαθεν). The learning process is thus "in the days of his flesh" (ἐν ταῖς ἡμέραις τῆς σαρκὸς); it occurs during his earthly sojourn (v. 7). The obedience referred to in this passage is coupled with the incarnate Son's experience of suffering; it is not something that is said to be true of the Son eternally, nor is it said to be intrinsic to the identity of the Son or his relationship to his Father. Whatever we might learn about the obedience and subordination of the Son from other passages, and whatever we might conclude about it theologically, what is clear in this passage is that the Son learned obedience through suffering.

Fourth, this passage shows us that he learned obedience *as Son* (v. 8). He does not leave or abandon his filial relation to learn obedience—indeed, how could he do so? Instead, it is precisely *as Son* that he learns this obedience through suffering. As Cockerill points out, "Christ's sonship did not cease while he was learning 'obedience.' When the pastor speaks of the human Son he is always referring to the eternal Son who has assumed humanity."[6] The suffering does not establish the Sonship; the force of the "although" (καίπερ) is concessive here. Nor does it even serve to demonstrate it (cf. 12:3–11). But neither does it negate it. Accordingly, for Hebrews obedience is not inimical to the filial relation. Jesus Christ learns obedience through suffering, and he does so precisely *as Son*.

Fifth, the process of learning obedience through suffering is closely related to the high priestly work of the Son. Cockerill is right when he says that "the Son has been set apart for a fully effective priesthood through complete obedience," and "this offering of total submission to God unto death is his sacrifice of priestly consecration."[7] The "fervent cries and tears" are the prayers of the Son who lived and died *for others*. Jesus Christ has been called or designated a high priest by God (v. 10), and it is in this capacity that he both learns obedience through suffering and becomes the cause or source (αἴτιος) of eternal salvation for all who obey him (v. 9). As a high priest, he acts not on his own behalf but on behalf of others (5:1; cf. 2:17), thus it is for others that he prays and for others that he learns obedience through suffering. His work is not for himself, for he is holy and pure in his innocence (7:26). His work is not for himself, because he has no need of such work (7:27; 10:4, 10). What he does is on behalf of others. And what he does is enough; it is final. "This doing of God's will is the sacrifice that does away

---

6. Cockerill, *Hebrews*, 247.
7. Ibid., 240.

with all previous sacrifices."[8] The Son learns obedience while suffering to be the source of our eternal salvation; he learns obedience not in place of our obedience but so that we can be obedient too (v. 9). As Cockerill concludes, "By his obedience Christ makes their obedience possible."[9]

KARL BARTH AND THOMAS AQUINAS ON THE OBEDIENCE OF THE SON

Karl Barth on the Eternal Subordination of the Son

Karl Barth is, of course, well aware of the straightforward New Testament statements that speak to the subordination, submission, or obedience of Jesus. After all, Jesus himself says that, "The Father is greater than I" (John 14:28). Barth is also surely aware of the traditional distinction between what might be called *functional* or *economic* subordination, on one hand, and *ontological* subordination on the other hand. But while he clearly rejects Arian and Socinian views, he is reticent to avail himself of the traditional distinction. Instead, he thinks that submission or subordination belongs to the very nature of the Trinity. He sees the "dignity of Jesus, the Lordship of Jesus and the superiority of Jesus" as real but also as "basically different and subordinate compared to that of the Other who is properly called θεός."[10] He goes on to say that "what is beyond question is that the κύριος Ἰησοῦς Χριστός is separate from and subordinate to θεὸς πατήρ."[11] While these statements are somewhat short of finally decisive (Barth is here referring to the Son *as incarnate*), he further offers a ringing affirmation of the view that this subordination is more than merely functional within what is sometimes referred to as the "economic" Trinity. For, as Barth says, we must "affirm and understand as essential to the being of God the offensive fact that there is in God Himself an above and a below, a *prius* and a *posterius*, a superiority and a subordination."[12] To be clear, Barth speaks here of something that is "essential to the being of God," and it is obvious that he holds to a kind of hierarchy within the Trinity. The Son simply *is* the one who is obedient; the Son is the one "who is himself this act of obedience."[13] For "according to the New Testament, it is not the being of the man Jesus which has this character"

8. Ibid., 242.
9. Cockerill, *Hebrews*, 445.
10. Barth, *Church Dogmatics* I/1:385.
11. Ibid., 385.
12. Barth, *Church Dogmatics* IV/1:200–201.
13. Barth, *Church Dogmatics* II/2:106.

of obedience.[14] No, "on the contrary," in the New Testament it is the Son of God who is described as the servant.[15] Thus the Son is obedient "not accidentally and incidentally . . . But necessarily and, as it were, essentially."[16] Indeed, Barth highlights the element that he labels "the most offensive fact of all;" this is the fact that there is "a below, a *posterius*, a subordination that . . . belongs to the inner life of God."[17] The Triune God is "both a First and a Second, One who rules and commands in majesty and One who obeys in humility. The one God is both the one and the other."[18]

It is worth noting that not all so-called "Barthians" agree with him on this point. Thomas F. Torrance, for instance, takes a very different approach both in affirming the full equality of the Son with the Father and in refusing to concede that the subordination in the biblical portrayals of the incarnate Son are to be read back into the intra-Trinitarian divine life. He rather gently critiques and then rejects the "element of 'subordinationism' in [Barth's] doctrine of the Holy Trinity."[19] Torrance follows his reading of Gregory of Nazianzus in rejecting relations of "superiority and inferiority or 'degrees of Deity' in the Trinity" as "quite unacceptable, for to 'subordinate any of the three Divine Persons is to overthrow the Trinity.'"[20] Thus "the statement of Jesus 'My Father is greater than I' is to be interpreted not ontologically but soteriologically, or economically . . . In other words, the subjection of Christ to the Father in his incarnate economy as the suffering and obedient Servant cannot be read back into the eternal hypostatic relations and distinctions subsisting in the Holy Trinity."[21] Paul D. Molnar concludes that "this is not just a patristic insight but a biblically based patristic insight," thus "there is for Torrance no way that scripture can be read to imply subordinationism within the immanent Trinity."[22]

Returning to Barth, he clearly interprets the subordination of the Son in an eternal sense. He insists that the subordination of the Son somehow belongs to the person of the Son *qua* Son in the life of the immanent Trinity. He insists on this point while also resolutely insisting that both modalism (of the classical Sabellian variety) and subordinationism (especially of the

---

14. Barth, *Church Dogmatics* IV/1:164.
15. Ibid.
16. Ibid.
17. Ibid., 201.
18. Ibid., 202.
19. Torrance, *Karl Barth*, 131–32.
20. Torrance, *Christian Doctrine of God*, 179.
21. Ibid., 180.
22. Molnar, *Divine Freedom*, 324.

Arian and other anti-Nicene varieties) are theologically mistaken and indeed disastrous.

Thomas Aquinas on the Son's Missional Obedience

Thomas Aquinas consistently interprets the Christ of Hebrews through the lens of Niceno-Constantinopolitan and Chalcedonian orthodoxy. He understands the Christology of Hebrews as distinctly "two-natures" Christology, and this clearly informs his interpretation throughout. Contemporary exegetes may criticize Aquinas for reading orthodoxy *back into* the text, but, as Daniel Keating argues, "in most cases" his strategy "casts light on the text and helps to resolve genuine tensions within the letter itself."[23] For not only does the text depict Jesus "as a vulnerable human being who was tempted" and "who was driven to cry out to the Father with tears" while learning obedience through suffering, it also "contains some of the strongest assertions of the eternity and divinity of Christ in the New Testament."[24] In other words, the incarnate Son is fully human without ceasing to be fully divine, and we are to read the witness of Hebrews accordingly.

Turning to his understanding of the Son's "learned obedience," Aquinas is representative of a great deal of the Christian tradition in his consideration of the subordination and obedience of the Son. On his view, the missions are to be clearly distinguished from the processions, and obedience and subordination pertain only to the mission of the Son as the incarnate Redeemer. In other words, he will have nothing whatsoever to do with any notion of subordination and obedience that is either eternal or necessary. Explicitly echoing Augustine, he says that

> It is not without reason that Scripture mentions both, that the Son is equal to the Father and the Father is greater than the Son, for the first is said on account of the form of God, and the second is said on account of the form of a servant, without any confusion. Now the less is subject to the greater. Therefore in the form of a servant Christ is subject to the Father.[25]

Importantly, it is the *incarnate* Son who is subordinate to the Father. This is the case because it is the *incarnate* Son who has *the form of a servant*. Appealing to his account of the communication of attributes, Aquinas then says that as "we are not to understand that Christ is a creature simply

---

23. Keating, "Thomas Aquinas," 99.
24. Ibid.
25. Aquinas, *Summa Theologica* III, q. 20, a.1.

[*simpliciter*] but only in his human nature . . . so also are we to understand that Christ is subject to the Father not simply [*simpliciter*] but in his human nature."[26] As the editors of the Blackfriars edition express the point:

> It is, then, the divine Word that is subject to the Father—but, it must be added at once, the divine Word precisely and exclusively as subsisting in a human nature. The relation of the divine Word to the Father in the Trinity is free from any trace of subordination; but, having once assumed a human nature, the Son can perform those actions which express subordination.[27]

So Aquinas is strikingly clear that all acceptable senses of subordination must be attributed to the person of the Son *qua-human nature*. Indeed, Aquinas is so certain of this point that he will even insist that the incarnate Son (in his human nature) is subject *to himself*![28] As Thomas Joseph White puts it, "the voluntary human obedience of the Son in temporal history implies a dynamic subordination of his human will to the agency of his transcendent will which he shares with the Father."[29]

Indeed, the unity of the incarnate Son with the Father is of such strength and intensity that Aquinas also insists that Christ enjoys the beatific vision during his earthly career. White explains the point as follows: "Christ as man possessed the immediate, intuitive knowledge of his own deity, the divine life with the Father and the Spirit."[30] This does not mean for Aquinas that Christ had nothing to learn. To the contrary, Aquinas holds that Christ in his human nature surely does have "empiric" or acquired knowledge of human matters.[31] But it does mean that the incarnate Son is never without direct, filial awareness of his divinity and relationship to his Father.

BARTH'S GAMBIT: A THEOLOGICAL ANALYSIS

As we can see, both Aquinas and Barth affirm that Jesus Christ is subordinate to the Father in some sense. But where Aquinas follows the broadly traditional line of attributing this subordination to the Son *kata sarka* and

---

26. Ibid.
27. Aquinas, *One Mediator*, 112–13.
28. Aquinas, *Summa Theologica* III, q.20, a.2.
29. White, *Incarnate Lord*, 303.
30. Ibid., 237.
31. When I say "Aquinas," I mean the Aquinas of the *ST*. As Thomas himself notes, by the writing of the *ST* he has changed his mind (from earlier comments on Lombard's *Sentences*). See *Summa Theologica* III. q12. a2.

forma servi, to the *incarnate* Word, to the Word *qua* humanity, Barth insists that the subordination is proper to the being or divinity of the Triune God.[32] Beyond the observation that these positions are different in some important respects, just what are we to make of their views?

Barth, Consistency, and Monotheism

Barth clearly holds that the subordination of the Son to the Father is somehow internal to the life of the Triune God. "We can say quite calmly," he says, that God "exists as a first and a second, above and below, *a priori* and *a posteriori*."[33] He is well aware that his view will prompt criticism; thus he insists that to "grasp" his point we "have to free ourselves from two unfortunate and very arbitrary ways of thinking."[34] Nonetheless, several puzzles and problems attend Barth's view.

First, it is not hard to see the appearance of inconsistency between what Barth says here and what Barth says elsewhere about the distinction of the divine persons. Barth is well known for his vehement opposition to any doctrine of the Trinity according to which there are multiple divine "centers of consciousness." As he puts it,

> By Father, Son, and Spirit we do not mean what is commonly designated to us by the word "persons." This designation was accepted—though not without opposition—on linguistic presuppositions which no longer obtain today. It was never intended to imply—at any rate in the theological tradition—that there are in God three different personalities, three self-existent individuals with their own self-consciousness, cognition, volition, activity, effects, revelation, and name. The one name of the one God is the threefold name of Father, Son, and Holy Spirit. The one "personality" of God, the one active and speaking divine Ego, is Father, Son, and Holy Spirit. Otherwise we should obviously have to speak of three gods.[35]

The notion that there are multiple divine subjects or agents is rejected by Barth as "mythology, for which there can be no place in a right relationship of the doctrine of the Trinity as the doctrine of the three modes of being

---

32. As Sumner nicely characterizes Barth's position ("Obedience and Subordination," 131).
33. Barth, *Church Dogmatics* IV/1:201–2.
34. Ibid., 202.
35. Ibid., 204–5.

of the one God...."[36] Instead, "Christian faith and the Christian confession has one Subject, not three. But he is the one God in self-repetition, in the repetition of his own and equal divine being, and therefore in three different modes of being—which the term 'person' was always explained to mean."[37]

We should note that Barth mixes several distinct claims together. He lumps "three divine personalities" with "three self-existent individuals," and he further conflates both notions with any account of the divine persons according to which they are (or possess) any distinct agency. But it is less than obvious that these come as a kind of package deal that must taken together and then either accepted or rejected accordingly. If there is a relationship of mutual entailment between three "self-existent individuals" and what we might refer to as distinct divine speech-agents, then it is not an *obvious* one. Surely any proponent of orthodox Trinitarian theology would deny that there are three self-existent divine individuals! But to deny this is not to deny that there are three divine speakers or agents, three who know one another.

Questions abound. Is Barth really rejecting the modern psychological definition of person—or is he really assuming it and then insisting that there can only be one such "Ego" within God? Is it really true that an I-Thou relationship within the Trinity would imply multiple deities? Indeed, is not this exactly what the New Testament demands?[38] What does it mean to deny that the divine persons have distinct "activity?" Consider the *opera ad extra*. While Barth is right that the tradition has insisted that these are "always undivided," it is also true that this divine action may be such that it sometimes reaches it terminus on one or another of the divine persons. Thus it is beyond dispute that only the Son became incarnate, for "one of the Trinity suffered in the flesh."[39] Or consider the *opera ad intra*; the generation of the Son is the work of the Father only and not the agency of the Son or Spirit.

If Barth means only that the divine persons are not *self-existent individuals*, then surely he is right. But if he means that they are not distinct in knowledge or agency at all, then it is hard to see how he might be correct about this. At any rate, it is hard to see how his account of intra-Trinitarian subordination is internally consistent with what he says elsewhere about the personhood of God. But pressing beyond the issues of the appearance of inconsistency, some critics raise further concerns at this point. For instance, Thomas Joseph White worries that Barth's doctrine "renders obscure

---

36. Ibid., 65. See also *Church Dogmatics* I/1:348–68.
37. Barth, *Church Dogmatics* IV/1:205.
38. See my summary in *Two Views*, 117–27.
39. See Barth himself on this point, *Church Dogmatics* I/1:397.

the confession of the unity of the divine will and power in God."[40] For according to classical Trinitarian theology, the Father and Son share exactly one will; on Barth's proposal, on the other hand, the Father always wills that the Son obey and the Son always obeys (albeit in willing agreement). Darren O. Sumner responds on Barth's behalf at this juncture by making three points. First, he says, Barth's account of the subordination of the Son "continues to operate under" his strident critique of any version of "social Trinitarianism."[41] Second, he thinks that Barth "would not be quick to grant the presumption that the act of obedience necessarily entails two willing agents."[42] I cannot see how Sumner's first point does anything but heighten the sense that there is an internal contradiction in Barth's theology, and his second point also fails to provide help. Perhaps it is true that Barth would not have been quick to grant that the problematic conclusion is entailed by his view. But that seems irrelevant to the main point; someone's reluctance to admit that P entails Q is irrelevant to the issue of whether or not P actually entails Q. Sumner's third rejoinder (to White's critique) is perhaps more promising but surely more perplexing, for he appeals to Barth's "actualistic ontology." According to the "revisionist" interpretation of Barth's "actualism" (especially as defended by Bruce L. McCormack),[43] God elects to be Triune and incarnate and thus is never (at least proleptically) without his humanity. According to this view, the divinity and humanity are in a "mutually conditioning relation" that is eternal.[44] Whether this revisionist interpretation of Barth aids his view or brings it to ruin is a question of intense debate.[45] We need not, however, finally resolve that hotly contested matter to see further worries about Barth's view.

Suppose that the "revisionists" are wrong: In that case, I take it that the correct reading of Barth's view would be

> (~R) the will of the eternal Son *qua* Son is eternally and necessarily subordinate to the Father.

Or suppose that the revisionists are right. Then Barth's view would be

---

40. White, *The Incarnate Lord*, 280.

41. Sumner, "Obedience and Subordination," 140.

42. Ibid., 141.

43. See especially McCormack, "Grace and Being," 92–110. Also important is McCormack, "With Loud Cries and Tears," 37–58.

44. Sumner, "Obedience and Subordination," 141–42.

45. Hunsinger, *Reading Barth*; Molnar, *Faith*; and Dempsey, *Trinity and Election*.

(R) the will of the eternal Son *qua humanity* (or, perhaps, *qua the Son's humanity-conditioned deity*) is eternally and necessarily subordinate to the Father.[46]

If (~R) is the right way to take Barth, then we are left to wonder why his view would not qualify as (what he labels) "the worst and most extreme expression of tritheism" and "mythology." Indeed, we are left to wonder why his theology would not be hoist on its own petard. If (R), on the other hand, is the correct reading of Barth, then it seems that its merits are pretty well camouflaged. For if (R) is right, and if the subordination of the Son belongs to the life of the immanent Trinity, then it seems that we are left with two options. Either the creation of humanity is necessary for God (so that the Son could have a human will with which to condition his divinity) or the Trinity is contingent. Surely the second option would be unpalatable to Barth, so we are left with the first. But does not this option lead straight to panentheism?[47]

Barth and the Threat of Ontological Subordination: The Authority of the Father

A second problem is potentially more serious. Do not Barth's claims about an "above and below" within the Trinity not entail some kind of *ontological* (rather than merely functional or economic) subordinationism? Surely this would be problematic for any Christology that wishes to maintain contact with classical orthodoxy. Barth recognizes the appearance of a problem, and he understands that it would indeed be a serious one. But he denies that this is really a problem for his view. He rejects the assumption that "there is necessarily something unworthy of God and incompatible with His being as God in supposing that there is in God a first and a second, an above and a below, since this includes a gradation, a degradation, an inferiority in God, which if conceded excludes the *homoousia* of the different modes of the divine being."[48] So while Barth recognizes the appearance of a serious threat to orthodoxy, he refuses to concede that there really is

---

46. See Sumner, "Obedience and Subordination," 141–42.

47. For a helpful analysis of some of these issues, see Diller, "Is God *Necessarily* Who God Is?," 209–20.

48. Barth, *Church Dogmatics* IV/1:202. Vanhoozer appears to hold a similar position: after claiming to see "some textual evidence" for eternal submission (in John 5:30; 8:28), he concludes: "[S]uffice it to say that there is nothing necessarily demeaning in suggesting that God the Son is eternally, yet *freely*, obedient to God the Father" (*Remythologizing Theology*, 255, 256n59).

such a problem. At one level he admits that the concern is plausible: "that all sounds very illuminating."[49] But his retort is swift. "Is it not an all too human—and therefore not a genuinely human—way of thinking?"[50] "What is the measure," he wants to know, "by which it measures and judges? Has there really to be something mean in God for Him to be the second, below? Does subordination in God necessarily involve an inferiority, and therefore a deprivation, a lack?"[51] Instead, he asks, "why not rather a particular being in the glory of the one equal Godhead, in whose inner order there is also, in fact, the direction downwards, that has its own dignity? Why should not our way of finding a lesser dignity and significance in what takes the second and subordinate place (the wife to her husband) need to be corrected in light of the *homoousia* of the modes of the divine being?"[52]

Barth's protests notwithstanding, the concerns are serious, and the threat seems real. White worries that Barth's Christology would "make problematic the affirmation of a divine immutable omnipotence present in the incarnate Son."[53] If the Father has authority necessarily and eternally while the Son does not, then it surely seems that they are of different essences. Even Hunsinger says that on Barth's own premises, "obedience is constitutive of the Son's essential deity," and that "obedience belongs to the Son's eternal essence."[54] But if obedience is part of *the Son's* "essential deity" and "belongs to *the Son's* eternal essence" in contradistinction to the Father, then it will be hard to avoid the conclusion that the Son has a different essence. If Barth is right that the Son is obedient "necessarily" and "essentially," then obedience is part of the Son's essence.[55] But if the Father is

---

49. Barth, *Church Dogmatics* IV/1:202.
50. Ibid., 202.
51. Ibid.
52. Ibid. Barth's appeal to gender and nuptial relations at this point is somewhat puzzling. Exactly what role the appeal to marital relations is to play here is less than obvious, for Barth wants to offer a genuinely theological correction of common notions of husband-wife relations while also drawing upon common relationships between husbands (who, apparently, are authoritative and thus analogous to the Father) and wives (who, apparently, are subordinate and thus analogous to the Son) to support his claim that the Son can be necessarily subordinate to the Father though still equal to him. Moreover, it is not at all clear just how this appeal to gender relations might cohere with his resolute denial of any *vestigium trinitatis*. Molnar (*Faith*, 337) asks if Barth himself has not "conceived of the Trinity in an all-too-human way," and he concludes that Barth "has illegitimately read back into the Godhead the order he thinks he found in male-female relations."
53. White, *Incarnate Lord*, 280.
54. Hunsinger, *Reading Barth*, 113.
55. Barth, *Church Dogmatics* IV/1:164.

not obedient "necessarily" and "essentially"—and for Barth the Father most decidedly is *not* obedient at all (much less necessarily and essentially)—then obedience is not part of the Father's essence. Thus the Father and Son are not, *and cannot be, homoousios*. No wonder, then, that even someone as sympathetic to Barth as Molnar admits that Barth "creates a major problem here by introducing hierarchy into the divine being."[56] White concludes that there is "an inevitable discord between [Barth's] affirmation that the eternal, wise, and omnipotent God became human, and [his] affirmation that there is obedience within the very life of God that characterizes the person of the Son as distinct from the Father."[57] More could be said, but it should be obvious that there are deep problems for Barth's view of the obedience and subordination of the Son.[58]

Barth and Hebrews 5

Beyond these general theological concerns—troubling though they are in their own right—we come to the question of how Barth's view relates to the teaching of Heb 5. Barth does not engage in extended exegesis of this passage, but he does offer some indication of his views.[59] He thinks that the "days of his flesh" refer to Jesus' passion and especially to his death.[60] He is certain that the "loud cries and tears" are an "insufficiently noticed" commentary on Gethsemane.[61] He also says that this is a reference to Jesus' cry of dereliction from the cross.[62] And, of course, he is sure that the obedience of the Son is necessary and essential to the Son. This much is obvious. But when we move beyond what Barth says explicitly about this passage and read Heb 5 while asking what it means for his general view of Christ's

---

56. Molnar, *Faith*, 331.

57. White, *Incarnate Lord*, 280. White suggests that a more "benign" interpretation of Barth is to take this in reference only to the mission of the Son (rather than the procession); he also recognizes that this seems to be at some distance from the most plausible reading of Barth and an even greater distance from the McCormackian "revisionist" account of Barth.

58. For somewhat more technical treatments of these problems, see, e.g., McCall, *Which Trinity?*, 175–88; McCall and Yandell, "On Trinitarian Subordinationism"; McCall, "Gender and the Trinity."

59. He mentions this passage several times in the *Church Dogmatics* I/1:386–87; I/2:158; II/2:666; III/2:327–29, 337, 462; IV/1:164–65, 193–96; IV/2:95, 250, 606–7; IV/3:395.

60. E.g., Barth, *Church Dogmatics* III/2:562.

61. Barth, *Church Dogmatics* III/2:337; cf. *Church Dogmatics* IV/2:95, 250.

62. E.g., Barth, *Church Dogmatics* I/1:386; *Church Dogmatics* I/2:158.

subordination, two main considerations emerge. First, in Hebrews we see that Jesus "*learned*" obedience. On Barth's view, however, obedience and submission are intrinsic to the Son's identity. To be Son is to be "below," the *posterius*, the "Second," the one who "obeys in humility." But if to be the Son is to be obedient, if there is no possibility that the Son is not obedient, then what does it even mean to assert that he *learned* obedience? We do not know, and Barth's Christology gives us little guidance here.[63]

Second, we should remember that he learned obedience *although* he was Son. The noun is anarthrous here (as it is in 1:2), and surely this testifies to the quality of his filial relation.[64] When we see this combined with the concessive force of καίπερ, we can see that the force of this statement "is that Jesus is not an ordinary Son, who might be expected to learn through suffering (12:4–11), but the eternal Son."[65] As Luke Timothy Johnson notes, the statement here comes as something of a surprising reversal. We would expect someone to be obedient *because* he is a son, and we indeed are easily tempted to say "because" for καίπερ. But this would be a mistake, he says, because the concessive that is used here actually sets up a *contrast*.[66] Thus William L. Lane concludes that "discussion of the obedience of the Christ is qualified by the affirmation that Jesus is inherently and intrinsically the Son of God, whose essential sonship is a fact wholly apart" from the fact that he learned obedience through suffering.[67] There is no hint here that obedience is constitutive of his Sonship. Hebrews does not lead us to conclude that the filial relationship is based upon that obedience, or even that it entails that obedience. He is obedient *although* he is Son. Accordingly, it is hard to see how Barth's account of the subordination of the Son as necessary and eternal can be consistent with what is stated in Heb 5.

---

63. In *Church Dogmatics* I/1, Barth echoes both Heb 5 and Phil 2 in reminding us that the obedience was the obedience of suffering and death on a cross (387). By *Church Dogmatics* I/2, Barth says that "Jesus Christ's obedience consists in the fact that He willed to be and was only this one thing with all its consequences, God in the flesh, the divine bearer of the burden that man as sinner must bear" (156). He also notes that "the New Testament has nowhere attempted to describe this 'learning'" (158).

64. Bruce, *Hebrews*, 104.

65. Attridge, *Hebrews*, 152. Cf. Koester, *Hebrews*.

66. Johnson, *Hebrews*, 147.

67. Lane, *Hebrews 1–8*, 120.

OBEDIENCE AND THE BEATIFIC VISION: RECONSIDERING AQUINAS'S VIEW

We have seen that Thomas Aquinas takes a very different view of the subordination and obedience of the Son. The obedience and subordination of the Son is to be understood only with reference to the economy of salvation. As such, it pertains only to the mission of the Logos and not to the procession *per se*. For while the divine missions are, of course, consistent with the divine processions, they are not to be confused or conflated. Nor can we reduce the processions to the missions. The subordination of the Son is for us and our salvation; it is "a dynamic subordination of his human will" to the one divine will that is shared with the Father.[68] Accordingly, Aquinas avoids the problems that are raised by Barth's view. The point here is not that Aquinas merely has different resources than Barth to deal with the problems, rather, the point is that he does not run into these problems at all.

But if Aquinas avoids the problems that come with Barth's view, does his own view not encounter other problems? Here Heb 5 is very important, and reflection on it might raise some potential criticisms of Aquinas's view. First, there is a general concern that such Christology would try to import something into this text that is not really present. Aquinas himself appeals to Heb 5:8 as an example of Christ's "empiric" or acquired knowledge that he has in virtue of the incarnation.[69] However, Cockerill warns us not to assume too much when reading this text, and especially not to "import the preexistence-humiliation-exaltation schema from Phil 2:6–11 into this passage."[70] He says that the author of Hebrews "certainly assumes the incarnation here, but he says nothing about the preexistent act of obedience by which he became incarnate. God's declaration of sonship and priesthood in vv. 5–6 did not occur in the Son's preexistence but at his exaltation. Verses 7–8 describe the obedient course of his human life. This earthly obedience is integral to both the theological development and pastoral purpose of Hebrews. It is by this obedience that Christ becomes the 'source' of salvation and thus the one who enables the obedience of his people. His obedience is also their example and encouragement."[71] A canonically-informed reading of the text, however, would find what *is* stated here in Heb 5 to be entirely consistent with what Paul teaches in Phil 2 (and elsewhere). And, as Cockerill points out, this text actually "assumes the incarnation" while directly

---

68. White, *Incarnate Lord*, 303.
69. Aquinas, *Summa Theologica* III q.9, a.4.
70. Cockerill, *Hebrews*, 242n62.
71. Ibid.

addressing "the obedient course of his human life" as "earthly obedience." In sum, one need not read all of Aquinas's Christology *into* the teaching of Heb 5 to see that it is consistent with that teaching at this point.

Another potential problem for Aquinas's Christology might come from reflection on the statements that Jesus "offered up prayers and petitions with fervent cries and tears" (5:7) and "learned obedience" (5:8). Is the teaching of Heb 5 consistent with Aquinas's steadfast belief in the beatific vision? What could it mean to say that he "learned" obedience (or anything else) if he is omniscient? And what should we make of his "fervent cries and tears" if he really enjoys the beatific vision?

When considering the issue of Christ "learning" obedience, it is hard to see that there is any more of a problem here than there is anywhere else in Aquinas's doctrine of the hypostatic union (and, in particular, his view of the distinction of the natures).[72] He offers an account of the acquisition of knowledge in Christ. Aquinas's doctrine is not, of course, beyond dispute, and his critics (both medieval and modern) are not convinced that his view is finally defensible (his defenders, of course, are convinced that it is). Full consideration of such matters is beyond the scope of the current discussion, but it is hard to see how there might be more of a problem with respect to his learning obedience than there is with him learning anything else. And when we remember that the issue is of learning *obedience*, the message of Hebrews comports nicely with Aquinas's view. As Cockerill notes, the author of Hebrews "is not speaking of a heavenly obedience but of an abandonment to God that occurred when the Son was experiencing all the impairments of a humanity like our earthly humanity."[73]

But what about the "fervent cries and tears" of our Lord? How does this teaching cohere with the conviction that the one who cries out in this way enjoys uninterrupted and untarnished communion with God? In light of this clear teaching in Hebrews, just what are we to make of Aquinas's belief that Christ enjoyed the beatific vision? Two observations are important here. First, we need to see that it seems entirely possible to accept Aquinas's general doctrine of the incarnation (including the metaphysics of the doctrine) without committing ourselves to all the details—and particularly so with respect to his belief in the beatific vision. Many other theologians, especially those in the Reformed tradition, take this option by agreeing with a broadly Thomist (or, more minimally, a concretist) account of the metaphysics of the incarnation while also steering clear of the claims about

---

72. For more on Aquinas's metaphysics of the incarnation, see especially Stump, *Aquinas*, 407–26; Stump, "Aquinas's Metaphysics," 197–218.

73. Cockerill, *Hebrews*, 243.

the beatific vision.⁷⁴ It seems entirely possible to agree with what he says about the subordination of the Son without also adopting his account of the beatific vision.

Second, it is important not to assume too quickly that Aquinas's doctrine must be inconsistent with this text. Aquinas is, of course, well acquainted with the passage, and he even appeals to it to demonstrate that Christ has acquired knowledge (as well as knowledge that is infused into his human soul). On his "two natures" interpretation of the "learning," Aquinas says that "although Christ knew by simple recognition [*simplici notitia*] what obedience is, he nonetheless learned from the things he suffered."⁷⁵ John Calvin is convinced that there is "no doubt" that the loud cries are the prayers from Gethsemane and the cry of dereliction from the cross. He interprets the εὐλαβείας (of v. 7) as terror before the righteous judgment of God (rather than as the reverence that is appropriate to human encounter with God). Jesus is under the curse of God, and he knows it.⁷⁶ P. E. Hughes agrees but goes even further, on his interpretation, Jesus fears not only death by execution but also "something other and deeper," and this "other and deeper" fear is truly terrifying. It is nothing short of the "disintegrating experience of separation from God" as Christ is "torn away from his Father."⁷⁷ On Aquinas's view, by contrast, Christ's beatific vision gives him the clearest and brightest access to the beauty and goodness of God—the beauty and goodness that the man Jesus Christ shares in the hypostatic union.

If the interpretation of Calvin and Hughes is right, then there indeed seems to be a problem for Aquinas's Christology at this point; it really does look like it would run afoul of the teaching of Hebrews. But is the Calvin-Hughes interpretation correct? There are reasons to doubt that it is. Here are three. First, it is far from obvious that we should interpret the "reverence" or "fear" this way. There are easier and more direct ways to communicate anxiety, dread, or terror; φόβος is at hand and ready for use, but the author of Hebrews does not employ it here. And, as Patrick Gray argues, all uses of εὐλάβεια in the New Testament are "unequivocally positive" and appear in reference to devout and pious worshipers.⁷⁸ Certainly it is used positively in Hebrews with reference to Noah (11:7), and overall "there is more than ample precedent for viewing the description of Jesus in Heb 5:7 as some-

74. E.g., Turretin, *Institutes*, 354.

75. Aquinas, *Hebraeos*, 117.

76. Calvin, *Hebrews*, 64–65.

77. Hughes, *Hebrews*, 183. I say "goes even further" because Calvin will nonetheless say that "at no time" is the Son "deprived of God's mercy and help" (*Hebrews*, 64).

78. Gray, *Godly Fear*, 203.

thing other than a picture of cowering fear in the face of death."[79] As Thomas R. Schreiner concludes, "reverence" is a better term than either anxiety or fear.[80] And, importantly, reverence is entirely consistent with the beatific vision. Indeed, how could one have the beatific vision and *not* be reverent? One could be reverent without the beatific vision, but it is hard to see how one could have that vision and not be reverent. Second, it is far from clear that the cry of dereliction is even in view here. As Ben Witherington III points out, the *multiple* prayers mentioned here in Hebrews do not line up neatly with *the* cry of dereliction.[81] Finally, and much more importantly, to conclude that Christ cries out in terror because he anticipates being "torn apart" from his Father both over-reads the cry of dereliction and is itself inconsistent with the Christian doctrine of God (as I have argued elsewhere).[82] In sum, it is hard to think that there is a significant obstacle to Aquinas's view here in this passage.

But does enjoyment of the beatific vision still somehow damage Christ's soteriological suitability? Is there reason to think that somehow the beatific vision would disqualify the incarnate Son? On Aquinas's view of the incarnation, the human nature of Christ is united with the divine nature, but it is not replaced or overwhelmed by it. The human nature, though unstained by sin, nonetheless relates to the divine as human. Christ is thus able to cry out in solidarity and sympathy with his fellow humans. Moreover, it is precisely *because* his human nature is unsullied by depravity and self-centered sin that he is able to *completely and fully* identify with those to whom he is joined. It is because he is so radically *unselfish* that he is able to "sympathize" so fully as high priest and offer himself so completely for the sins of the world. It is because he is divine as well as human that he is able to be the "source" of salvation, for no one who is merely human can qualify as Savior who reunites us to God. And it is because he is the one who is human and divine—and thus the one who enjoys and is sustained by the unbroken loving communion shared with the Father (the beatific vision)—that he is able to fully sympathize with us in our weaknesses while also uniting us to God. He is able to be the High Priest, the one who is able to save us from death, because he is both human and divine—and he has the beatific vision precisely because he is the man who is fully divine.

---

79. Ibid.
80. Schreiner, *Hebrews*, 163.
81. Witherington, *Letters*, 201.
82. See McCall, *Forsaken*.

CONCLUSION

We have arrived at the point where we can see that while Barth's account of the subordination of the Son both encounters several weighty theological objections and sits awkwardly with the teaching of Heb 5:7–10, Aquinas's Christology avoids these problems and coheres well with this passage. While there may be some remaining questions about the overall suitability of some of the more controversial aspects of Thomistic Christology, such questions sit lightly to the central issues at hand. In other words, it is entirely possible to take what Aquinas says about the incarnation more generally and about subordination in particular without committing oneself to what may be more questionable aspects of Aquinas's doctrine.

Even the most casual reader will recognize that my sentiments are somewhat more with Aquinas rather than Barth on this matter. But we should also see and appreciate the magnificent insights offered by Barth. We should remember that his discussion of the subordination of the Son comes in the context of an extended and insightful discussion of hamartiology. Barth refuses to consider sin apart from a properly Christological center; for Barth it is not "clear how it can be otherwise than that a doctrine of sin which precedes Christology and is independent of it should consciously or unconsciously, directly or indirectly, move in the direction of [idolatry]."[83] Thus he insists upon starting with Christ; in direct opposition to traditional ways of thinking about sin he insists that "in opposition to [such ways] we maintain the simple thesis that only when we know Jesus Christ do we really know that man is the man of sin, what sin is, and what it means for us."[84] What we do learn about sin in light of Christ is not at all flattering:

> Man wants only to judge. He thinks he sits on a high throne, but in reality he sits only on a child's stool, blowing his little trumpet, cracking his little whip, pointing with frightful seriousness his little finger, while all the time nothing happens that really matters. He can only play the judge. He is only a dilettante, a blunderer, in his attempt to distinguish between good and evil, right and wrong, acting as though he really had the capacity to do it. He can only pretend to himself and others . . .[85]

This is because sin, "in its totality is pride."[86] It is pride and "sloth" (disobedience as a manifestation of unbelief), and it takes many forms: stupidity,

---

83. Barth, *Church Dogmatics* IV/1:365.
84. Ibid., 389.
85. Ibid., 446.
86. Ibid., 414. He also admits that "pride" is a "very feeble word to describe" the

inhumanity, dissipation, inordinate care about trivialities.[87] And while pride manifests itself as trying to be like God, it only does so by trying to take the place of a "god" that does not exist. The sad error is that this idolatry only yields a "god" who is "self-centered."[88] But in direct and starkest contrast to such sin, in God incarnate we see not a pitiful and terrifying caricature of God but the God truly revealed in Jesus Christ. And in Christ we see that

> God is for himself, but he is not only for himself. He is in a supreme self-hood, but not a self-contained self-hood, not in a mere divinity . . . God is *a se* and *per se*, but as the love which is grounded in itself from all eternity. Because he is the triune God, who from the first loved us as the Father in the Son and turned to us by the Spirit, he is God *pro nobis* . . . God is not egoistic in this revelation and defense of his honor and glory, nor is he concerned about the satisfaction of his needs. As God he does not need . . .[89]

I take these to be marvelous insights from Barth. Barth is wrong to designate this humility and condescension as somehow unique to *the Son's deity*; the better way is to see this as Christ's revelation of the self-giving love of *the Triune God*. Frankly, his view needs correction: it is not merely *the Son* who is capable of condescension, humility, and self-sacrifice. It is *the Triune God* who is revealed by Jesus Christ as the God who condescends in self-giving love in the incarnation of the Son. Such correction is possible, and in fact it seems to cohere closely to Barth's own methodological commitments. Jesus Christ is revelatory *of God*, after all. Properly corrected, this powerful truth is one that is consistent with Aquinas's overall Christology. But it is one that finds particularly forceful articulation from Barth. Hopefully we can learn from both theologians. Hopefully they will help us to read Hebrews better. And hopefully—by God's grace—we can better know God as Father and walk in holy obedience to him.[90]

---

human condition; "the correct word is perhaps megalomania" (437).

87. Barth, *Church Dogmatics* IV/2:404–5.

88. Barth, *Church Dogmatics* IV/1:422.

89. Ibid., 422, 452.

90. I wish to take this opportunity to express my profound gratitude to Gary Cockerill for his mentorship, investment, and friendship. This has been an exercise in "theological interpretation of Scripture." Theological exegesis is what Gary has been doing for decades, and I am deeply grateful to him for doing it with such sustained rigor, deep virtue, and passionate devotion. I am even more grateful for his exemplary ministry and scholarship, and more thankful yet for his friendship.

BIBLIOGRAPHY

Aquinas, Thomas. *The One Mediator.* Vol. 50 of *Summa Theologiae.* Edited by Colman E. O'Neill. New York: Blackfriars, 1965.
———. *Summa Theologica.* Translated by the Fathers of the English Dominican Province. New York: Benzinger Bros., 1948.
———. *Super Epistolam B. Pauli ad Hebraeos Lectura.* Edited by J. Mortensen and E. Alarcon. Translated by F. R. Larcher. Lander, WY: Aquinas Institute for Sacred Doctrine, 2012.
Attridge, Harold. *The Epistle to the Hebrews.* Minneapolis: Fortress, 1989.
Barth, Karl. *Church Dogmatics.* 14 vols. Edited by Geoffrey W. Bromiley and T. F. Torrance. Translated by G. T. Thomson et al. Edinburgh: T. & T. Clark, 1936–1969.
Bruce. F. F. *The Epistle to the Hebrews.* Grand Rapids: Eerdmans, 1964.
Calvin, John. *The Epistle of Paul the Apostle to the Hebrews and the First and Second Epistles of St. Peter.* Edited by David W. Torrance and Thomas F. Torrance. Translated by William B. Johnson. Calvin's Commentaries 12. Grand Rapids: Eerdmans, 1963.
Cockerill, Gareth L. *The Epistle to the Hebrews.* NICNT. Grand Rapids: Eerdmans, 2012.
Dempsey, Michael, ed. *Trinity and Election in Contemporary Theology.* Grand Rapids: Eerdmans, 2011.
deSilva, David A. *Perseverance in Gratitude: A Socio-Rhetorical Commentary on the Epistle "to the Hebrews."* Grand Rapids: Eerdmans, 2000.
Diller, Kevin. "Is God Necessarily Who God Is?" *SJT* (2013) 209–20.
Gray, Patrick. *Godly Fear: The Epistle to Hebrews and the Greco-Roman Critiques of Superstition.* Atlanta: SBL, 2003.
Holmes, Stephen R., et al. *Two Views on the Doctrine of the Trinity.* Edited by Jason S. Sexton. Grand Rapids: Zondervan Academic, 2014.
Hughes, P. E. *Commentary on the Epistle to the Hebrews.* Grand Rapids: Eerdmans, 1977.
Hunsinger, George. *Reading Barth with Charity: A Hermeneutical Proposal.* Grand Rapids: Baker Academic, 2015.
Johnson, Luke Timothy. *Hebrews: A Commentary.* Louisville: Westminster John Knox, 2006.
Keating, Daniel. "Thomas Aquinas and the Epistle to the Hebrews: 'The Excellence of Christ.'" In *Christology, Hermeneutics, and Hebrews: Profiles from the History of Interpretation,* edited by Jon C. Laansma and Daniel J. Treier, 84–99. New York: T. & T. Clark, 2012.
Koester, Craig R. *Hebrews: A New Translation and Commentary.* New York: Doubleday, 2001.
Lane, William L. *Hebrews 1–8.* WBC. Nashville: Nelson, 1991.
McCall, Thomas H. *Forsaken: The Trinity and the Cross, and Why It Matters.* Downers Grove, IL: IVP Academic, 2012.
———. "Gender and the Trinity Once More: A Review Article." *TJ* (2015) 263–80.
———. *Which Trinity? Whose Monotheism? Philosophical and Systematic Theologians on the Metaphysics of Trinitarian Theology.* Grand Rapids: Eerdmans, 2010.
McCall, Thomas H., and Keith E. Yandell. "On Trinitarian Subordinationism." *Philosophia Christi* (2009) 339–58.

McCormack, Bruce L. "Grace and Being: The Role of God's Gracious Election in Karl Barth's Theological Ontology." In *The Cambridge Companion to Karl Barth*, edited by John B. Webster, 92–110. Cambridge: Cambridge University Press, 2000.

———. "'With Loud Cries and Tears': The Humanity of the Son in the Epistle to the Hebrews." In *The Epistle to the Hebrews and Christian Theology*, edited by Richard Bauckham et al., 37–68. Grand Rapids: Eerdmans, 2009.

Molnar, Paul D. *Divine Freedom and the Immanent Trinity: In Dialogue with Karl Barth and Contemporary Theology*. London: T. & T. Clark, 2002.

Molnar, Paul D. *Faith, Freedom, and the Spirit: The Economic Trinity in Barth, Torrance, and Contemporary Theology*. Downers Grove, IL: IVP Academic, 2015.

Schreiner, Thomas R. *Hebrews*. BTCP. Nashville: B&H, 2015.

Stump, Eleonore. *Aquinas*. New York: Routledge, 2003.

———. "Aquinas's Metaphysics of the Incarnation." In *The Incarnation: An Interdisciplinary Symposium on the Incarnation of the Son of God*, edited by Stephen T. Davis, Daniel Kendall, and Gerald O'Collins, 197–218. Oxford: Oxford University Press, 2002.

Sumner, Darren. "Obedience and Subordination in Karl Barth's Trinitarian Theology." In *Advancing Trinitarian Theology: Explorations in Constructive Dogmatics*, edited by Oliver D. Crisp and Fred Sanders, 130–46. Grand Rapids: Zondervan Academic, 2015.

Torrance, Thomas F. *The Christian Doctrine of God: One Being, Three Persons*. Edinburgh: T. & T. Clark, 1996.

Torrance, Thomas F. *Karl Barth: Biblical and Evangelical Theologian*. Edinburgh: T. & T. Clark, 2001.

Turretin, Francis. *Institutes of Elenctic Theology, Volume Two*, translated by George M. Giger. Philipsburg, NJ: Presbyterian and Reformed, 1992.

Vanhoozer, Kevin J. *Remythologizing Theology: Divine Action, Passion, and Authorship*. Cambridge: Cambridge University Press, 2010.

Vanhoye, Albert. *Structure and Message of the Epistle to the Hebrews*. Rome: Editrice Pontifico Instituto Biblico, 1989.

White, Thomas Joseph. *The Incarnate Lord: A Thomistic Study in Christology*. Washington, DC: Catholic University of America Press, 2015.

Wiley, H. Orton. *The Epistle to the Hebrews*. Kansas City: Beacon Hill, 1959.

Witherington, Ben, III. *Letters and Homilies for Jewish Christians: A Socio-Rhetorical Commentary on Hebrews, James, and Jude*. Downers Grove, IL: IVP Academic, 2007.

9

Early Methodist Theology in the Book of Hebrews[1]

CHRISTOPHER T. BOUNDS

AD FONTES IS A recurring theme in Christian theology. The Protestant Reformation used it to bring renewed focus on the Scriptures after a period of moral and theological drift in medieval Roman Catholicism. Anglicanism made it a rallying cry for a return to Ante-Nicene, Nicene and Post-Nicene biblical exegesis to settle seventeenth and eighteenth century doctrinal disputes.[2]

One of the greatest strengths of any Christian theological tradition is its foundational *fontes*. They fortify it by providing a trajectory for theological development, while protecting it from doctrinal novelty. Historic Christian theology welcomes any growth as maturation of its seminal and embryonic ideas, while spurning doctrinal innovation changing its substance or *essentia*. Only by a tradition's disciplined and frequent return to its sources can it discern the difference. Sources therefore provide an anchor preventing theological drift as doctrine develops in thought.

The Wesleyan theological tradition unfortunately has a history of neglecting its *fontes*. In the Methodist Episcopal Church's Christmas

---

1. I am honored to have this opportunity to honor my good friend, spiritual mentor, and dearly loved brother in Christ, Rev. Dr. Gary Cockerill. He exemplifies the best of our Wesleyan-Holiness tradition: a heart and mind infused with the holy love of God and neighbor.

2. See Lane, *Laudians*, 12; Tracy, "Ad Fontes," 76–93; Turnbull, *Anglican and Evangelical?*, 10.

Conference of 1784, John Wesley's *Standard Sermons, Explanatory Notes on the New Testament*, and "General Rules" were adopted as doctrinal standards. General Conferences in 1808 and 1832 fortified their status by giving them constitutional protection.[3] American Methodism, however, and its progeny in the Holiness Movement quickly set them aside, effectively ignoring them. While John Wesley and early British Methodists were recognized and venerated, they were not read and studied. His writings and the literature of early Methodism remained dormant for over a century.[4]

The 1935 release of George Croft Cell's *The Rediscovery of John Wesley* marked the beginning of a renaissance in Wesley and early Methodist studies. Albert Outler at Southern Methodist University's Perkins School of Theology, Frank Baker at Duke Divinity School, and Edwin Lewis and Stanley Hopper at Drew University's Theological School provided oversight to a burgeoning generation of scholars focused on early Methodist *fontes*, producing significant dissertations, monographs, journal articles and popular books. Their work helped Wesleyans reconnect with their origins, leading to theological reinvigoration and propelling Wesleyan studies into the twenty-first century.[5]

With this as a backdrop, my essay is an exercise in Wesleyan *ad fontes* as expressed in explanatory notes and commentaries on the book of Hebrews from early Methodist theologians: Joseph Benson, Adam Clarke, Joseph Sutcliffe and John Wesley. While researchers have focused on Wesley and his theological heirs' sermons, journals, hymns, letters and treatises, their scholarly treatment of Scripture has not received the same attention. Because early Methodists generally did not write volumes of systematics, their theology is embedded in sustained reflection on the Bible.[6] Hebrews, more specifically, has been selected for our focus because they believed it to be the book where the "principal doctrines of the gospel are more expressly asserted and more fully explained than in any other of the inspired writings."[7] Their reflection here sheds light on what early Wesleyans shared theologically with historic Christianity, as well as their distinctive doctrinal emphases.

---

3. See Oden, "What Are 'Established Standards of Doctrine'?," 41–62.

4. See Cell, *Rediscovery*, 4–50.

5. See Collins, *A Wesley Bibliography*, 20–225. Note the explosion of articles, books, and dissertations on Wesley after 1935.

6. An exception is Richard Watson.

7. Benson, *Commentary*, 6:503.

BASIC OVERVIEW OF EARLY METHODISTS ON THE BOOK OF HEBREWS

Early Methodist commentators on the book of Hebrews followed the early church fathers in ascribing authorship to the apostle Paul. His audience was Jewish Christians experiencing "poverty, affliction and persecution," faced with the temptation to apostatize and return to the religious practices of Judaism.[8] He writes to confirm them in the faith and practice of the gospel by showing how Christianity is the OT dispensation's fulfillment and end. Jesus Christ is superior to the patriarchs, prophets and priests of Israel, even higher than the angels; he is "an uncreated Being, infinitely greater than all others, whether earthly or heavenly."[9]

More specifically, Hebrews opens with a clear declaration of Jesus Christ's preeminence and majesty (1:1-3). Christ is then showed to be greater than the angels (1:4—3:1), greater than Moses (3:2—4:13), greater than Aaron and all high priests. Because he is seated presently at the right hand of God's throne, his sacrifice offered for the sins of the whole world is sufficient in a way Jewish sacrifices are not, and he remains a perpetual High Priest, offering his life unto God for all generations. The new covenant established in Christ is superior to the old, offering better promises: a true atonement for sin and the inscription of the law upon human hearts, not tablets of stone (4:14—10:18). These Jewish Christians are then exhorted to remain faithful to Christ, persevere to the end, hold fast their confession, continue to assemble together, beware of apostasy, and follow the example of their eminent ancestors (10:19—12:29). The epistle concludes with an expectation to continue in love and affection for one another, a caution to be careful of false teaching, an exhortation to cleave to Christ and not avoid persecution, a call to submit to their teachers, and a benediction that the "God of peace" make them "perfect in every good work to do his will" (13:1-24).[10]

---

8. Benson, *Commentary*, 6:503; Clark, *Commentary*, 677; Sutcliffe, *Commentary*, 246; Wesley, *Explanatory Notes*, 276.

9. Clark, *Commentary*, 682.

10. While there are some nuances in understanding, this represents a basic overview of Hebrews found in these early Methodist commentators. See Benson, *Commentary*, 6:508-10; Clark, *Commentary*, 677-83; Wesley, *Explanatory Notes*, 276-78.

THEOLOGICAL THEMES FOR EARLY METHODISTS IN THE BOOK OF HEBREWS

Early Wesleyans followed the general practice of Anglican divines by communicating theology in hymns, liturgies, sermons and explanatory notes on Scripture for the spiritual benefit of the church. While they did not produce a magisterial treatment of Christian doctrine like John Calvin's *Institutes of the Christian Religion* in the Reformed tradition or Philip Melanchthon's *Loci Praecipui Theologici* in the Lutheran tradition, they did address substantively key Christian doctrines and Wesleyan distinctives through this Anglican practice.

Initial work on the book of Hebrews by these Methodists provided a venue for such theological expression because it was "by far the most important and useful of all the apostolic writings," one in which "all of the doctrines of the Gospel are in it embodied, illustrated, and enforced in a manner most lucid."[11] In their commentaries and explanatory notes on Hebrews, doctrines central to Christianity and Methodism were taught and issues critical to spiritual life explored: Jesus Christ, new covenant versus old covenant, salvation and atonement, the necessity of obedience, apostasy, Christian perfection, and bodily resurrection in new creation.

Jesus Christ

Central to the book of Hebrews for early Methodists is the recognition that Jesus Christ is fully divine, explicitly rejecting any Arian or adoptionist heresies.[12] Based on the epistle's opening statements (1:1–3) they assert the Son of God to be the same substance as the Father, proceeding from the Father, while being distinct in person from the Father. As God, the Son is uncreated, eternal and co-exists with the Father. His deity is established further by the call for all God's angels to worship him (1:6)—if Christ is not God, then angels are guilty of idolatry—and by the psalmist's declaration about the Son, "Your throne, O God, will last for ever and ever" (1:8). They confess the language of the Nicene Creed: the Son is the same nature as the one in whom he has his source "God of God, Light of Light."[13]

---

11. Clarke, *Commentary*, 681.

12. Benson, *Commentary*, 6:515; Clarke, *Commentary*, 691–94; Sutcliffe, *Commentary*, 246–52.

13. Wesley, *Explanatory Notes*, 281. For full treatment of this opening declaration of the Son's deity, see Benson, *Commentary*, 6:511–19; Clarke, *Commentary*, 686–89; Sutcliffe, *Commentary*, 252–55; Wesley, *Explanatory Notes*, 279–82. It should be noted that, while Clarke affirmed the eternal deity of Jesus Christ and his divine personhood,

Adam Clarke provides an extensive discussion of the divine nature in his reflection upon Heb 11:6 ("anyone who comes to him must believe that he exists and that he rewards those who earnestly seek him."). He teaches that God's nature must be unoriginated and immaterial, contingent upon nothing else. Attributes of deity are without cause as well; if God produced his own attributes, God would have acted before he existed. They are perfect and infinite; to be otherwise would mean the divine nature is capable of improvement.[14]

Clarke then explores specific attributes: omnipresence (God exists everywhere in the same manner as he does anywhere), simplicity (God is an uncompounded substance, "identically the same everywhere, not consisting of *parts*, for these must be distinct and independent, nor of *whole*, for this is the aggregate of parts, nor of *magnitude* or *quantity*, for these signify a composition of parts"), omniscience (God's knowledge extends to all that can be known), omnipotence (God has all power, extending to all that can be done), free will (God is at liberty to exercise power or limit his power according to what is right), goodness (God desires to give happiness to others), wisdom, mercy, justice and truth (God always makes right use of his power and knowledge).[15] Each of the divine attributes "concur and combine, so all the works of his hands must bear the impress" of the natural and moral attributes.[16]

Early Methodists also recognize in Hebrews the full humanity of Jesus Christ, rejecting any Docetic or Apollinarian tendencies in Christianity. He is divine person, who at a point in time became incarnate, assuming full human nature in the created order (Heb 2:9–18). In their reflection upon Heb 4:15 and 5:7–8, they define the Son's humanity as a physical body with a rational soul. Through his earthly life and ministry, Christ participated in normal physical, spiritual, mental and emotional development, as well as the limitations attendant to human nature. Accordingly, Joseph Benson argues that the Son experienced "various weaknesses, and the faculties of the soul, of course being influenced thereby. While in his childhood he is said

---

he did not believe he was eternally the Son of God. He only became the Son in the incarnation. Clarke rejected the idea that Christ was "eternally begotten" by the Father for two primary reasons: the Scriptures never state Christ was "eternally" begotten and that the idea leads too easily to Arianism, which believed "there was a time when the Son was not," that the Father precedes the Son in existence. Instead, Clarke saw Jesus Christ as the "eternal logos" of the Father. See his full discussion of the issue in his commentary on Heb 1:8 (691–94).

14. Clarke, *Commentary*, 770–71.
15. Ibid., 771–72.
16. Ibid., 772–73.

to have increased in wisdom . . . as the powers of the mind were gradually unfolded, and subjects, through the medium of his senses, were presented to his contemplation. And if he increased in wisdom, he must of course increase in love to God and man, and all other graces and virtues, though always perfectly free from every defilement of sin, internal or external."[17]

Following orthodox Christology stated in the Council of Chalcedon (AD 451) and the Councils of Constantinople II (AD 553) and III (AD 681), these Methodists understood Christ's humanity to be free from original and actual sin.[18] Therefore, the body he assumed was "perfectly tempered; it was free from all morbid action, and consequently from all irregular movements."[19] Jesus' human soul was free from any kind of sin and experienced no "irregular temper," nothing contrary to his divine person. Through his human nature, however, the Son had a "lively feeling of our infirmities; of our wants, weaknesses, miseries, dangers" (Heb 4:15).[20] In his humanity, Christ experienced the fear of death, but not as one who fears final judgment, but as one who pays the price for the human offence against infinite justice (5:7). Ultimately, they interpreted Christ's humanity as God's way of being human.

Because Jesus Christ is the theandric one, fully divine and fully human, united in the person of the Son, he is able to be the ultimate High Priest.[21] Early Wesleyan commentators believed Heb 5:1–4 provides an overview of the appointment, duties and qualifications of a high priest: he is one set apart from the tribe of Levi of the family of Aaron; he is ordained to that office for the benefit of Israel; he mediates between God and humanity; he offers gifts (free-will offerings) as expressions of gratitude for divine kindness, and animal sacrifices to atone for sin; and finally, he feels compassion for the weaknesses and misery of others.[22] Accordingly, Christ is superior to any other high priest because he is God's Son, the same nature as the Father, appointed by the Father to this office for the whole human race. He offers his human life as the only sufficient atonement for sin. He conquers death and ascends into heaven where he presides as a human High Priest

---

17. Benson, *Commentary*, 6:571–72.

18. Ibid., 6:564, 572; Clarke, *Commentary*, 698, 700, 715; Sutcliffe, *Commentary*, 258–60; Wesley, *Explanatory Notes*, 286, 312.

19. Clarke, *Commentary*, 715.

20. Benson, *Commentary*, 6:564.

21. Ibid., 6:542, 562, 566–74; Clarke, *Commentary*, 717, 739–41, 756; Sutcliffe, *Commentary*, 269–71; *Explanatory Notes*, 285–86.

22. Benson, *Commentary*, 6:566–67; Clarke, *Commentary*, 716–17; Sutcliffe, *Commentary*, 269–70; Wesley, *Explanatory Notes*, 295.

in perpetuity without successor, sympathizing and interceding for all who share his human nature.[23]

New Covenant Verses Old Covenant

As the perfect High Priest, the incarnate Son mediates a greater covenant, established upon better promises (Heb 8:6). Early Methodists saw in Hebrews a clear contrast between the old covenant made with Israel and the new one inaugurated by Jesus Christ for the church. The old demanded perfect obedience to the law from life's inception, even though humanity is powerless to keep it. Because of Adam and Eve's fall in the Garden, all are slave to sin and bear sin's guilt. The old was used by God to demonstrate Israel's inability to fulfill the covenant and to prepare them for a better one (8:7–9). The old was "temporal and earthly," although it pointed out spiritual and eternal things. It existed only as a "shadow" (10:1), but was impotent to provide real pardon from sin, significant sanctification and "title" to eternal life.[24]

The new covenant mediated by Christ, however, provides true absolution of sin and furnishes grace to all believers, enabling them to walk in obedience to the moral law, as described in the Gospels, loving God with their entire lives and their neighbor as themselves (Heb 7:22–28).[25] In Christ's new covenant God puts his laws into human minds and writes them on their hearts (8:10). Adam Clarke describes life under the new covenant as formation in "the principles of law, truth and holiness"; with a "fully enlightened" understanding "to comprehend them"; and to have "affections, passions and appetites . . . purified and filled with holiness and love to God and man"; leading to "willing" obedience in life and "feeling that love is the fulfilling of the law."[26]

Joseph Sutcliffe, expounding on Heb 8:8–10, declares the glories of the new covenant. Christ works as High Priest to "reimpress" upon human hearts what first existed in human innocence: the moral image of God. Because of original sin the moral image has been devastated, placing another law in human hearts, causing enmity between God and humanity. Through the moral image's renewal in Christ's priestly office, the "heart becomes the ark in which the tables of the law are deposited . . . Obedience is not

---

23. Wesley, *Explanatory Notes*, 295.

24. Benson, *Commentary*, 6:564, 572; Clarke, *Commentary*, 698, 700, 715; Sutcliffe, *Commentary*, 258–60; Wesley, *Explanatory Notes*, 286, 312.

25. Benson, *Commentary*, 6:600–604; Clarke, *Commentary*, 738–42; Sutcliffe, *Commentary*, 280–82; Wesley, *Explanatory Notes*, 308–10.

26. Clarke, *Commentary*, 741.

rendered merely on the ground of its authority, but also from the perception of the excellency of its requirements . . . and happiness is found in conformity to its precepts."[27] To become like God is the driving passion of believers because of the new covenant enacted by Christ.

Salvation and Atonement

As already intimated, the heart of the new covenant is redemption. Early Methodist commentators on Hebrews believed only the Son of God as theandric High Priest can enact salvation.[28] To do so, Christ must be fully human. In statements reminiscent of Gregory Nazianzus' maxim, "The unassumed is unhealed," these Wesleyan exegetes point to the redemption of human nature through the Son's participation in it.[29] It is not just what the Son of God does through human nature that redeems humanity, walking in faithful obedience to the Father as a second Adam, fulfilling the law of God, but his very union with it. On the most obvious level, humanity experiences victory over death through Christ's bodily resurrection. By the Son taking his physical body through death and resurrection, human nature shares in his victory over the grave. On another level, the power and hold of the enemy over the human soul is broken through the Son's human soul.[30] More specifically, Adam Clarke teaches that through his body Christ provides support for all physical trials and infirmities, and through his soul he cleanses all spiritual unrighteousness and fills with the Holy Spirit.[31]

Only through his human nature, furthermore, is Christ qualified to make atonement for sin. In the office of High Priest, Christ offers his own unblemished humanity through the shedding of blood as a sufficient sacrifice for all sin and sinners (7:27). His expiation of sin comes through the experience of suffering and death, the price for humanity's transgression

27. Sutcliffe, *Commentary*, 281.

28. Benson, *Commentary*, 6:535; Clarke, *Commentary*, 697–701; Sutcliffe, *Commentary*, 258–61; Wesley, *Explanatory Notes*, 286–88.

29. Gregory Nazianzus, "To Cledonius against Apollinaris," 218. Specifically speaking of Jesus Christ, Nazianzus states, "If anyone has put his trust in him as a man without a human mind, he is really bereft of mind, and quite unworthy of salvation. For that which he has not assumed he has not healed, but that which is united to his Godhead is also saved. If only half Adam fell, then that which Christ assumes and saves may be half also; but if the whole of his nature fell, it must be united to the whole nature of Him that was begotten, and so be saved as a whole."

30. Benson, *Commentary*, 6:253; Clarke, *Commentary*, 700–701, 715; Sutcliffe, *Commentary*, 257–59; Wesley, *Explanatory Notes*, 287

31. Clark, *Commentary*, 715. See also Sutcliffe, *Commentary*, 259; and Wesley, *Explanatory Notes*, 288, 293.

of God's law. After death, Christ bodily rises from the dead, ascends into heaven and appears before God as a man in the sacerdotal office for the human race (8:1–2).[32] Unlike Levitical high priests, he does not leave the holy of holies after making atonement, but abides at God's throne "as a continual priest, in the permanent act of offering his crucified body unto God, on behalf of all succeeding generations of mankind."[33]

To bring salvation, Christ's humanity must be united with his divine nature. All early Methodist theories of the atonement expressed in commentaries on Hebrews require it. While the commentators had different ways of describing redemption through ransom and penal substitutionary perspectives on the atonement, perhaps, there is no greater example of the necessity of theandric union than those holding to a satisfaction view. Following Anselm's theory, these Wesleyans believed human sin to be an infinite offence against God for which no finite human can atone.[34] Because perfect humanity is joined with deity, however, in the incarnate Son of God, Christ's human sacrifice on the cross becomes an infinite act of atonement for human sin against God. Adam Clarke writes, "God willed not the sacrifices under the law, but he willed that a human victim of infinite merit should be offered for the redemption of mankind. That there might be such a victim, a body was prepared for the eternal Logos; and in that body he came to do the will of God, that is, to suffer and die for the sins of the world."[35]

Obedience Necessary for Final Salvation

As early Methodists read and comment on Hebrews, their synergistic understanding of salvation comes to the fore. While Christians are saved by divine grace through faith, cooperation with ongoing grace through obedience is seen as crucial to final salvation. In exploring the reasons why the Israelites did not enter "rest" in Canaan (3:19), they recognized it was not the result of a divine decree, or any deficiency of divine grace and counsel, but unbelief leading to disobedience, resulting in hardness of heart and dullness of mind.[36]

32. Wesley, *Explanatory Notes*, 295.
33. Clarke, *Commentary*, 739.
34. Benson, *Commentary*, 6:611–22; Clarke, *Commentary*, 754. For an excellent discussion of Anselm's satisfaction view of the atonement and subsequent historical appropriation, see O'Collins, *Christology*, 297–315.
35. Clarke, *Commentary*, 754.
36. Benson, *Commentary*, 6:548–49; Clarke, *Commentary*, 707–8; Sutcliffe, *Commentary*, 262–63; Wesley, *Explanatory Notes*, 90. It should be noted that while Clarke acknowledges unbelief, he argues for something more fundamental to unbelief: the

They believed the description of Jesus Christ in 5:9 as the "author of eternal salvation unto all that obey him" to be strong evidence of their understanding.[37] Faith in Jesus Christ must be joined with obedience. Christ is the perfect High Priest by offering himself as the sacrifice for sin, obtaining forgiveness and eternal life for those who obey him.[38] Clarke writes that through his death and resurrection Christ has purchased for humanity an "endless glory; but in order to be prepared for it, the sinner must, through the grace which God withholds from no man, repent, turn from sin, believe on Jesus as being a sufficient ransom and sacrifice for his soul, receive the gift of the Holy Ghost, be a worker together with him, walk in conformity with the divine will through divine aid, and continue faithful unto death, through him, out of whose fullness he may receive grace upon grace."[39]

The necessity of obedience is picked up again in the caution against backsliding and apostasy found in Heb 6. Early Methodists warn of the dangers of negligence and laziness, forerunners of all mortal sin. Faithfulness to God and diligence in the means of grace (understood to be works of piety and mercy) are required to nourish the walk of obedience. While Christians may be buffeted by the storms of this life, as they continue in faithful obedience, God will give them sufficient grace to persevere to the end, enabling them to see God even as Jesus Christ does now (6:18–20).[40]

Apostasy

The necessity of obedience for final salvation in Hebrews is intertwined with the warning of apostasy. Early Wesleyan reflection here is significant. The first hint of this mortal sin is flagged in Heb 2:1, where Christians are told to be careful of letting sound teaching "at any time . . . slip." Methodist commentators pick up this note of caution and explore how Christian faith can be lost at any time—in peace and prosperity, in persecution and adversity, or in times of peculiar temptation. While "falling from grace" happens for

---

Israelites were unpersuaded and their unbelief was a result of their stubborn minds.

37. Benson, *Commentary*, 6:572–73; Clarke, *Commentary*, 719; Wesley, *Explanatory Notes*, 297.

38. Wesley, *Explanatory Notes*, 297.

39. Clarke, *Commentary*, 719.

40. Benson, *Commentary*, 6:581. John Wesley ("Minutes of Several Conversations," 322–24) gives examples of works of piety among the instituted means of grace: prayer, reading the Scriptures, Holy Communion, fasting, and Christian conferencing. He also gives works of mercy, which consisted of rules for ordering the Christian life: "doing no harm" and "doing good" such as feeding the hungry, clothing the naked, visiting those in prison, etc.

many reasons, the discussion typically centers around five: a love of or attachment to the world, a "corrupt passion or vile affection" for sin, adherence to false doctrine, incitement to division among devout Christians, or lack of participation in the divinely appointed means of grace, both public and private.[41]

What is implied in Heb 2 becomes explicit in 3:2–19, where the church is given a twofold exhortation; they are not to harden their hearts or provoke God through unbelief as the Israelites did in the wilderness, resulting in personal destruction and forfeiture of Canaan's "rest." Early Methodist commentators saw here direct evidence that believers could "fall from the grace of God and perishing everlastingly." How does apostasy happen? By Christians succumbing to the deception of sin through willful consent, by recalcitrance of heart developed through the practice of sin, by unbelief fed though internal questioning of God's truth, leading to even greater unbelief manifested in vocal opposition to the Gospel, and finally, by the departure of the Holy Spirit, leaving people with a reprobate mind and apostate.[42] How do people defend against such mortal sin? By the pursuit and experience of Christian perfection, having the sinful heart cleansed with the pure love of God and neighbor.

In Heb 4:7–14 the danger of abandoning Jesus Christ is examined again through the Israelites' loss of Canaan's rest through rebellion against Moses. Early Wesleyan reflection on this passage identified different types of "rest": the seventh day Sabbath of God, the land of Canaan promised to the Israelites, the present blessings of the Gospel, and eternal glory. More specifically, "rest" here addresses the experience of present salvation in life, which is preparatory for heaven (4:9).[43] Present rest for Christians includes "peace and joy, the solid and satisfying happiness consequent on pardon and holiness ... the renovation of our nature, the love of God and of all mankind shed abroad in the heart, and that lively, well-grounded hope of eternal life."[44] However, Christians must work responsibly with God's ongoing grace if they are to enter ultimate rest. Clarke states, "We receive grace, improve grace, retain grace, if we are to obtain eternal glory," lest a person

---

41. Benson, *Commentary*, 6:527, 530–31; Clarke, *Commentary*, 694–95; Sutcliffe, *Commentary*, 257; Wesley, *Explanatory Notes*, 284.

42. Benson, *Commentary*, 6:542–53; Clarke, *Commentary*, 705–8; Sutcliffe, *Commentary*, 262–64; Wesley, *Explanatory Notes*, 289–91.

43. Benson, *Commentary*, 6:556–61; Clarke, *Commentary*, 709–11; Sutcliffe, *Commentary*, 265–67; Wesley, *Explanatory Notes*, 292–93.

44. Benson, *Commentary*, 6:554.

"fall off from the grace of God, from the Gospel and its blessings, and perish everlastingly" (4:11).[45]

Hebrews 6:4–8 shows the importance of Christians moving toward perfection, as discussed earlier, lest they lose the Holy Spirit's illuminating presence and become apostate, a state impossible from which to be renewed again.[46] According to early Methodist commentators, the apostate is not a person professing Christian faith or a backsliding Christian. Adam Clarke writes, "No man believing in the Lord Jesus as the great sacrifice for sin, and acknowledging Christianity as a divine revelation, is here intended, though he may have unfortunately backslidden from any degree of the salvation of God."[47] Instead, Hebrews has in mind people who have experienced salvation in Christ, had the witness of the Holy Spirit, been thoroughly instructed in the Christian faith ("enlightened") and have come to a place where they willfully reject the "whole Christian system, and its author, the Lord Jesus."[48] By their apostasy they "crucify to themselves the Son of God" (6:6).[49]

Hebrews 6:4–8 is reinforced later in 10:26–38, which identifies the consequence of deserting Christian faith: eternal death. "If we deliberately keep on sinning after we have received the knowledge of the truth, no sacrifice for sins is left" (10:26). Early Wesleyans took note of the immediate context: abandonment of the church (10:25). Because local congregations are the most significant means of God's grace, Christians who forsake them are backsliders, opening the door to apostasy's possibility. More specifically, 10:26 does not address directly a backslider or a Christian caught up in sin. While they are in spiritual danger, they are not hopeless. Rather, it speaks of the apostate. There is no sacrifice for apostasy since the one who makes the sacrifice for sin is completely rejected.[50]

---

45. Clarke, *Commentary*, 711.

46. Benson, *Commentary*, 6:577–80; Clarke, *Commentary*, 724–26; Sutcliffe, *Commentary*, 272–75; Wesley, *Explanatory Notes*, 299–301.

47. Clarke, *Commentary*, 724.

48. Ibid.

49. Clarke and Benson address the Calvinist Theodore Beza's exegesis and translation of this passage of Scripture, accusing him of contorting the plain sense of this passage to fit into the Calvinist system of predestination and the perseverance of the saints. See Benson's *Commentary*, 6:578 and Clarke's *Commentary*, 725.

50. Benson, *Commentary*, 6:631–33; Clarke, *Commentary*, 757–58; Sutcliffe, *Commentary*, 288–92; Wesley, *Explanatory Notes*, 318–19. While these early Methodists saw this sin as one of apostasy, they took opportunity to warn Christians of willful sin and exhorted them to continue in the means of grace. Representing this approach, Sutcliffe writes, "Our grand caution is against all wilful and presumptuous sins; and though the words refer especially to apostasy, all wilful sin must be dreaded as the most dangerous of calamities . . . the grand point is to be holy as he is holy. The means are connected

The final significant discussion of apostasy by early Methodist exegetes is Heb 12:14–15. Jewish Christians once again are admonished not to fall from the grace of God. In recognition of the many temptations and threats facing them, especially to revert back to Judaism, with its inferior covenant, sacrifices, rites and high priests, they are exhorted to persevere in Christianity without regard to the cost, even to the point of laying down their lives. Because Wesleyan commentators see this as the ultimate purpose for which Hebrews is written, they strongly urge readers to persevere to the end, not losing sight of their prize and hearing God say to them, "Well done, good and faithful servant, enter thou into the joy of thy Lord."[51]

Christian Perfection

John Wesley called the doctrine of Christian perfection "the grand depositum which God has lodged with the people called Methodists; and for the sake of propagating this chiefly God appeared to have raised" them up.[52] Early Methodists committed themselves to the doctrine, proclamation and experience of entire sanctification. Commentators on Hebrews saw in it abundant support for their teaching. Most importantly, they believed the personal experience of Christian perfection to be the best fortification against backsliding and apostasy. Commenting on the Israelites' failure to enter Canaan's rest and Jewish Christians facing a similar threat in Heb 3:2–19, Joseph Benson writes, "God has promised to purify the heart; and the blood of Jesus cleanses from all sin. It is therefore the highest wisdom of genuine Christians to look to God for the complete purification of their souls; this they cannot have too soon, and for this there cannot be too much earnest."[53]

While they recognized the negative attitude ("the violent outcry") of many in the Church to its most distinctive doctrine, Wesleyans saw the exhortation to "go unto perfection" (Heb 6:1) as the call to be saved from the power and nature of sin; and to be filled with the Spirit and with the power

---

to the end. Let us not forsake the public worship of Christ for that of the synagogue; or recreations, or company, for God is there. There his people pray, there we will be assisted in knowledge, and there we shall be blessed" (*Commentary*, 291).

51. Sutcliffe, *Commentary*, 309; see also Benson's *Commentary*, 6:667–68; and Clarke's *Commentary*, 779.

52. Wesley, "Letter to Robert Carr Brackenbury," 237–38. See Benson, *Commentary*, 6:253; Clarke, *Commentary*, 723, 738, 742, 776–77, 779, 784, 789; Sutcliffe, *Commentary*, 291, 306, 309; Wesley, *Explanatory Notes*, 308–10.

53. Benson, *Commentary*, 6:549.

of Christ to love God and neighbor.[54] Adam Clarke describes this sanctifying work of God more clearly in his description of what it means for God to inscribe his law upon human hearts (8:10): "All their affections, passions and appetites, shall be purified and filled with holiness and love to God and man; so that they shall willing obey the law, and feel that love is the fulfilling of the law . . ."[55]

Another way early Methodists defined Christian perfection was in terms of renewal in the moral image of God. As created perfect in the Garden, John Wesley understood the *imago Dei* in humanity to comprise three parts: the moral, natural, and political. Specifically, the moral image enabled humanity to enjoy true righteousness, holiness, love, and knowledge of God in the immediacy of a relationship with God. Because of Adam and Eve's sin, the moral image was completely destroyed in humanity, miring humanity in the "unceasing bent toward sinning." Wesley believed this to be the "essence" of humanity's sinful nature.[56] However, through the regenerating power of new birth Christians experience partial renewal in the moral image and through entire sanctification full restoration, grounding them in God's holy love, enabling joyful obedience to God.

Some early Wesleyans interpreted Heb 12:1 ("let us throw off everything that hinders and the sin that so easily entangles") as the problem of humanity's sinful nature, the corrupted moral image of God. It also points, however, to true hope in present life: Christians can be liberated from this "weight" by divine grace through the full renewal of the moral image. Later in 12:14 they directly connect this to "holiness," without which "no one will see the Lord," bringing heart purity to Christians and detachment from all lusts of the world, giving them every disposition necessary to enjoy the kingdom of God on earth and in heaven.[57]

These commentators believed there is no room for selfish agendas or self-focused living in the presence of God. Without holiness, therefore, there can be no delight in the kingdom of God. At this point they are prescient of C. S. Lewis, who powerfully illustrates their point in *The Great Divorce*. Lewis imagines a group of people in hell who are given the opportunity to experience heaven. They participate in its delights and share in the communion of saints. Surprisingly, they find life displeasing and uncomfortable. After a short time, they long for their previous lives; they desire a return to

---

54. Ibid., 6:575–77; Clarke, *Commentary*, 723; Sutcliffe, *Commentary*, 272–75; Wesley, *Explanatory Notes*, 299–300.

55. Clarke, *Commentary*, 741.

56. See Maddox, *Responsible Grace*, 67–83.

57. See Clarke, *Commentary* 741; Sutcliffe, *Commentary*, 309.

hell. Why? Because their hearts long for sin. They are therefore unsuited for heaven, unable to enjoy the Kingdom of God.[58] Early Methodists believed only the grace of Christian perfection can establish the heart in true holiness without which "no one will see the Lord," bringing joy in the experience of God's kingdom.

Wesleyan discussion of entire sanctification concludes with comments on the mention of "the righteous made perfect," in Heb 12:23 and on the prayer for Christians to be fitted "with everything good for doing his will" in 13:21. Perfection as seen through both passages implies a transformation of the soul, cleansed from all sin, which is the only way to be pleasing in God's sight (13:21). This inward purity results in outward conformity to God's will, enabling good works, made possible only by the blood of the everlasting covenant.[59]

In their reflection upon Christian perfection in the book of Hebrews, these early Methodist commentators expected Christian perfection to occur sooner rather than later in life. They recognized, however, that the conditions for its experience are varied and determined by God alone. Adam Clarke states, "There can be little difficulty in attaining the end of our faith, the salvation of our souls from all sin, if God carry us forward to it; and this he will do if we submit to be saved in his own way, and on his own terms."[60]

Bodily Resurrection and New Creation

While not a significant theme in Hebrews, early Wesleyan reflection on Hebrews addressed bodily resurrection and new creation at the end of the age. In the eighteenth century, John Wesley inherited from his Anglican tradition a medieval eschatology focused on a "spiritual" heaven. At death Christians are immediately ushered into a transcendent reality free of the physical world, obscuring traditional teaching of an intermediate state, bodily resurrection at Christ's second coming, and a new heavens and

---

58. Lewis, *The Great Divorce*, 65–68, 72.

59. Benson, *Commentary*, 6:672–73; 685–87; Clarke, *Commentary*, 782, 789; Sutcliffe, *Commentary*, 309–11; Wesley, *Explanatory Notes*, 329–30. The author of Hebrews speaks more to the sin from which Christian are absolved and liberated from its power (8:12). The first is unrighteousness (ἀδικία), which is defined as injustice or wrongdoing against God, another person or even oneself. Sin (ἁμαρτία) is seeking happiness apart from God and within the scope of divine law. Finally, there is iniquity (ἀνομία) or lawlessness, "not having, knowing, or acknowledging a law; having no law written" on the heart and living without restraint. See Clarke, *Commentary*, 742; Benson, *Commentary*, 6:603–4.

60. Clarke, *Commentary*, 723.

earth.[61] Wesley, however, rejected this model and shifted focus.[62] At Christ's second coming, the intermediate state of death will cease. The dead will be reunited with their bodies, now transformed and suited for their respective destinies through bodily resurrection.[63] After final judgment, the entire created order will be transformed and made incorruptible for "life everlasting," no longer subject to disease, decay and death.[64]

Wesley's theological heirs, as seen in early Methodist commentaries, generally followed his line of thought, recognizing the place of human nature and the entire created order in the eschaton through their reflection upon Heb 1:10–12; 4:7–14; 6:2; 10:28. Regarding humanity, they are keenly aware of the necessity of the human body to human nature as seen in their comments on Heb 6:2.[65] The human body is honored. Without bodily resurrection, even though humanity has conscious existence in an intermediate state, they are incomplete. Following the pattern of Christ's resurrection, the resurrected body is identical with the one that died, although with a change in its properties: it will not be a different body, but a different form of the same body. The resurrected body of the righteous will be perfectly suited for the "new creation," able to participate fully in it and enjoy union with God and fellow humanity.[66] While the language of Heb 1:11 may seem to indicate the destruction of the created order, they interpreted it and other similar passages to point to creation's renewal and perfection, participating in the final eternal rest to which Hebrews points.[67]

CONCLUSION

In summary and conclusion, the biblical commentaries by Joseph Benson, Adam Clarke, Joseph Sutcliffe, and John Wesley provide essential *fontes* from which to understand Methodist theology and evaluate Wesleyan doctrinal development. While they are not magisterial theological texts as

---

61. Maddox, *Responsible Grace*, 231–35. Here, Maddox is reliant upon McDannell and Lang, *Heaven*.

62. Wesley, "On Faith," 188–200.

63. Wesley, "The Resurrection of the Dead," 474–85.

64. See Maddox's discussion of Wesley's vision of animals in the "new creation" in *Responsible Grace*, 246–47, 253.

65. Benson, *Commentary*, 6:576–77; Clarke, *Commentary*, 623–24.

66. Benson, *Commentary*, 6:522, 529, 577; Clarke, *Commentary*, 710–11, 723–24, 765–66; Sutcliffe, *Commentary*, 259, 311; Wesley, *Explanatory Notes*, 282.

67. Benson, *Commentary*, 6:522; Clarke, *Commentary*, 691; Sutcliffe, *Commentary*, 259; Wesley, *Explanatory Notes*, 282.

found in other Christian traditions, they represent a distinctive Anglican approach to spiritual formation in the church, demonstrating an inner cohesion between thoughtful expression of historic Christian orthodoxy and distinctive Wesleyan themes.

These early Methodist theologians' work on the book of Hebrews, more specifically, exemplifies the heart and strength of Wesleyan theology: soteriology. They exhibit an acute concern for the doctrine, proclamation and experience of salvation. They ground redemption in the theandric union of the Son of God as the perfect High Priest who mediates a new covenant, delivering humanity from the guilt, power and nature of sin and establishing the law of love in their hearts. This "present rest" prepares for the final rest of heaven. Christians, however, must walk in obedience to God, cooperating with divine grace in the appointed means of grace to avoid falling away from Christ into apostasy, like the Israelites did in the wilderness. The best fortification against this mortal sin is to go on to perfection. If Christians persevere, they will experience eternal rest: a renovated created order brought fully into the life of God where the kingdom of God is fully experienced.

BIBLIOGRAPHY

Benson, Joseph. *Commentary of the Old and New Testaments*. 6 vols. Electronic ed. Rio, WI: Ages Software, 2002.

Cell, George Croft. *The Rediscovery of John Wesley*. New York: Holt, 1935.

Clarke, Adam. *Commentary on Romans to Revelation*. Vol. 6 of *Commentary Taken from the Holy Bible, Containing the Old and New Testaments*. New ed. Nashville: Abingdon, 1977.

Collins, Kenneth J. *A Wesley Bibliography*. 4th ed. Wilmore, KY: First Fruits, 2015.

Lane, Calvin. *The Laudians and the Elizabethan Church: History, Conformity and Religious Identity in Post-Reformation England*. New York: Routledge, 2013.

Lewis, C. S. *The Great Divorce*. New York: Macmillan, 1946.

Maddox, Randy. *Responsible Grace: John Wesley's Practical Theology*. Nashville: Kingswood, 1994.

McDannell, Colleen, and Bernard Lang. *Heaven: A History*. New Haven: Yale University Press, 1988.

Nazianzus, Gregory. "To Cledonius against Apollinaris." In *Christology of the Later Fathers*, edited by Edward R. Hardy, 215–24. Louisville: Knox, 1954.

O'Collins, Gerald. *Christology: A Biblical, Historical and Systematic Study of Jesus*. New York: Oxford University Press, 2009.

Oden, Thomas C. "What Are 'Established Standards of Doctrine'?: A Response to Richard Heitzenrater." *QR* 7 (1987) 41–62.

Sutcliffe, Joseph. *Commentary on 2 Corinthians—Revelation*. Vol. 5 of *Commentary on the Old and New Testaments*. Electronic ed. Rio, WI: Ages Software, 2002.

Tracy, J. D. "Ad Fontes: The Humanist Understanding of Scripture as Nourishment for the Soul." In *Christian Spirituality II: High Middle Ages and Reformation*, edited by Jill Raitt, Bernard McGinn, and John Meyendorff, 76–93. New York: Crossroad, 1987.

Turnbull, Richard. *Anglican and Evangelical?* London: Continuum, 2007.

Wesley, John. *Explanatory Notes on 1 Corinthians—Revelation*. Vol. 2 of *Explanatory Notes on the New Testament*. Electronic ed. Rio, WI: Ages Software, 2002.

———. "Letter to Robert Carr Brackenbury." In *The Letters of John Wesley: 1787–1791*, vol. 8 of *The Letters of John Wesley*, edited by John Telford, 237–38. London: Epworth, 1931.

———. "Minutes of Several Conversations." In *Addresses, Essays, Letters*, vol. 8 of *The Works of John Wesley*, edited by Thomas Jackson, 322–44. 1872. Repr., Grand Rapids: Baker, 1978.

———. "On Faith." In *Sermons IV: 115–151*, vol. 4 of *The Bicentennial Edition of The Works of John Wesley*, edited by Frank Baker, 184–202. Nashville: Abingdon, 1987.

———. "The Resurrection of the Dead." In *Sermons*, vol. 7 of *The Works of John Wesley*, edited by Thomas Jackson, 474–85. 1872. Repr., Grand Rapids: Baker, 1978.

Bibliography of of Gareth Lee Cockerill

BOOKS

Christian Faith in the Old Testament: The Bible of the Apostles. Nashville: Nelson, 2014.
The Epistle to the Hebrews. NICNT. Grand Rapids: Eerdmans, 2012.
Cockerill, Gareth L., et al. *Four Views on the Warning Passages in Hebrews*. Edited by Herbert W. Bateman IV. Grand Rapids: Kregel, 2007.
Guide for Pilgrims to the Heavenly City. Pasadena, CA: William Carey Library, 2002.
Tracy, Wes, Gary Cockerill, Donald Demaray, and Steve Harper. *Reflecting God*. Kansas City: Beacon Hill, 2000.
Hebrews: A Bible Commentary in the Wesleyan Tradition. Indianapolis: Wesleyan, 1999.

EDITED BOOKS

Harper, A. F., et al., eds. *The Wesley Bible: A Personal Study Bible for Holy Living*. Nashville: Nelson, 1990.

JOURNAL ARTICLES

"The Truthfulness and Perennial Relevance of God's Word in the Letter to the Hebrews." *BSac* 172 (2015) 190–202.
"Structure and Interpretation in Hebrews 8:1–10:18: A Symphony in Three Movements." *BBR* 11 (2001) 179–201.
"The Better Resurrection (Heb 11:35): A Key to the Structure and Rhetorical Purpose of Hebrews 11." *TynBul* 51 (2000) 215–34.
"Hebrews 1:6: Source and Significance." *BBR* 9 (1999) 51–64.
"To the Hebrews/to the Muslims: Islamic Pilgrimage as a Key to Interpretation." *Missiology* 22 (1994) 347–59.
"Melchizedek or 'King of Righteousness.'" *EvQ* 63 (1991) 305–12.
"Jesus and the Greatest Commandment in Mark 10:17–22: A Test Case for John Wesley's 'Theology of love.'" *AS* 40 (1985) 13–21.
"Heb 1:1–14, 1 Clem 36:1–6 and the High Priest Title." *JBL* 97 (1978) 437–40.

REVIEW ARTICLES

Review of *You Are My Son: The Family of God in the Epistle to the Hebrews*, by Amy L. Peeler. *JETS* 58 (2015) 413–16.

Review of *Hebrews*, by David L. Allen. *JETS* 55 (2012) 202–5.

Review of *Cosmology and Eschatology in Hebrews: The Setting of the Sacrifice*, by Kenneth L. Schenck. *JETS* 52 (2009) 171–73.

Review of *Understanding the Book of Hebrews: The Story Behind the Sermon*, by Kenneth L. Schenck. *JETS* 47 (2004) 730–31.

Review of *Hebrews*, by George H. Guthrie. *ATJ* 32 (2000) 146–47.

Review of *Interpreting the Epistle to the Hebrews*, by Andrew H. Trotter, Jr. *RBL* 1 (1999) 383–85.

Review of *The Gospel According to Mark: An Introduction and Commentary*, by R. Alan Cole. *JETS* 37 (1994) 430–31.

Review of *Hebrews: A Call to Commitment* by William L. Lane. *JETS* 37 (1994) 436–37.

Review of *Proleptic Priests: Priesthood in the Epistle to the Hebrews*, by John M. Scholer. *JBL* 112 (1993) 171–73.

Review of *Eschatology and the New Testament: Essays in Honor of George Raymond Beasley-Murray*, edited by W. Hulitt Gloer. *JETS* 35 (1992) 103–4.

Review of *The Melchizedek Tradition: A Critical Examination of the Sources to the Fifth Century A.D. and in the Epistle to the Hebrews*, by Fred L. Horton. *Interpretation* 31 (1977) 328–29.

DISSERTATION

"The Melchizedek Christology in Heb. 7:1–28." PhD diss., Union Theological Seminary, 1976.

Ancient Document Index

OLD TESTAMENT

Genesis

1–2	49
1:26–28	9
2	57
2:2	40, 44–45
3	56
8:21	101, 109
14	57–58
22:2	78–79
22:12	78
22:16	78
22:22	78, 80

Exodus

4:22–23	78, 97
4:22	99
15:17	102
16:8–9	25
16:9–10	23
16:12–21	23
16:12	25
16:23	102
19	107
19:6	99, 107
19:22	102–3
23:20	77
24	102
24:1–9	79
24:1	102
24:2	103
24:9–11	23
24:9–10	102
24:12–15	79
24:16	79
25:28	109
26:33	102
28–30	102
28–29	107
28:3	102
28:31	100
28:38	100
28:39	100
28:41	102
29	101
29:18	101, 109
29:25	101, 109
29:30	100
29:36	100
29:41	109
30:20	100
31:3	64
33–34	70
34	70
34:29–35	79
34:30	79
35:18	100
35:31	64
36:34	100
38:27	100
39:11–12	100
40:9–10	100

Leviticus

1–5	101
1:9	101, 109
1:13	101, 109

Leviticus *(continued)*

1:17	101, 109
2:2	101, 109
2:9	101, 109
2:12	101, 109
3:5	101, 109
3:11	101, 109
3:16	101, 109
4:31	101, 109
5:5	21
6:10	104
6:15	101, 109
6:21	101, 109
8:11	100
8:21	101, 109
8:28	101, 109
9	24
9:7	103
9:8	103
16:10	21
16:21	21
17:4	101, 109
17:6	101, 109
21:21	103
21:23	103
23:13	101, 109
23:18	101, 109

Numbers

1:50	100
3:6	100
3:31	100
4:3	100
4:9	100
4:12	100
4:14	100
4:23–24	100
4:26	100
4:30	100
4:35	100
4:37	100
4:39	100
4:41	100
4:43	100
5:9	100
8:22	100
8:26	100
12:1–8	70
13:1—14:45	40
15:3	109
15:5	109
15:7	109
15:10	109
15:13–14	109
15:24	109
16:9	100
18:2	100
18:6–7	100
18:7	109
18:21	100
18:23	100
28:2	109
28:6	109
28:8	109
28:13	109
28:24	109
28:27	109
29:2	109
29:6	109
29:11	109
29:13	109
29:36	109
35	32

Deuteronomy

1:31	97
4:24	104
5:23–29	24
5:28	25
6:4–9	xvii
8:5	97–98
9:3	104
10:8	100
11:11	60
14:1	97
17:12	100
18:3	101
18:5	100
18:7	100
18:15	80
28:14	60
32:6	97
34:10–12	70

Joshua

5:13–15	24–25

22:27	100

2 Samuel

7:2	97
7:11	97
7:12–13	86
7:13	97
22:20	78–80

1 Kings

1:50	32
2:28	32
7:34	100
8:11	100

1 Chronicles

6:17	100
15:2	100
16:4	100
16:37	100
21:26	104
23:13	100
23:28	100
23:32	100
26:12	100
28:12	64
28:13	100

2 Chronicles

5:14	100
8:14	100
11:14	100
13:10	100
23:6	100
29:11	100
31:2	100

Ezra

6:14	64

Nehemiah

10:36	100

Psalms

1	88–89
2	58, 78, 84–90
2:1–6	87
2:1–2	89
2:1	86
2:2	78, 87, 89–90
2:6–7	88
2:6	88
2:7	76, 78–80, 84–86, 89, 91–92
2:7a	88
2:8	72, 89
2:9	87
2:10–11	88
2:11	89–90
2:12	88–89
8	2–13, 56–58, 60, 71, 73, 84
8:5–7	7, 9, 11
8:5	7
8:6	6
8:7	7, 10
8:7a	9, 11
20:3	101
39:7	100
40:6–8	92
45	71, 84
50:14	104
51:17	104
95	48, 57–59, 106
95:7–11	40, 43
95:7–8	48
95:11	58
102	70, 84
103:13	97
109	4, 7
109:1	7–8
110	56, 58, 71, 84, 112
110:1	60
110:4	57, 61
141:2	104

Proverbs

3:11–12	98
21:3	104

Isaiah

5	81
5:1–7	60
40:3	77
42:1	78–80
42:2	79
43	98
43:6	98
61:6	99

Isaiah *(continued)*

63:16	97, 99
64:8	97
65:17–25	3

Jeremiah

3:4	97
3:19	97
3:22	97
31	56, 58, 60, 106
31:9	97
31:20	97
31:31–34	34
52:18	100

Ezekiel

11:18–19	60
16:19	109
20:28	109
34	60
36	60
40:46	100
42:14	100
43:19	100
44:11	100
44:15–17	100
44:19	100
44:27	100
45:4–5	100

Daniel

12:10	86

Hosea

1:10	98
11:1–4	97

Joel

1:9	100
1:13	100
2:17	100
2:28–32	34

Malachi

1:6	97
2:10	97
3:1	77, 81
3:17	97–98
4:5–6	81

NEW TESTAMENT

Matthew

3:17	78
4:10	104
4:18–22	107
5	90
5:17–19	58
6:9	99
7:15	60
11:27	67
15:4–5	100
21:16	3
26:28	76
27:43	133
28:19	xix

Mark

1:1	77–78, 82–83
1:2–3	79
1:3	77
1:4	77
1:7–8	77
1:7	80
1:9–11	80
1:9	77
1:10	79
1:11	77–79, 81, 90
1:16–20	107
2:1—3:12	80
2:24	80
2:26	80
3:4	80
3:11	79
3:20–30	80
5:7	79
5:8	79
7:1–23	80
7:10–11	100
8:31—9:1	79
9:2–8	79
9:7	80–81, 90
9:8	80
9:12–13	81
10:2	80
10:45	108

11:25	99	5:12	34
12:1–12	81	6:1–6	107
12:6	81, 90	6:8	34
12:12	81	7:7	104
12:14	80	7:38	5, 84
13:32–42	132	7:42	104
14:61	81	7:53	5
14:62	81	7:55–56	34
15:34	133	8:6–8	34
15:37	82	8:13	34
15:39	77, 82	9	34
		10	34

Luke

		10:44–48	63
1:74	104	13:33	89
2:37	104	14:23	108
4:8	104	15:2	108
6:36	99	15:8	63
23:46	133	24:14	104
24:45–47	64	26:7	104
		27:23	104

John

Romans

1:1–18	70, 90		
1:1	122	1:7	99
1:2	122	1:9	104
1:3	122	1:25	104
1:5	126–27	4	127
1:14	122–23	4:3	127
1:34	90	4:4	127
1:35–51	107	4:13	56
3:16	127	5:8	127
5:30	133	6:2–8	128
8:28	133	6:23	127
13–17	123	7:4	128
13:13	123	8	34
14:9	71	8:14–16	105
14:20	99	8:15–16	99–100
14:25–27	65	9:4	100
14:28	133, 135	9:26	100
16:12–15	65	11:36	72
20:17	99	12:1	100
20:29–31	127	15	109
		15:16	100, 109

Acts

		15:27	100
1:1	65	16:16	109

1 Corinthians

2:1–13	34		
2:16–21	34	3:17	101
2:22	63	6:19	101
4:25–26	89		
4:29–33	34		

1 Corinthians (continued)

10:1–13	60
12–14	34
13:1–2	60
13:9–12	34
13:10	70
15	10
15:25	7
15:27	3, 7

2 Corinthians

2:14	109
2:15	109
2:16	109
3:7–18	70
3:18	34
5:17	34
5:21	126
7:15	90
9:12	100
12:1–12	34
12:1–6	63

Galatians

3:1–5	34
3:2–5	63
3:19	5, 84
4:1–7	101
4:5–6	105
4:6–7	99–100
4:6	34
6:2	90

Ephesians

1–3	34
1	10
1:5	100
1:20	7
1:22	3, 7
4:30	101

Philippians

1:1	109
2	145–46
2:5–11	123, 133
2:6–11	146
2:6	133
2:7	133
2:8	133
2:9	73
2:12	90
2:15	101
2:17	101, 109
3:3	104
4:18	101

Colossians

1:15–20	124
1:15–18	72

1 Thessalonians

1:5–6	34

1 Timothy

3	107
5	107

2 Timothy

1:3	104
4:6	109

Titus

1	107

Hebrews

1–4	61
1:1—4:13	61
1	84–85
1:1–14	85
1:1–4	4, 54–55, 62, 71–72, 85, 90
1:1–3	125, 156, 157
1:1–2	11, 64, 70
1:1–2a	9, 83
1:1	66
1:2–13	4
1:2–3	70
1:2	6, 8, 11–12, 58–59, 91, 106, 145
1:2a	4, 7–8, 10, 84
1:2b–4	69, 84
1:2b	8
1:3	56–57, 63, 70–71
1:4—3:1	156
1:4–14	7–8, 84
1:4	5, 7, 10, 73, 84
1:5—2:18	8, 84
1:5–14	56, 84

Ancient Document Index

1:5–13	8	2:15	60
1:5	59, 70, 84, 89, 91, 106	2:16	56, 61
1:6	157	2:17–18	57, 59
1:8–9	71	2:17	4, 43, 96, 101, 112, 134
1:8	70, 157–58	2:18	11–12, 112
1:10–12	9, 70, 169	3	38–42, 51, 106
1:10	70	3:1—4:11	23
1:11	169	3:1–6	59, 61, 70, 85, 90
1:13	7–8, 26, 56	3:1	4, 43, 64, 96, 101–02, 106
1:14	4–5, 7, 56, 96, 101	3:2—4:13	156
2–4	34	3:2–19	164, 166
2	10, 56, 164	3:2	70
2:1–4	33, 64	3:3	85
2:1–3a	84	3:4	70
2:1	5, 7, 33, 163	3:5–6	9, 85
2:2	5	3:5	58, 70
2:3	5, 7, 33, 56, 63–64, 111	3:6	43, 96
2:4	63–64, 106	3:7—4:11	37–38, 40, 43–45, 48, 50–51, 55, 57
2:5–18	55–56		
2:5–9	71	3:7	48, 63–64, 67, 91, 106
2:5–8	5, 8, 56	3:12–15	59
2:5	5–8, 10–11, 56–57, 72	3:12	4, 43
2:6–9	12	3:13–14	60
2:6–8	8, 10, 12	3:13	43, 48, 91
2:6–8a	7	3:14	34
2:6	8, 11	3:15	43, 48, 91
2:6b–8a	9	3:17	128
2:6b	7–8, 10	3:18–19	59
2:7	9, 12	3:19	43, 47, 162
2:8–9	35, 59, 62	4	38–42, 49, 51, 102, 106
2:8	8–10, 12	4:1–11	57
2:8a	7	4:1	20, 40
2:8b	9	4:2	46, 58, 64, 73
2:9–18	158	4:3	20, 37, 43–44, 48, 58
2:9–10	20, 22, 32, 49	4:3b–5	45
2:9	10–13, 58, 70, 125	4:3b–4	45
2:9a	8	4:4	44
2:10–18	56	4:6	40, 43, 47, 58, 64
2:10–11	9, 11–12, 57	4:7–14	164, 169
2:10	4, 7–12, 72, 96	4:7	48, 59, 91
2:11–14	4	4:9	20, 40, 42–43, 164
2:11–12	4, 9, 12–13, 43	4:10	44, 46
2:11	57, 96	4:11	38, 43, 49, 165
2:12–13	20, 62–63	4:12–13	54, 58, 63, 71
2:13–14	96	4:14—10:25	72
2:13	61	4:14—10:18	156
2:14–15	60, 106	4:14–16	12–13, 17, 20–23, 25, 32, 105
2:14	12, 56–57, 70		

Hebrews *(continued)*

4:14–15	101
4:14	22, 25, 49
4:15–16	26
4:15	112, 125, 133, 158, 159
4:16	25, 30, 50, 102, 112
5:1—10:18	61
5	96, 131–32, 144–47
5:1–4	159
5:1	134
5:4–5	113
5:5–6	146
5:5	59, 90, 101, 131
5:7–10	131, 150
5:7–9	4, 11
5:7–8	4, 146, 158
5:7b–8	126
5:7	12, 59, 76, 132–34, 147–48, 159
5:8–9	10
5:8	4, 13, 133–34, 146–47
5:9	13, 58, 134–35, 163
5:10	101, 133–34
5:11—6:20	55, 57
5:11–6:12	57
5:12–14	33
5:12	65
5:14	56, 70
6–10	34
6	163
6:1	44, 166
6:2	60, 169
6:4–8	165
6:4–5	33, 60–61
6:4	63, 106
6:6	165
6:7–8	60
6:8	56
6:10	58, 62
6:11	18, 34, 62
6:12–20	59
6:12	4, 33, 96, 111
6:13–20	31, 57
6:13–18	9
6:13–14	31
6:14	61
6:17–20	27
6:17–18	31
6:17	4, 9
6:18–20	22, 31–32, 163
6:18–19	112
6:18	31–32
6:19–20	8, 20–22
6:19	31–32
6:20	20, 31, 101
7–10	17
7	102, 105, 125
7:1–10	59, 70
7:1–3	65
7:3	65
7:5	43
7:11–12	58
7:11	58
7:14	105
7:19–22	31
7:19	50, 58, 102
7:21	31
7:22–28	160
7:25	21, 26, 102, 112
7:26—8:1	101
7:26	134
7:27	134, 161
7:28	4, 9–10, 58
8	56, 106, 126
8:1–2	126, 162
8:2	49
8:3	101
8:5	58, 70, 104
8:6	160
8:7–9	160
8:8–12	34
8:8–10	160
8:9	56
8:10	58, 160, 167
8:12	168
9:1	100
9:1–10	28
9:6–14	28
9:6–10	70
9:6	100
9:7	101
9:8	19, 64
9:9	58, 62, 104
9:10	11, 59
9:11–14	126
9:11	101

Ancient Document Index   183

9:12	11, 20	10:26–38	165
9:14	44, 58, 62, 102, 104, 106	10:26	165
9:15	4, 11, 56, 96	10:27	58
9:18–21	28	10:28	169
9:19b–22	76	10:29	63
9:20	102	10:32–39	12
9:22	58	10:32	33, 41
9:23	59	10:33	41, 62
9:24	20, 70	10:34	41
9:25	20, 28	10:36	41
9:26	59	10:39	111
9:27	56, 58	11	58, 110
9:28	62	11:1—12:4	30
10	102, 106, 126	11:1	61, 62
10:1–4	28	11:3	63
10:1	58–59, 70, 160	11:6	21, 102, 158
10:2	62, 104	11:7	111, 148
10:4	134	11:8–19	59
10:5–18	62	11:8	96
10:5–10	64	11:9–10	56
10:5	70	11:10	56
10:7	133	11:11–12	60–61
10:9	133	11:12	61
10:10	102, 134	11:18–19	61
10:11–15	72	11:19	58, 60
10:11–12	126	11:22	111
10:13	26	11:23–29	59, 111
10:14	12, 27, 58–59, 102	11:32–38	18
10:15–17	34	11:32	2, 111
10:15	64, 67, 106	11:35	60
10:18–22	112	11:40	58
10:18	58, 73	12	103
10:19—12:29	156	12:1–11	12
10:19—12:22	61	12:1–4	22, 32
10:19–39	60	12:1–2	20, 30
10:19–25	105	12:1	111, 167
10:19–23	17, 20–22, 26, 28–29, 32	12:2	8, 11, 13, 58–59, 62, 70
10:19–20	27–28, 95	12:3–11	134
10:19	28, 43, 50, 102	12:3	33
10:20	28	12:4–11	60–61, 145
10:21	29	12:4	41
10:22	13, 27, 62, 102	12:5–11	9, 96
10:23	13, 41, 50	12:5–8	4
10:24–25	13	12:5	96, 106
10:24	50, 62	12:7	41
10:25–29	50	12:10–17	25
10:25	62, 165	12:12–13	111
10:26–39	18	12:12	41

Hebrews *(continued)*

12:14–15	166
12:14	167
12:19	4
12:22–24	21–22, 25, 29, 34, 56
12:22	50, 102
12:23	30, 58, 96, 168
12:24	30
12:25–29	54, 57, 62–63, 71–72
12:25–27	67
12:25	73
12:28	59–60, 104
13:1–24	156
13:1–3	62
13:7	111
13:8	59, 91
13:9–16	59
13:10	104–5, 112
13:12	126
13:13–14	59
13:14	56, 73
13:15–16	60
13:16	62, 104
13:17	111
13:20	58, 60
13:21	168
13:22	4, 12, 43, 111

1 Peter

1:1–2	106
1:2	98, 107
1:3	98, 106
1:4	98
1:11	107
1:14–17	98
1:14–15	98
1:17	98
1:22–23	98
2:2	97
2:5	97–98
2:9–10	97
2:9	96–98, 106
2:10	98
2:21–25	108
3:9	98
4:10–11	107
4:10	107
4:12–19	107
4:17	98
5	108
5:4	108
5:5	108
5:6	107

2 Peter

1:17	90
2:1–22	90
2:20–22	60

1 John

1:5–6	126
2:23	71
3:1	99
3:2	34

Jude

5	60

Revelation

1:1	109
1:6	98, 105
1:11	110
1:19	110
1:20	110
2:1	110
2:8	110
2:12	110
2:18	110
2:26–27	90
3:1	110
3:7	110
3:12	99
3:14	110
4:4	110
5	99
5:5	110
5:8	110
5:9–10	99
5:9	110
5:10	105, 110
5:11–14	110
7:3	99
7:13–14	110
7:15	104
11:15	90
11:16	110
11:18	90

12:5	90
17:18	90
19:4	110
19:15	90
19:19	90
20:6	99
21:3	99
22:3	104

APOCRYPHA

Judith
4:14	100
16:16	109

1 Maccabees
10:42	100

Sirach
24:15	109
45:15	100
50:15	109

PSEUDEPIGRAPHA

Apocalypse of Moses
13.2–6	3
39.2–3	3

1 Enoch
14.24–25	27
48.8–10	87

3 Enoch
5.10	2

4 Ezra
6.46	2
7.28	87
13.32	87
13.38	87

Jubilees
1.27	84
1.29	84
2.1	84

Liber antiquitatum biblicarum
13.8–9	3
26.13	3

Psalms of Solomon
2.32	87
13.9	98
17	87
17.22	87
17.23–24	87
17.29	87
17.32	87
17.37	87
18.7	87

Sibylline Oracles
3.663–71	87
8	87
8.248	87
frag. 3.13–14	2

DEAD SEA SCROLLS

CD
11.20–21	103

1QS
3.17–18	2

3Q2
	86

4Q174
1.10–12	86
1.18–2.1	86
2.4–6	86

4Q246
2.1	86
11Q7	86

JOSEPHUS

Antiquities
15.136	84

Jewish War
5.219	23

PHILO

De Abrahamo
98	103

Flaccus
53	32

De gigantibus
53–60	103

De migratione Abrahami
92	103

De specialibus legibus
1.243	103

De vita Mosis
2.224	103

TARGUMS

Targum Psalms
2	88
2:7	78
2:7b	88
2:12	88

RABBINIC WRITINGS

Babylonian Talmud (b.)

ʿAbodah Zarah
3a–b	89

Berakot
7b	89
9b–10a	89

Sanhedrin
92a	89

Sukkah
52a	89

Yoma
4b	89

Jerusalem Talmud (y.)

ʿAbodah Zarah
2.1.1	88

Berakot
5.1.6	89
30b	89

Taʿanit
2.2.2	89

Midrash Rabbah

Genesis Rabbah
14.7	89
19.7	3
44.8	89

Exodus Rabbah
1.1	89
51.5	88

Leviticus Rabbah
12.5	89
27.2	89

Numbers Rabbah
9.9	89
10.4	89

Esther Rabbah
7.23	89

Song Rabbah
7:3 §3	89

Midrash Tanḥuma

Genesis
11:1 (Noah 24)	89
11:3 (Noah 28)	88
11:7 (Noah 28)	89
14 (Lek-Leka 12)	88
18:17 (Wayyera 9)	89
20:1 (Wayyera 24)	88

Leviticus
22:28 (Emor 18)	89

Other Rabbinic Writings

Mekilta

Exodus
15:9–10 (Šir. 7.64)	89

Midrash Mishle (Proverbs)
1.3	89
11:25	89

Midrash Tehillin (Psalms)
2.2	89
20.2	89
64.1	89
8.7	3
83.2	88
92.10	88
100.3	89
118.12	89
120.7	89
149.6	88

Pesiqta de Rab Kahhana
9.11	89
S 2.2	88

Pirqe Rabbi Eliezer
§18	88
§28	88

Seder Eliyahu Rabbah
18 (107)	89

Soperim
1.16b	89
4.37a	89
16.41a	89

GRECO-ROMAN WRITINGS

Aeschylus

Supplices
190	32

Herodotus

Histories
1.26	32

Plutarch

fragments
178	34

Solon
12.1	32

De superstitione
166e	32

www.ingramcontent.com/pod-product-compliance
Lightning Source LLC
Chambersburg PA
CBHW051739230426
43670CB00012B/2085